To Joanie

Enjoy your culinary experience in the Del manner

Brully Bass

THE
HOTEL
DEL CORONADO
COOKBOOK

THE HOTEL DEL CORONADO COOKBOOK

Beverly Bass

PELICAN PUBLISHING COMPANY
Gretna 1998

First printing, July 1993
Second printing, February 1998

Library of Congress Cataloging-in-Publication Data

Bass, Beverly.
    The Hotel del Coronado cookbook / Beverly Bass.
        p.   cm.
    Includes index.
    ISBN 0-88289-912-0
    1. Cookery.   2. Menus.   3. Hotel del Coronado (Coronado, Calif.)
I. Hotel del Coronado (Coronado, Calif.)   II. Title.
TX714.B375   1993
641.5'09794'98—dc20   92-43542
                                                        CIP

Manufactured in China

Published by Pelican Publishing Company
1101 Monroe Street, Gretna, Louisiana 70053

To Henry Loudermilk, a friend, who took two years out of his life to assist and to encourage me in the preparation of this book as a legacy for Barry Thein, my son. To Julia Loudermilk, his wife, who never complained of the endless hours he devoted to my project.

To Ken, my husband, who helped in every way to make a life-long dream come true. Without his constant love and understanding, my manuscript would have never been completed.

To my mother, Lillian Kantor, who shared with me her unusual creativity in culinary arts and inspired me to pursue a career in the hospitality field.

Contents

1   A Cook's Tour

From the Crown Room's Scampi Tashi Opal and the Prince of Wales' homemade ice cream to the Ocean Terrace's Pepper-Smoked Breast of Ranch Chicken with Curry-Dijon Dressing, you will be taken on a behind-the-scenes tour of the restaurants and kitchens of the Hotel del Coronado.

2   Presidential Cuisine

Menus and recipes prepared for presidents and dignitaries are featured, together with details of the advance planning and protective measures that take place when a president of the United States decides to dine at the Hotel del Coronado. Richard Nixon's Mexican-American selection of Sea Bass and Prime Sirloin Mexicana, Ronald Reagan's Médaillons of Alaskan Salmon, and President Carlos Salinas de Gortari's favorite, Filet of Mahimahi with Poached Scallops and Tri-Pepper Wine Sauce, are just a sampling of the presidential cuisine served at the Del.

3   Cocktail Buffets

Cocktail Buffets are here for all occasions—Valentine's Day, Super Bowl Sunday, or the Academy Awards celebrated at home. Hors d'oeuvres and canapés may be served as a prelude to a meal or as a fanciful, stand-alone cocktail buffet as in Rejoice and Reciprocate. Look for Vegetable Strudel with Tomato-Basil Relish, Grilled Swordfish and Salmon Canapés, and Coconut Shrimp with Tomatillo Relish.

4   Brunches for Festive Occasions

Brunch, an American creation, is one of the most versatile forms of entertaining. Special brunches for New Year's Day, Easter, Mother's Day, and the award-winning Sunday Brunch, which has earned the Del first place in San Diego County, are both easy to cook and incomparably delicious.

5   Tying the Knot at the Del

The marriage of food and beverage at the Del adds to the romance of weddings. Here are recipes for a rehearsal dinner, a wedding breakfast that includes Smoked Salmon Pinwheels with Strawberries filled with Boursin Cheese and Caviar, a luncheon wedding of classic Lobster Salad and Swiss Cheese Puffs, as well as a more formal elegant reception for which the executive chef prepared a signature creation of Ballotine of Chicken with Pistachio Nuts. Additionally, the Del's Strawberries and Cream Wedding Cake, which has become a favorite of brides and grooms, is featured here.

Acknowledgments

To Executive Chef Jay Pastoral, whose talent for painting a picture on a plate gave life to this long-awaited collection of recipes from the Hotel del Coronado.

To Glen Hoag, who designed and created the floral arrangements and backdrops.

To Dave Siccardi, my photographer, whose eye for perfection produced the exquisite photography.

To Edie Greenberg, my food stylist and dear friend, whose innate talent is reflected in the backgrounds and placement of every item featured in the photographs.

To Irene Weber, who mentally prepared every recipe in this book.

To Judith Bond from the public relations department of the Hotel del Coronado, whose in-depth knowledge of the hotel's archives made the historical renderings a unique addition.

To Jackie McDaniel for her efficient secretarial assistance on the word processor.

To Jim Shaffer of Neiman-Marcus in San Diego, for his assistance in providing the exquisite table settings featured in the photographs.

To Judy Smith, owner of the Dining Room Shop in La Jolla, for the use of select table settings in Brunches for Festive Occasions and the Beach Bash.

*Early drawing of the hotel showing the numerous chimneys. Originally nearly
every room had a fireplace, but a steam heating system was installed in
1897, and the fireplaces were gradually replaced (thereby reducing the risk of
the hotel being destroyed by fire).*

Introduction

Sitting on the white sandy beaches of Coronado, California, encompassed by a panoramic view of San Diego Bay, the city skyline, and the Pacific ocean; the Hotel del Coronado opened its doors to its first guests on February 19, 1888. The vision of Elisha Babcock and H. L. Story, which had come to fruition after eleven months of construction by Chinese laborers, is known today as the Grand Old Lady by the Sea.

Throughout its century of service, sumptuous food and beverage presented with elegance have played a major part in making the Hotel del Coronado a national landmark. The hotel has been the meeting place for presidents, kings, princes, and film stars. Every such occasion has provided the opportunity to create new and exciting menus and recipes, which are captured here in authentic detail for the first time in book form.

Almost any day at the hotel is an occasion of culinary delight—from happy hours to banquets, weddings, and the hotel's award-winning Sunday brunch. Traditionally festive days such as Thanksgiving, Christmas, New Year's Day, Easter, and Mother's Day have always been celebrated with palate-pleasing fare. At the Hotel del Coronado, imaginative dishes have been prepared for Valentine's Day and Fourth of July as well; but the most extravagant and extraordinary recipes were created for the hotel's own One Hundredth Anniversary Centennial weekend celebration.

The recipes featured in this book were created and served at the Hotel del Coronado during the 1980s—one of its most exciting decades—when the hotel celebrated its 100th anniversary. These recipes are original and have never before been published. They have been prepared and served at the hotel by Executive Chef Jay Pastoral and his culinary team.

You will be able to create the excitement and originality of the Hotel del Coronado in your own kitchen by following the recipes in this book. You can easily prepare and serve meals such as those served to former presidents Richard Nixon and Ronald Reagan and many other dignitaries. The recipes are set out in an easy-to-follow step-by-step format to make it possible for even the least experienced cook to reproduce them successfully. Last minute preparation has been minimized, so your guests can enjoy the pleasure of your company at your own party. Many of the dishes can be assembled or cooked either the day before or earlier in the week, requiring only minimum preparation at the time of serving.

The Hotel del Coronado Cookbook includes over 350 carefully tested recipes that have been served at the Grand Old Lady by the Sea.

CHAPTER ONE

A Cook's Tour

A Cook's Tour is a look at the Hotel del Coronado as a whole from the cook's perspective, followed by a sampling of the restaurant specialties. From the outside, the Hotel del Coronado looks like an extended gingerbread house—all turrets and cupolas. A long front porch on the beach side once held comfortable rocking chairs where Victorian ladies enjoyed the fresh air and watched the bathers, discreetly out of the sun. The old-fashioned lobby is carpeted in a rich burgundy that was fashionable at the turn of the century. A lacy wrought-iron elevator still lifts guests up to their floors in the original building, and the lights in the haunted room—number 3312—still mysteriously turn off and on when the room is occupied. Visitors have been known to request an immediate room change after perceiving items moving about the room on their own power. Some say that the ghost is of an anguished woman who died in the hotel. Whatever haunts this room keeps the maids on their toes; they rarely look forward to cleaning it and insist on not tidying it up alone.

On the inside, let's first give a few brief statistics. The hotel has seven hundred guest rooms, accommodating a total of approximately fourteen hundred guests—a thousand of whom are likely to be hungry at any one time. Meeting rooms and

A Prince of Wales Gourmet Dinner. Center: Roast Salmon in Pine Nuts with Sloe Gin and Beurre Blanc Sauce. Left: Fois Gras in Riesling and Golden Raisin Sauce. Right: Crayfish Bisque. Top: Chocolate Mousse Duet with Raspberry Coulis.

banquet rooms can accommodate approximately forty-eight hundred persons at one time. Additionally, the restaurants of the hotel can accommodate approximately fifteen hundred persons. All this adds up to as many as seventy-three hundred guests in the hotel at one time, all wishing to eat. To satisfy their collective appetites, there are forty-six areas in the hotel where food can be served, not including the individual guest rooms. Of these areas, several are restaurants serving the public:

- Crown Room
- Poolside Deli & Bar
- Ocean Terrace
- Burger Bar
- Ocean Terrace Grill
- Prince of Wales
- Del Deli

Behind the restaurants and other places that serve food is the cook's domain, where food is prepared by a staff of nearly two hundred. Since this is the cook's tour, let's take a brief look at the cook's domain before we go on to the restaurants. The main kitchen, which is located behind the Crown Room, prepares food for the Crown Room, banquets, and room service. The main kitchen is huge and is subdivided into specialized areas for grilling and broiling meat, fish, and fowl. Large vats known as a *bains-marie* steam all the Del's fresh vegetables. There is a pantry area for the preparation of salads, desserts, canapés, hors d'oeuvres, and all cold items. The main kitchen is supported by subareas for vegetable preparation, a butcher shop, scullery, large walk-in

Hotel bakery staff (left) *and kitchen staff* (right) *on opening day, February 18, 1888.*

refrigerators, freezers the size of an average living room, and storage areas for the chef's daily food orders. The second kitchen, which is located in another part of the hotel, serves the Ocean Terrace for breakfast and lunch. At three in the afternoon, it is transformed into a gourmet kitchen serving the Prince of Wales restaurant for dinner. Supporting the kitchens is a large subterranean bakery that turns out breads, rolls, pastries, cakes, and other delicacies. A large storeroom complex issues food items to the kitchens to meet the needs of the day. Delivery trucks juggle their arrival times to avoid traffic jams when they deliver all the provisions to the receiving area. Enough of the cook's domain. Now let's go to the restaurants to sample the specialties of each. Enjoy.

The Crown Room

It was in the Crown Room during a royal visit that Edward, prince of Wales, was introduced to Wallis Simpson, the wife of a local Coronado naval officer. Outside this historic dining room, L. Frank Baum sat in a rattan rocking chair, contemplating the Pacific Ocean, and wrote *The Wizard of Oz.* Unbelievably, he took time out to design the crown chandeliers that hang from the ceiling of this majestic room. Constructed of sugar pine, the ceiling is joined by dowels and contains not a single nail. At the hotel's centennial birthday celebration on February 18, 1988, the chef decided to duplicate the chandeliers in nougatine studded with candy jewels. He planned to make seven hundred of them as dessert for the gala dinner, but gave up after the tenth, figuring that seven hundred would take another century to make. The recipes for Eggs in Brioches, Crown Cordon Bleu Salad, and Scampi Tashi Opal from that famous room are adapted here for home kitchens.

An early view of the dining room, now known as the Crown Room because of its crown-shaped chandeliers designed by Wizard of Oz *author L. Frank Baum.*

Eggs in Brioches

6 individual brioche rolls
6 slices Muenster cheese
6 eggs
Salt and pepper to taste
3 tbsp. chives, chopped
   (for garnish)

1. Cut top off from each brioche; set aside. Hollow out each brioche, leaving a ¼-inch-thick shell.

2. Line brioches with slices of muenster cheese. In a 12-inch round microwave-safe baking pan, arrange brioches in a circle 1-inch apart.

3. Break 1 egg into each brioche; pierce egg yolk with toothpick. Cook covered in microwave on high (100% power) for 4 to 5 minutes, until almost set.

4. Let brioches stand, covered loosely with waxed paper, for 2 to 3 minutes, until whites are opaque. If eggs require additional cooking time, cook on high for 15 seconds at a time until done. Season with salt and pepper.

5. Transfer to warm serving plate. Garnish with chopped chives.

Serves 6.

Crown Cordon Bleu Salad

1 head romaine lettuce, washed
   and dried
2 oz. Danish bleu cheese,
   crumbled
2 oz. prosciutto ham, cut into
   julienned strips
2½ oz. red wine vinegar
4 oz. olive oil
Juice of 2 lemons
2 tsp. freshly ground black
   pepper

1. Cut romaine into bite-size pieces; set aside.

2. In a small mixing bowl, mix bleu cheese and prosciutto ham; set aside.

3. In a large mixing bowl, place the red wine vinegar and whisk in olive oil, lemon juice, and black pepper.

4. Fold in bleu cheese and prosciutto ham. Add romaine and toss thoroughly until all leaves are coated. Divide salad into four portions and serve on chilled salad plates.

Serves 4.

Scampi Tashi Opal

Scampi:

2 oz. olive oil
14-16 (about ½ lb.) jumbo shrimp
2 tbsp. garlic, peeled and chopped
2 oz. red wine
6 oz. Opal Basil Cream Sauce
  (recipe follows)
½ cup leeks, washed and cut into
  julienned strips
2 opal basil top leaves
8 tbsp. pistachio nuts, chopped

1. In a large skillet, heat oil. Add shrimp and briefly sauté. Add garlic, continue cooking for 2 minutes, then add red wine and bring to a simmer.
2. Add Opal Basil Cream Sauce, bring to a simmer. Remove shrimp and keep warm; set aside.

Opal Basil Cream Sauce:

1 tbsp. olive oil
¼ cup garlic, peeled and chopped
1 bay leaf
3 tsp. black peppercorns
2 cups opal basil stems
2 pt. burgundy wine
2 pts. cream

1. In a medium-size saucepan, heat oil. Sauté garlic, add bay leaves, peppercorns, opal basil stems, and Burgundy wine. Reduce by ¾.
2. Add cream and reduce by ⅓. Strain sauce into the top of a double boiler and keep warm.

To Assemble:

1. Divide shrimp and place them in a circle on each of two plates.
2. Evenly spoon sauce over shrimp. Place leeks in center of the plate.
3. Place basil leaf in the middle of leeks and sprinkle chopped pistachio nuts over top of shrimp.

Serves 2.

The Ocean Terrace

With the Pacific Ocean in the background, guests in the Ocean Terrace restaurant look down on tennis players sparring back and forth. Joggers and exercise enthusiasts gather for breakfast, along with families from near and far. From the breakfast menu, Hawaiian French Toast is a favorite. Thick slices of Hawaiian sweet bread are coated with egg batter and shredded coconut, then cooked and served with pineapple-macadamia syrup.

Lunch offers Pepper Smoked Breast of Ranch Chicken with Curry-Dijon Dressing, and a favorite of pasta lovers is the Lemon-Pepper Fettuccine Topped with Shrimp, Snow Peas, and Yellow Tomato Sauce. The Terrace Club Sandwich is for those on the go. Lunch in the Ocean Terrace is casual, and relaxed guests can be seen clad in anything from tennis shorts to beachwear.

The menu matches the indoor-outdoor ambiance of the restaurant. You can duplicate the experience on your patio with a barbecue and a good appetite.

Boardwalk along the beach around the turn of the century.

Hawaiian French Toast with Pineapple-Macadamia Syrup

Toast:

1 loaf Hawaiian sweet bread
8 eggs
⅔ cup canned cream of coconut
½ cup shredded coconut
½ cup milk
¼ cup rum
Pinch of salt
⅓ cup butter or margarine, divided

1. Slice bread into eight 1-inch slices, then cut each slice in half.
2. In a medium-size mixing bowl, whisk together the eggs, cream of coconut, shredded coconut, milk, rum, and salt.
3. In a large skillet, place half the butter, and heat until melted. Dip bread slices into egg mixture, coating each side. Cook in skillet until golden brown, about 2 minutes on each side. Repeat procedure with remaining butter and bread.
4. Transfer to a warm serving plate and serve with warmed pineapple-macadamia syrup.

Syrup:

2 cups maple syrup
1 cup fresh or canned crushed pineapple, including juice
¾ cup macadamia nuts, chopped

1. In a small saucepan, combine maple syrup with crushed pineapple. Add nuts, stir, and simmer over low heat until mixture is thoroughly heated.
2. Transfer to a small pitcher.

Serves 4.

Pepper-Smoked Breast of Ranch Chicken with Curry-Dijon Dressing

Chicken:
1 large onion, chopped
4 6-oz. skinless chicken breasts
Salt
Crushed black pepper
2 cups water
2 cups chablis wine
8 baby carrots
4 cups mixed greens, chopped
1 cucumber, peeled, seeded, and sliced
4 hard-cooked eggs, cut into wedges
2 medium-size tomatoes, cut into wedges
4 sprigs fresh basil (for garnish)

Curry Dijon Dressing:
4 egg yolks
2 tbsp. Dijon-style mustard
2 tsp. curry powder
1 tsp. salt
1 tsp. white pepper
1 tsp. garlic powder
2 tbsp. fresh lemon juice
1 cup virgin olive oil

1. Preheat oven to 350 degrees.
2. Place chopped onions in a large skillet, then lay chicken breasts on top of the onions and sprinkle salt and crushed black pepper over chicken. Add 2 cups water; cover and pan-poach for 5 minutes.
3. Remove chicken breasts from poaching liquid and transfer to a 13 x 9 x 2-inch baking pan. Add wine and bake at 350 degrees for about 10 minutes, or until chicken breasts are fork tender.
4. Remove from oven and transfer chicken breasts to a plate. Cool and refrigerate for 1 hour before serving. (Recipe may be prepared up to this point the day before.)
5. Peel baby carrots, leaving 1 inch of green on top. In a medium-size saucepan, add enough water to cover baby carrots. Cook until tender, about 12 minutes. Cool, drain, and set aside.

1. In a medium-size mixing bowl, whisk together egg yolks, mustard, and curry powder. Add salt, pepper, garlic powder, and lemon juice. Blend thoroughly.
2. Whisk in olive oil in a slow stream. Blend all ingredients until smooth.

To Assemble:
1. Place 1 cup of greens on each of four plates.
2. Cut chicken breasts into fine slices and fan in center of plate. Arrange cucumber slices, egg, and tomato wedges on both sides of plate. Garnish each plate with two baby carrots and a sprig of basil.
3. Spoon dressing over salads.

Serves 4.

Lemon-Pepper Fettuccine Topped With Shrimp, Snow Peas, and Yellow Tomato Sauce

¾ lb. lemon-pepper fettuccine
2 tbsp. olive oil, divided
6 oz. snow peas, stringed and cut into julienned strips
Yellow Tomato Sauce (recipe follows)
1½ lb. medium-size shrimp, peeled and deveined
Salt and pepper to taste
6 oz. oyster mushrooms, sliced
3 shallots, peeled and chopped
3 tbsp. Riesling wine
Juice of 1 lemon

1. In a dutch oven, bring 2 quarts of water to a rolling boil, then cook lemon-pepper fettuccine *al dente*. Rinse with cold water and toss with 1 tablespoon olive oil to prevent sticking; set aside.

2. Blanch snow peas by quickly immersing them in boiling water. Remove immediately to ice water; drain and reserve.

3. Prepare Yellow Tomato Sauce (recipe follows). Reserve and keep warm.

4. Season shrimp with salt and pepper. In a large skillet, heat remaining tablespoon of olive oil. Sauté shrimp rapidly over high heat until shrimp are no longer translucent. Remove from heat; set aside.

5. In same skillet, sauté mushrooms and shallots. Return shrimp to skillet, then add snow peas. Stir wine into mixture and simmer over low heat.

6. While shrimp are cooking, plunge the cooked pasta into boiling water for 15 to 30 seconds. Drain pasta in a colander and transfer to a large mixing bowl.

Note: Lemon-pepper fettuccine is available at local Italian markets.

Yellow Tomato Sauce:
2 tbsp. virgin olive oil
2 tbsp. red bell pepper, finely chopped
2 tbsp. yellow bell pepper, finely chopped
1 clove garlic, peeled and minced
1 shallot, finely chopped
¼ tsp. chili powder
6 large yellow tomatoes, blanched and chopped
3 tbsp. dry vermouth
12 cilantro leaves, coarsely chopped
1 tbsp. dried oregano
1 tbsp. dried thyme
Salt and pepper to taste

1. In a large skillet, heat 1 tablespoon of the olive oil. Sauté red and yellow peppers, then move them to the side of the skillet.

2. Add remaining tablespoon of olive oil and sauté the garlic and shallot. Add chili powder, tomatoes, and vermouth. Simmer for 25 minutes.

3. Purée the mixture in a blender, then return it to the skillet. Add cilantro, oregano, thyme, and season to taste with salt and pepper. Keep warm.

To Assemble:
1. Add lemon juice to shrimp mixture, then toss together.
2. Ladle sauce over drained fettuccine and fold into shrimp mixture. Divide fettuccine among six plates.

Serves 6.

6 slices sourdough bread, toasted
2 oz. mayonnaise
2 lettuce leaves, washed and dried
8 oz. cooked turkey breast, sliced
1 medium-size tomato, cut into
   4 slices
2 oz. alfalfa sprouts
4 slices bacon, crisply cooked and
   drained
½ avocado, peeled and pitted,
   cut into 6 slices

1. Spread two slices of sourdough toast with mayonnaise. Place 1 lettuce leaf on each slice, then layer each with 4 ounces of sliced turkey.

2. Place a slice of sourdough toast on top of turkey on each, then spread with additional mayonnaise. Top each with 2 slices of tomato, alfalfa sprouts, 2 slices of bacon, and 3 slices of avocado.

3. Place slice of sourdough toast on top, then cut each sandwich diagonally in half and in half again.

Serves 2.

The Ocean Terrace Grill

Kissed by a warm sea breeze, the Ocean Terrace Grill is *al fresco* dining at its best. This informal late lunch and early dinner restaurant provides its guests with Red Hot Coronado Chicken Wings, King Salmon Sandwiches, and Scallop Brochettes.

This brochure from around 1904 was directed to those ''freezing in the east'' while we are ''picking roses in the west.''

Red Hot Coronado Chicken Wings with Bleu Cheese Dipping Sauce

Chicken:
24 chicken wings, disjointed (instructions follow)
1 cup olive oil
⅛ cup Cajun spice
¼ cup butter or margarine, melted
1 tsp. Tabasco sauce

1. Preheat oven to 375 degrees. Light barbecue grill.
2. Coat chicken wings with oil, sprinkle with Cajun spice, and place them on a cookie sheet. Bake for 25 minutes.
3. While chicken wings are baking, combine melted butter or margarine with Tabasco sauce in a small mixing bowl.
4. Remove chicken wings from oven. Dip wings in sauce and coat evenly. Place on a barbecue (coals should be hot) for about 1 minute on each side, just enough time to mark wings and set the sauce. (Chicken wings may be returned to the oven for 10 minutes instead of cooking on a barbecue.)

To disjoint chicken wings:
1. Cut wings off at the joint (do not use the tips).
2. Loosen the meat away from the bone.
3. Pull back all the skin and meat.

Bleu Cheese Dipping Sauce:
1 tbsp. distilled white vinegar
1 tbsp. Worcestershire sauce
1 tbsp. olive oil
3½ cups mayonnaise
¼ cup milk
2 drops Tabasco sauce
½ lb. bleu cheese, crumbled

1. Mix all the ingredients together and transfer to a covered jar.
2. Refrigerate overnight. Yields 5 cups.

To Assemble:
1. Transfer chicken wings to a warm serving platter.
2. Serve with Bleu Cheese Dipping Sauce on the side.

Serves 6.

King Salmon Sandwich

Sandwich:
1 lb. king salmon
4 French rolls or 2 baguettes, sliced in half
4 tbsp. butter or margarine, divided
8 lettuce leaves, washed and dried
2 tomatoes, cut into 8 slices
1 medium-size red onion, sliced and lightly grilled or sautéed

Marinade:
1½ cups olive oil
½ cup fresh lemon juice
2 tbsp. fresh oregano, finely chopped
1 tsp. garlic powder
⅛ tsp. salt
1 tbsp. white pepper

1. In a medium-size mixing bowl, whisk all the marinade ingredients together. Slice salmon on the diagonal about ½ inch thick. Place salmon slices in a 9 x 9-inch baking pan, add marinade, and marinate for 30 minutes.

2. Barbecue salmon on a hot grill, or sauté in a large nonstick skillet, for about 7 to 8 minutes on each side, until salmon is lightly browned and tender.

3. Spread 1 tablespoon of butter or margarine on both halves of a French roll or baguette.

4. Place 2 salmon slices on one half of each roll. Place 2 lettuce leaves and 2 tomato slices on remaining halves. Place grilled red onions over both halves.

5. Serve open faced.

Serves 4.

Scallop Brochettes

6 oz. butter or margarine, softened
2 oz. garlic salt
16 large scallops (about ¾ lb.)
12 oz. pancetta, thinly sliced
1 medium-size red onion
1 green bell pepper
1 yellow bell pepper
8 large fresh mushrooms (about ¾ lb.)

1. In a small mixing bowl, combine butter or margarine with garlic salt. Set aside.

2. Wrap scallops with pancetta. Cut onion into eight pieces, and cut each pepper into eight pieces.

3. Thread scallops and vegetables on four 10-inch bamboo skewers, beginning and ending with a mushroom. Brush skewers with garlic butter. Barbecue over medium heat for about 12 to 15 minutes, turning skewers so all sides cook evenly. Do not allow pancetta to burn.

4. Remove scallops and vegetables from skewers and serve with Confetti Coleslaw (see recipe).

Note: Pancetta, an Italian bacon roll with peppercorns, may be found in most Italian delicatessens.

Serves 4.

The Del Deli

During its early days, the hotel kept its water supply inside the four-foot-thick walls of a huge cistern. The cistern was later converted into a twenty-four-hour authentic Eastern-style deli. A typical bill of fare gives special prominence to Larry's Chicken Soup with Matzo Balls and Meat Knishes. These recipes are good to use for part of a Passover dinner or to fullfill a yearning for a New York deli treat.

A 1923 Model T Ford laundry truck was restored by the grandson of the man who drove the truck for the Del. Instead of giving him a watch when he retired, the hotel gave him the truck. For years, it stood in open air and was used to store garden tools.

Larry's Chicken Soup

1 3- to 3½-lb. chicken, cleaned
2 medium-size carrots, coarsely chopped
2 stalks celery, cut in half
2 sprigs parsley, including stems
2 bay leaves
1 onion, peeled and cut in half
1 turnip, peeled and quartered
1 parsnip, peeled and quartered
1 tbsp. coarsely ground black pepper
2 tsp. salt
1 tsp. garlic salt
¼ tsp. dried thyme
1 chicken bouillon cube

1. In a large stock pot or dutch oven, combine chicken, carrots, celery, and parsley. Add water to cover by about 3 inches, then bring to a simmer over medium heat. Skim off froth as it rises to the surface. Reduce heat and simmer for 30 minutes.

2. Add all the remaining ingredients. Partially cover stock pot or dutch oven, and simmer for an additional 30 minutes, or until whole chicken is cooked. Remove all vegetables and set whole chicken aside.

3. Allow broth to cool; then cover and chill overnight. When ready to serve, skim and discard layer of fat that has formed on the surface. Add white meat of the cooked chicken to the soup; then reheat and serve.

Note: Extra cooked chicken may be used for a chicken salad.

Serves 6.

Matzo Balls

4 tbsp. butter or margarine,
  at room temperature
4 eggs, slightly beaten
2 tsp. salt
¾ cup matzo meal
¼ cup matzo cake meal
4 tbsp. strained chicken broth
  (from Larry's Chicken Soup)
4 qt. water
1 tbsp. salt

Note: Matzo meal and matzo cake meal are available at most supermarkets during Passover.

1. In a medium-size mixing bowl, whisk together butter or margarine and eggs until thoroughly blended.
2. In a small mixing bowl, stir together the two teaspoons salt with matzo meal and matzo cake meal. Stir the matzo meal mixture into the egg mixture. Add chicken broth and stir until the mixture is blended together. Cover and refrigerate for 30 minutes.
3. In a dutch oven, bring 4 quarts of water and 1 tablespoon of salt to a boil. Form rounded teaspoons of matzo mixture into balls and place on a plate. Drop the matzo balls one-by-one into the salted boiling water. Cover and simmer for 2 hours without lifting the lid. Matzo balls will expand.
4. Remove dutch oven from heat and allow the matzo balls to cool in the poaching liquid. Remove with slotted spoon and place one or two in bottom of each soup bowl before ladling Larry's Chicken Soup into bowls.

Yields about 20 matzo balls.

Meat Knishes

1 lb. lean brisket
¼ cup water
1 tbsp. butter or margarine
1½ cups onions, finely chopped
2 tsp. salt
1 tsp. freshly ground black pepper
1 tsp. garlic salt
4 sheets frozen puff pastry,
  defrosted according to
  package directions
2 eggs, lightly beaten

Note: Puff pastry can be found in the frozen section of most supermarkets.

1. Preheat oven to 325 degrees.
2. Place brisket and water in an ovenproof baking pan. Cover and bake for about 2 hours, or until fork tender. Turn brisket occasionally. Remove from oven, cool brisket, and finely chop.
3. In a small skillet, melt butter or margarine. Sauté onions until they are limp. Add salt, pepper, and garlic salt. Mix thoroughly, then add chopped brisket.
4. Lay puff pastry sheets on a lightly floured cutting board. Cut into 5-inch squares. Place a 4-ounce scoop of meat mixture in the center of each square. Fold up flaps and corners of dough to seal meat mixture. Turn dough over and work into a flat round form approximately ¾ inch thick.
5. Place knishes on nonstick cookie sheets and brush top and sides with beaten eggs (egg wash). Bake for 20 to 25 minutes until golden brown. Brush additional egg wash on knishes every 5 to 7 minutes while baking. Serve hot.

Serves 4.

Poolside Deli & Bar

An olympic-size swimming pool sets the scene at the Poolside Deli and Bar, where the Del's guests luxuriate, sipping and swimming in the relaxed atmosphere. In between dips and sips, they munch on California Pitas and "What's the Good Bird," a sandwich layered high with turkey, shaved ham, and Monterey Jack cheese. Cocktails known as Poolside Smashers are served by the pool to ensure that the guests are refreshed both externally and internally.

This 1925 brochure contains photographs of the indoor swimming pool, the "casino" (now called the International Room), the front of the hotel, and the ballroom.

California Pita

1 tbsp. vegetable oil
2 thin slices yellow onion
1 thin slice green bell pepper
4 oz. chicken, sliced
1 oz. soy sauce
1 6-inch pita bread
1 leaf green lettuce
2 thin slices tomato
1 oz. alfalfa sprouts
3 thin slices avocado, peeled
3 oz. sour cream

1. In a small skillet, heat vegetable oil and sauté onion slices, green bell pepper, and chicken for about 3 minutes, or until chicken is fork tender. Add soy sauce and stir for 30 seconds.

2. Split pita bread, but do not cut through. Place green leaf lettuce, tomato slices, alfalfa sprouts, avocado slices, and sour cream inside the pita pocket. Add the cooked onions, green bell pepper, chicken, and soy sauce mixture.

Serves 1.

What's the Good Bird

2 slices New York rye bread
1 tbsp. mayonnaise
1 tbsp. wine-grain mustard
2 leaves green lettuce, shredded
2 thin slices tomato
2 oz. shaved cooked ham
2 oz. shaved cooked turkey
1 oz. Monterey Jack cheese

1. Spread 1 slice of rye bread with mayonnaise. Spread the other slice with wine-grain mustard.

2. Place shredded lettuce on bread slice coated with mayonnaise. Layer tomato slices, ham, turkey, and cheese on top of shredded lettuce. Cover with remaining slice of rye bread. Cut in half.

Serves 1.

Poolside Smashers

The Del-Light:
1¼ oz. light rum
3 oz. sweet frozen strawberries
(in syrup)
3 oz. cranberry juice
1 fresh strawberry

1. Fill blender container with ice to the 10-ounce mark. Add rum, frozen strawberries, and cranberry juice. Blend at maximum speed for 1 minute, or until a frozen (slush) consistency is achieved.
2. Pour into a 12-ounce glass. Add a straw and a fresh strawberry for garnish.

Serves 1.

Coronado Mimosa:
5 oz. brut champagne, chilled
2 oz. cranberry juice, chilled
1 lemon twist

1. Place two ice cubes in a 9-ounce fluted champagne glass. Add champagne and cranberry juice.
2. Garnish with lemon twist. (If desired, the ice cube may be omitted.)

Serves 1.

Melon Punch:
1 oz. Midori liqueur
½ oz. triple sec
5 oz. pineapple juice
¼ oz. Myers dark rum
1 wedge fresh pineapple

1. Fill a 12-ounce glass with ice. Add Midori and triple sec. Fill remainder of glass with pineapple juice and stir.
2. Float Myers dark rum on the top. Add a straw and garnish with a wedge of fresh pineapple.

Serves 1.

Casino menu for January, 1931.

Burger Bar

Overlooking the Pacific Ocean from a vantage point atop the Promenade Deck is the Burger Bar, the Del's answer to fast-food service. Guests line up and place their orders for giant beef burgers (a special recipe that compares to no other) and Crispy-Fried Onion Rings.

Hotel brochure from 1925.

The Del's Beef Burger

2 lb. lean ground beef
1 egg, slightly beaten
1 tsp. Dijon-style mustard
2 tsp. ketchup
1 tbsp. diced green chiles
2 tbsp. Worcestershire sauce
1 tsp. salt
1 tsp. pepper
8 Kaiser rolls, cut in half
mustard and ketchup (for
   condiments)

1. In a large mixing bowl, combine all the ingredients except condiments. Form mixture into eight patties.
2. Grill or broil patties four inches from heat for about 10 minutes on first side, then 4 minutes on second side.
3. Remove from heat and serve on Kaiser rolls with small bowls of mustard and ketchup.

Serves 8.

Crispy Fried Onion Rings

4 large Spanish onions
4½ cups all-purpose
   flour, divided
2½ tsp. baking powder
2 tsp. salt
½ tsp. white pepper
½ tsp. garlic salt
4 cups buttermilk
4 eggs, separated
Vegetable oil

1. Peel onions, then cut into ½-inch slices and separate into rings. Place onion slices in a paper bag with 2 cups flour. Shake until rings are coated.
2. In a medium-size mixing bowl, combine remaining 2½ cups flour, baking powder, salt, white pepper, garlic salt, and buttermilk. Stir in egg yolks, mixing thoroughly.
3. Beat egg whites at room temperature until stiff peaks form; then fold into batter. Dip onion rings in batter.
4. In a dutch oven, add vegetable oil to depth of 1½ to 2 inches. Heat oil to 375 degrees, then fry onion rings in small batches, turning once, until golden brown.
5. Drain on paper towels and serve immediately.

Serves 8.

Prince of Wales

The Prince of Wales is a gourmet restaurant with its own kitchen and staff. Here the chef has developed one-of-a-kind recipes, experimenting with new combinations of ingredients. Some popular successes include Crayfish Bisque and Roast Salmon in Pine Nuts with Sloe Gin and Beurre Blanc Sauce. With an ice cream machine that cost only twenty-five dollars at a local department store, he also created a luscious dessert combination—Blackberry Ice Cream with Blackberry Brandy Sauce. The gourmet cuisine at the Prince of Wales, prepared with a harmony of flavors and tasteful beauty, is meticulously planned and the service is impeccable. The recipes featured here are recommended for the experienced cook.

The Prince of Wales (pictured here at thirteen years old) visited the hotel in 1920. Here he met Coronado housewife Wallis Warfield Spencer (later Simpson) for whom he later abdicated the throne of England.

Crayfish Bisque

4 cups Chablis wine
32 live crayfish
16 red pearl onions
1 spaghetti squash
8 dried morel mushrooms
3 tbsp. unsalted butter
1 medium-size sweet red onion, chopped
1 medium-size carrot, chopped
1 bunch parsley (stems only), washed
Salt
1 pinch dried thyme
3 bay leaves
1 tbsp. whole black peppercorns
3 cups heavy cream
White pepper
4 sprigs parsley (for garnish)
4 sprigs thyme (for garnish)

1. In a medium-size saucepan, bring 2½ cups of wine to a boil and blanch 28 of the crayfish. Reserve broth. Remove meat from shells and set aside. Reserve shells and head for bisque.

2. Blanch pearl onions in boiling water for one minute, then transfer onions to a strainer and pour ice water over them. Remove root end and squeeze outer skins off. Set aside.

3. Cut squash in half crosswise. Reserve one half for other use. Place squash half in a saucepan with boiling water and cook for 10 minutes. Scrape pulp out of squash and set it aside.

4. Place mushrooms in ¾ cup of warm water for 20 to 30 minutes to soften.

5. In a large saucepan, melt half the butter over low heat. Add onion, carrot, and parsley. Sprinkle lightly with salt. Sauté, stirring occasionally, until vegetables are soft but not brown, about 10 minutes.

6. Add remaining wine, thyme, bay leaves, peppercorns, and remaining crayfish shells and broth from Step One. Cook on medium heat for 15 minutes. Add cream, lower heat to simmer, and cook for about 15 minutes or until liquid has been reduced by about one-third. Mixture should coat the back of a spoon. Remove four whole cooked crayfish. Set aside for garnish.

7. Strain bisque through a sieve set over a large mixing bowl. With a wooden spoon, mash the heads and shells in the sieve to break them up and extract their juices. Discard heads and shells. Return bisque to a saucepan, reheat and season with salt and pepper.

Note: Dried morel mushrooms are available in Asian markets and some supermarkets.

To Serve:
1. Divide bisque into four soup bowls.
2. Arrange ¼ of the squash, 2 mushrooms, and 4 pearl onions in each bowl. Garnish with 1 crayfish, 1 sprig of parsley, and 1 sprig of thyme. Serve immediately.

Serves 4.

Probably the most memorable dinner and ball held at the Hotel Del Coronado was during the 1920 visit of the Prince of Wales, who would later become King Edward VIII and then the Duke of Windsor.

Foie Gras in Riesling and Golden Raisin Sauce

Foie Gras:

4 profiteroles or cream puffs (recipe follows)

1 tsp. olive oil

8 1-oz. slices fresh duck liver

3 tsp. fresh garlic, peeled and chopped

3 tsp. golden raisins

1 cup Riesling wine

3 oz. heavy cream

3 oz. Demi-Glacé (see recipe)

Salt and pepper to taste

2 large shiitake mushrooms, sliced with stems removed

4 sprigs oregano (for garnish)

1. In a large heated skillet, heat olive oil, then add liver and sear on each side for about 20 seconds. Liver should be medium-rare. Add chopped garlic and raisins, then deglaze skillet with wine for about 10 seconds. Remove liver to a plate.

2. To the same skillet, add cream and Demi-Glacé. Simmer until sauce has reduced to coat the back of a spoon. Add salt, pepper, and shiitake mushrooms.

Profiteroles:

1 cup water

5 tbsp. butter, cut into small pieces

Pinch of salt

1 cup flour

4 eggs

1. Preheat oven to 400 degrees.

2. In a heavy saucepan, bring water, butter, and salt to a boil. As soon as mixture begins to boil, remove saucepan from the heat.

3. Add flour all at once and mix quickly. Return the saucepan to the heat and thicken the paste, stirring continuously with a wooden spoon. It takes about 1 minute for the pastry to leave the sides of the saucepan. When this occurs, remove mixture from the heat and quickly blend in 2 eggs, stirring briskly. Add remaining eggs, one at a time, continuing to stir until a smooth paste is obtained.

4. Transfer the pastry to a pastry bag fitted with a plain nozzle that is ½ inch in diameter. Pipe small pastry balls 1½ to 2 inches in diameter onto a lightly oiled baking sheet. Space them so they do not stick to each other as they swell during cooking.

5. Place in the oven and bake for about 15 minutes, or until the profiteroles have turned golden. Allow them to cool with the oven switched off and the door open.

Note: Profiteroles may be prepared ahead of time and they freeze well.

Yields about 12.

To Assemble:
1. Remove top portion of profiterole and set the bottom portion in a soup plate. Place mushroom mixture in profiterole bottom and replace top.
2. Place 1 slice of liver to the side of profiterole and spoon sauce over the liver. Garnish with fresh oregano.

Serves 4.

Roast Salmon in Pine Nuts with Sloe Gin and Beurre Blanc Sauce

Salmon:
8 oz. pine nuts
2 oz. blue cornmeal
1 tsp. dried oregano
1 tsp. parsley, chopped
¼ tsp. salt
¼ tsp. freshly ground black pepper
4 6-oz. salmon fillets
2 oz. Dijon-style mustard
2 tsp. olive oil

1. Preheat oven to 350 degrees.
2. Place pine nuts on a cookie sheet and bake for about 7 minutes while watching carefully. Coarsely chop 2 ounces of the pine nuts. Set aside.
3. Place remaining 6 ounces of pine nuts in a food processor with the cornmeal, oregano, and parsley. Process for about 30 seconds (mixture should be coarse), then transfer mixture from the processor to a medium-size mixing bowl. Add the 2 ounces of coarsely chopped pine nuts, salt, and pepper.
4. Brush salmon fillets with Dijon-style mustard, then dip in pine nut mixture. Place the olive oil in a medium-size bowl, then roll the fillets in the oil just to coat them.
5. Increase oven heat to 375 degrees. Place fillets in a greased baking pan and bake for approximately 10 to 15 minutes.

Sloe Gin and Beurre Blanc Sauce:
4 oz. sloe gin
2 oz. lemon juice
2 oz. chablis wine
2 large fresh peaches, peeled, pitted, and chopped
2 oz. shallots, peeled and chopped
4 oz. unsalted butter, cold and cubed
Salt and pepper to taste

1. In a medium-size skillet, combine sloe gin, lemon juice, wine, chopped peaches, and shallots. Cook over medium heat and reduce volume by three-fourths.
2. Strain mixture into another saucepan, add butter, and whisk over a very low heat. Add salt and pepper to taste. Sauce should be slightly thinner than a purée.

To serve:
1. Spoon 2 ounces of sauce onto each of four dinner plates.
2. Remove the salmon from the oven and place one fillet on the sauce on each plate.

Serves 4.

Chocolate Mousse Duet with Raspberry Coulis

Mousse:

8 oz. semi-sweet chocolate
3 tbsp. confectioners' sugar
3 tbsp. rum
3 egg yolks
1¼ cups heavy cream

1. Melt chocolate in the top of a double boiler.
2. Add confectioners' sugar, rum, and egg yolks, one at a time. Stir until mixture has thickened, then remove from heat. Let cool.
3. Whip heavy cream. Add to slightly cooled chocolate mixture.
4. Place mixture in a bowl and cover. Let cool in refrigerator for 1 hour.

Raspberry Coulis:

2 12-oz. bags frozen unsweetened raspberries, thawed
½ cup sugar
¼ cup raspberry jam

1. Purée all ingredients in a food processor.
2. Strain mixture through a fine sieve into a small bowl. Cover and refrigerate.

Note: Raspberry Coulis may be prepared two days ahead if left covered and refrigerated.

Sugar Cookies:

½ cup (1 stick) butter or margarine
1 cup plus 2 tbsp. sugar
2 eggs, beaten
2 tsp. vanilla
2 cups pastry flour
1½ tsp. baking powder
¼ tsp. salt

1. Preheat oven to 350 degrees.
2. In a medium-size mixing bowl, cream butter or margarine, 1 cup of the sugar, and beaten eggs. Add vanilla.
3. In a small mixing bowl, sift flour, baking powder, and salt. Add to cream mixture and blend thoroughly.
4. Refrigerate for 3 hours. Make 2 rolls out of the dough and slice into cookies ⅛ inch thick. Place on cookie sheet, sprinkle with 2 tablespoons sugar, and bake for 8 minutes. Watch carefully, so cookies do not brown.

Yields 36 cookies.

To Assemble:

1. Place mousse in a pastry bag with a star tip.
2. Spoon about 3 tablespoons of Raspberry Coulis onto one side of each of four dessert plates. Add 1 sugar cookie on the other side of plate. Pipe mousse onto sugar cookie.

Serves 4.

Blackberry Ice Cream with Blackberry Brandy Sauce

Blackberry Ice Cream:
1½ cups frozen unsweetened blackberries, thawed
1½ cups sugar
½ cup blackberry brandy
1 egg
1 egg yolk
2 cups whipping cream
1 cup milk
½ tsp. vanilla extract

1. In a bowl, mix berries with 1 cup sugar and brandy. Let stand 3 hours.
2. Beat egg, egg yolk, and remaining ½ cup sugar to blend. Add cream, milk, and vanilla; then stir until sugar dissolves. Blend berry mixture into cream.
3. Refrigerate mixture until it is cold, then freeze it in an ice cream maker according to manufacturer's directions. Freeze in covered container several hours to mellow flavors.

Yields about 1 quart.

Blackberry Brandy Sauce:
1 cup frozen unsweetened blackberries, thawed
½ cup sugar
⅓ cup blackberry brandy

1. Mix berries, sugar, and brandy in heavy medium-size saucepan. Let stand 2 hours.
2. Bring mixture to boil, stirring frequently. Reduce heat and simmer until syrupy, stirring occasionally for about 10 minutes. Cool completely.

Note: Blackberry Brandy Sauce may be prepared a day ahead and chilled.

Yields about 1½ cups.

To serve:
1. If ice cream is frozen solid, let soften in refrigerator before serving. Scoop into bowls.
2. Drizzle Blackberry Brandy Sauce over ice cream. Serves 6.

CHAPTER TWO

Presidential Cuisine

"President Nixon wants the Crown Room on September third!"

Late one afternoon in August of 1970, the night manager of the Hotel del Coronado received an inquiry. The conversation began as follows: "This is Mr. Bull at the White House. I wonder if the Crown Room might be available on September third for a dinner that President Nixon wants to host for the President of Mexico?" So began the preparations for the formal state dinner held by President Richard M. Nixon of the United States, honoring President Gustavo Diaz Ordaz of Mexico—the second state dinner ever to be held outside the White House in Washington D.C., and the first time that the Del wined and dined two sitting presidents at once. Also present were former president Lyndon B. Johnson and future president Ronald Reagan, then governor of California.

The Del had hosted nine other U.S. presidents beginning with Benjamin Harrison in 1891, and including William McKinley, William Howard Taft, Woodrow Wilson, Franklin D. Roosevelt (on numerous visits), Dwight D. Eisenhower, John F. Kennedy, Jimmy Carter, and Ronald Reagan. In 1983, when George Bush was vice-president, he enjoyed playing tennis with the Del's general

Ronald Reagan's Minisummit Luncheon. Center: *Médaillons of Alaskan Salmon on Dill Beurre Blanc Sauce, Gingered Baby Carrots, Parisienne Potatoes, Lattice of Green Beans.* Upper Left: *Chilled Avocado Soup with Caviar Dot.* Upper Right: *Hearts of Palm Salad Layered on Radicchio and Butter Lettuce Leaves Topped with Herb Vinaigrette Dressing and Sprinkled Toasted Pine Nuts.*

manager and jogging on the beach to keep his trim physique.

In preparation for the Nixon Gustavo Diaz Ordaz dinner, Washington went to work with the Del's staff to ensure that necessary security precautions were taken. Appropriate doors were padlocked in all areas the presidents would visit during their thirteen-hour stay, all windows were secured, and even the mailbox was sealed to prevent a bomb from being planted.

President Nixon arranged to have special White House china flown in (ivory with a green band and the presidential seal). Giant telephone switchboards with hot lines to Washington and Moscow were installed.

Approximately 100,000 people lined the streets of Coronado to cheer the president's motorcade as it drove to the hotel. In the crush of handshaking at the hotel, President Nixon lost one of his cuff links, which was never to be found.

President Nixon served as master of ceremonies, sharing speeches with former president Lyndon Johnson, who was a close personal friend of Diaz Ordaz. Whether you were a Nixon fan or not, you will enjoy the recipes of this once-in-a-lifetime pageant.

Another very special day for the Hotel del Coronado was when Jimmy Carter became the ninth U.S. president to visit the hotel. President Carter's visit occurred during a whirlwind tour of Southern California that included a speaking engagement at the eightieth annual convention of the AFL Building and Construction Trades Department in San Diego. As part of his welcome, a morning reception was held at the hotel, arranged by the supervisors of San Diego County. In President Carter's address, he recalled his early days in San Diego as a young naval officer. More than 350 people attended the reception, sipping fresh orange-cantaloupe juice from scooped-out orange shells while waiting to shake the president's hand as he circled the well-guarded ballroom.

Some twelve years after Nixon's visit, President Ronald Reagan hosted a minisummit conference with President Miguel de la Madrid of Mexico on October 18, 1982. A luncheon in the Coronet Room attended by international notables was followed by the minisummit in room 3253, which has been since renamed the Summit Suite.

A team of 150 White House security specialists set up protective measures. All outdoor areas through which President Reagan would walk from his limousine to the hotel were tented. Inside the hotel, the tenting continued from the suite where the minisummit meeting was held to the Coronet Room where the luncheon was served. The executive chef and his culinary team were not allowed to prepare any portion of the menu until a team of five security agents were in place to observe and to taste every item that was to be served to the president. The president's decaffeinated coffee was prepared by a presidential aide, who carried the ingredients in a suitcase. The heavy Coronet chandelier suspended directly over the presidential table was provided with additional support to ensure the president's safety. Before the luncheon, a security agent performed a Tarzan act by swinging on the chandelier to test the strength of its supports.

PRESIDENTS AT THE HOTEL DEL CORONADO

Top left: PRES. WOODROW WILSON

Top right: PRES. FRANKLIN D. ROOSEVELT

Botton left: PRES. BENJAMIN HARRISON

Several of the thirteen U.S. presidents that have visited the Hotel del Coronado during, before, or after their terms of office include Woodrow Wilson, F. D. Roosevelt, and Benjamin Harrison.

During a whirlwind tour through Baja California in September of 1991, President Carlos Salinas de Gortari of Mexico affirmed his national commitment to protect the dolphins by making Mexican tuna fishing 'dolphin-free.' He began and ended his visit in Mexico at Tijuana's international airport. He then flew into San Diego, where a police motorcade took him across the Coronado bay bridge to the Hotel del Coronado for a six-hour visit with Governor Pete Wilson of California.

You can prepare a presidential dinner of elegance with your choice of Nixon's Prime Sirloin Mexicana, Reagan's Médaillons of Alaskan Salmon, or Salinas' Mahi Mahi topped with Poached Scallops.

President Richard M. Nixon

President Richard M. Nixon selected the Hotel del Coronado for a dramatic state dinner because he knew that there was no dining room in America that equaled the Crown Room in scale, aesthetic beauty, and elegance. This was the largest state dinner ever held in the hotel. It was an ideal setting for the pomp and ceremony that President Nixon felt was necessary for him to host President Gustavo Diaz Ordaz of Mexico. The menu was a combination of the best of Mexican and American cuisines.

STATE DINNER MENU

Washington Chowder

Hearts of Artichoke Salad
Walnut Oil Dressing

Fillet of Sea Bass
Beurre Blanc Sauce

Prime Sirloin Mexicana
Español Sauce

Potato Fans

Colossal Asparagus in Lemon Butter

Lemon-Herb Jack Cheese Slices

Bombe Guadalupe

Washington Chowder

¼ cup bacon, chopped
3 tbsp. butter
½ cup celery, chopped
½ cup onion, chopped
¼ cup green bell pepper, chopped
2 bay leaves
½ tsp. crushed thyme
Salt and white pepper to taste
2 tbsp. flour
2½ cups Chicken Stock
    (see recipe)
½ cup russet potatoes, chopped
1 cup frozen whole kernel corn,
    defrosted
½ cup half-and-half

1. In a dutch oven, render bacon. Add butter, celery, onion, bell pepper, bay leaves, thyme, salt, and white pepper. Simmer for 5 minutes. Stir in flour and continue to cook, stirring for 3 minutes.

2. Add chicken stock, potatoes, and corn. Cover and simmer for 10 minutes, or until potatoes are tender. Season with additional salt and white pepper if necessary. Soup should be just somewhat thick in consistency.

3. Remove from heat and blend in half-and-half. Serve in soup bowls.

Serves 4.

Hearts of Artichoke Salad with Walnut Oil Dressing

Salad:
1 head butter lettuce
12 canned artichokes, drained
2 medium-size oranges
4 tbsp. minced walnuts
3 scallions (green part only),
    thinly sliced diagonally

Walnut Oil Dressing:
½ cup walnut oil
½ cup champagne vinegar
⅓ cup water
½ tsp. salt
⅛ tsp. freshly ground black
    pepper

1. Wash and dry lettuce, then core and separate head into twelve leaves.
2. Cut artichokes into thirty-six slices.
3. Peel oranges, remove pith, and separate into twelve segments.

Whisk together all the ingredients.

Yields about ⅞ cup.

To Assemble:
1. Arrange three leaves of butter lettuce on the left side of each of four salad plates. Place nine artichoke slices on top lettuce leaves on each plate.
2. Place three orange segments on the right side of each salad plate. Sprinkle top of orange segments with minced walnuts. Sprinkle scallions on top of artichoke slices.
3. Drizzle Walnut Oil Dressing over salad.

Serves 4.

Fillet of Sea Bass on Beurre Blanc Sauce

Sea Bass:
2 tbsp. butter or margarine
½ tsp. salt
¼ tsp. white pepper
½ tsp. fines herbes
4 4-oz. sea bass fillets
**2 lemons, cut into slices
   (for garnish)**
4 sprigs chervil (for garnish)

Beurre Blanc Sauce:
2 shallots, peeled and sliced
2 tbsp. chopped chives
⅔ cup dry vermouth
2 cups Fish Stock (see recipe)
1 cup heavy cream
1 tsp. salt
¼ tsp. white pepper

1. In a large skillet, melt butter or margarine. Sprinkle salt, white pepper, and fines herbes over sea bass, then place it in melted butter. Sauté over low heat for about 5 to 7 minutes, until fish is opaque. Do not allow it to color.

2. Carefully remove fillets from skillet, cover and keep warm. Add shallots to the skillet, then cover and cook over moderate heat, shaking the pan occasionally, until shallots are soft. Stir in chives, vermouth, and fish stock. Simmer until mixture is reduced to about ½ to ¾ cup. Stir in heavy cream and simmer until mixture is slightly thickened.

3. Transfer mixture to a blender, purée and season with salt and white pepper. Return sauce to skillet and reheat gently.

4. Divide sauce and spoon onto four dinner plates. Place warm fish on the sauce. Garnish with a lemon slice and sprig of chervil.

Serves 4.

Prime Sirloin Mexicana with Español Sauce

Español Sauce:
1 yellow bell pepper, chopped
1 green bell pepper, chopped
1 large onion, chopped
1 28-oz. can plum tomatoes
1 small green chile, minced
**½ cup (1 stick) butter or
   margarine**
**3 tbsp. cornstarch dissolved in
   3 tbsp. water**

1. Place chopped bell peppers in a small saucepan; add enough water to cover. Bring to a boil and cook for 10 minutes; strain and discard water.

2. Place chopped onion in same small saucepan; add enough water to cover. Bring to a boil and cook for 10 minutes; strain and discard water.

3. Empty can of tomatoes into a large saucepan; coarsely chop. Add green chile, butter or margarine, dissolved cornstarch, cooked peppers and onions. Simmer uncovered for 20 minutes. Set aside.

Note: Boiling the bell peppers and onions removes the acid bitter taste.

Steaks:

2 tbsp. olive oil
4 7-oz. New York strip steaks
1 tsp. salt
¼ tsp. freshly ground black
** pepper**
4 sprigs cilantro (for garnish)

1. In a large skillet, heat olive oil.
2. Season steaks with salt and pepper, then place in oil. Sauté steaks for about 6 to 10 minutes on each side for medium-cooked steaks (1-inch thick).

To Serve:
1. Spoon Español Sauce over steaks.
2. Garnish with cilantro sprigs.

Serves 4.

Potato Fans

2 russet potatoes
1 tbsp. butter or margarine,
** softened**
Salt and freshly ground black
** pepper to taste**
1¼ cups Chicken Stock, or as
** needed (see recipe)**

1. Preheat oven to 350 degrees.
2. Peel potatoes and cut in half lengthwise. Make parallel slices lengthwise, leaving the potatoes intact at the base, fan-style.
3. Place potatoes in a greased baking pan. Brush tops with butter or margarine. Season with salt and pepper.
4. In a small saucepan, bring chicken stock to a simmer, pour over potato fans. Bake in oven about 1 hour, until tender and golden brown.

Serves 4.

Colossal Asparagus in Lemon Butter

16 large asparagus spears
1½ tsp. salt
¼ cup butter or margarine, melted
⅛ cup fresh lemon juice

1. Cut away tough ends of asparagus stalks. If stalks are thick, peel lower few inches away with a vegetable parer. Wash asparagus spears, then tie them together with string.
2. Place asparagus standing upright in a tall pot or vegetable steamer; add boiling water and 1 teaspoon salt. Cook over medium heat for about 8 minutes (do not overcook). Drain and set aside.
3. In a small mixing bowl, combine ½ teaspoon salt, melted butter or margarine, and lemon juice.
4. Drain and separate asparagus, then pour lemon butter over them. Serve immediately.

Serves 4.

Lemon-Herb Jack Cheese Slices

8 oz. Monterey Jack cheese, at
   room temperature
1 tbsp. olive oil
1 tsp. lemon juice
1 tsp. oregano
4 leaves red kale lettuce or 8
   radicchio leaves
6 red seedless grapes, cut in
   half lengthwise
4 sprigs watercress (for garnish)
Water crackers

1. Slice cheese into twelve slices.

2. In a small mixing bowl, whisk olive oil, lemon juice, and oregano together. Dip cheese slices into mixture.

3. Place one red kale lettuce leaf or two radicchio leaves on each of four salad plates. Lay three cheese slices on each plate and top each cheese slice with a grape half.

4. Garnish with a watercress sprig and serve with water crackers.

Serves 4.

Bombe Guadalupe

½ cup golden raisins
1 8-oz. pkg. pitted dates, chopped
½ cup pistachio nuts, chopped
2 tbsp. amaretto liqueur or brandy
3 qts. pistachio ice cream,
   softened
1 cup Amaretti Di Saronno
   Italian cookies, crushed

1. In a large mixing bowl, combine raisins, dates, pistachio nuts, and amaretto liqueur or brandy. Let mixture stand at room temperature for 1 hour.

2. Fold ice cream into fruit mixture; then fold in ½ cup crushed cookies. Spoon mixture into a 3-quart mold. Cover and freeze overnight.

3. Loosen sides of mold with a knife and dip mold into a large bowl of very warm water. Immediately invert bombe onto a serving platter. Place bombe in freezer for 1 hour.

4. Pat remaining ½ cup of cookie crumbs over bombe. Serve immediately.

Note: Amaretti Di Saronno cookies may be found in most Italian markets or in the gourmet section of some supermarkets.

Serves 4.

President Jimmy Carter

Although President Jimmy Carter's visit lasted less than one hour, special preparations were made by the hotel, including the installation of new carpeting in the Grand Ballroom the day before the president arrived. All the woodwork in the ballroom was given a fresh coat of paint, so the Grand Lady by the Sea would again sparkle as she hosted the president of the United States. The pastry chef, with a crew of fourteen, prepared Heart Scones with Cinnamon Butter, Fudge Muffins, and other bakery delights.

Shortly before the president was to arrive, the secret service brought in specially trained guard dogs. The dogs promptly raced across the ballroom floor, sniffing and pulling just enough on the lace tablecloths to topple a pyramid of heart scones to the floor. However, everything was replaced and in perfect order by the time the president reached the hotel.

MENU

Orange-Cantaloupe Juice in Orange Shells

Blueberries and Honeyed Apricots

Lemon-Glazed Muffins

Pecan Rolls

Heart Scones with Cinnamon Butter

Fudge Muffins

Butter Crescents

The Del's Freshly Brewed Coffee

Best wishes to Beverly Bartelle,
Jimmy Carter

The author welcomes President Jimmy Carter to a reception held in the Grand Ballroom in 1979.

Orange-Cantaloupe Juice in Orange Shells

1 qt. freshly squeezed orange
  juice
1 cup ripe cantaloupe, peeled
  and cubed
1 tbsp. honey
1 tsp. orange peel, grated
8 orange shells

1. Combine orange juice, cantaloupe cubes, honey, and orange peel in a blender. Blend well.
2. Pour into 8 orange shells.

Note: See the recipe for Smashing Citrus Cocktails for the instructions to make orange shells.

Yields 16 ½-cup servings.

Blueberries and Honeyed Apricots

4 oz. fresh orange juice
2 tbsp. fresh lemon juice
2 oz. honey
8 ripe apricots, pitted and sliced
1 lb. blueberries, washed and
  drained

1. In a medium-size mixing bowl, blend together orange and lemon juices. Add honey and stir until it is dissolved. Add apricots and blueberries.
2. Refrigerate for 1 hour before serving.

Note: Blueberries and Honeyed Apricots may be prepared a day in advance.

Serves 8.

Pecan Rolls

3 eggs
⅔ cup sugar
½ tsp. plus ¾ cup butter or
  margarine, melted
1 cup sour cream
2 pkg. yeast sprinkled in ¼ cup
  warm water
1 tsp. salt
5 heaping cups all-purpose
  flour, sifted once
48 pecans
12 tsp. brown sugar

1. Beat eggs in a large mixing bowl. Stir in sugar, ½ teaspoon butter or margarine, and sour cream. Add dissolved yeast, mix thoroughly, then add salt and flour. Stir gently, cover, and refrigerate overnight.
2. The following morning, remove dough from refrigerator. Allow dough to rise for about one hour. Transfer to a lightly floured cutting board and knead until all bubbles are removed. Roll out dough to ½-inch thickness. Cut out rounds with a 2-inch cookie cutter.
3. Place 4 pecans, 1 tablespoon melted butter, and 1 teaspoon brown sugar in the bottom of each cup of a 12-cup muffin tin.
4. Place each round on top of pecan mixture and let rise at room temperature until more than double in size.
5. Bake at 350 degrees for 15 minutes; then reduce heat to 325 degrees and bake for 15 minutes more.
6. Remove from oven, invert tin to remove rolls, and allow to cool.

Yields 24 rolls.

Lemon-Glazed Muffins

Muffins:
2 cups all-purpose flour
⅓ cup sugar
2 tsp. baking powder
1 tbsp. lemon peel,
   grated
½ cup pecans, chopped
1 tsp. vanilla
¼ tsp. lemon extract
⅛ tsp. mace
¼ tsp. cinnamon
1 egg
1 cup milk
⅓ cup butter or margarine,
   melted
Lemon Glaze (recipe follows)

1. Preheat oven to 400 degrees.
2. In a large mixing bowl, combine flour, sugar, baking powder, lemon peel, and pecans.
3. In a small mixing bowl, beat together vanilla, lemon extract, mace, cinnamon, egg, milk, and butter or margarine. Add liquid mixture to flour mixture and stir until just moist.
4. Grease a twelve-cup muffin tin. Fill cups with batter about ⅔ full. Bake for 20 to 25 minutes. Remove muffins from oven and carefully spoon lemon glaze over the hot muffins.

Yields 12 muffins.

Lemon Glaze:
¼ cup plus 1 tbsp. freshly
   squeezed lemon juice
1 cup confectioners' sugar

In a small mixing bowl, stir lemon juice into sugar until smooth.

Yields about ¼ cup.

Fudge Muffins

1 lb. unsalted butter
8 oz. sweet baking
   chocolate
3½ cups sugar
2 cups all-purpose flour, sifted
2 tsp. baking powder
Pinch of salt
8 eggs
2 tsp. vanilla
4 cups pecans, coarsely chopped
36 pecans

1. Preheat oven to 350 degrees.
2. Line muffin tins with paper liners.
3. In the top of a double boiler, melt butter and chocolate together.
4. In a large mixing bowl, combine sugar, flour, baking powder, and salt. Stir in chocolate mixture. Add eggs and vanilla. Whisk just until ingredients are evenly moistened; do not overmix. Fold in chopped pecans.
5. Fill cups with batter about ⅔ full. Top each with 1 pecan. Bake muffins for about 25 to 30 minutes, or until cake tester inserted in center of muffins comes out clean. Cool on racks and serve.

Yields 36 muffins.

Heart Scones with Cinnamon Butter

4 cups all-purpose flour
1½ tsp. baking soda
1 tbsp. cream of tartar
½ tsp. salt
¼ tsp. nutmeg
1 tbsp. sugar
8 oz. (2 sticks) unsalted butter,
  chilled and cut into small pieces
1 cup currants
2 eggs, lightly beaten
1 cup buttermilk
2 egg yolks
2 tbsp. milk

1. Preheat oven to 425 degrees.
2. In a large mixing bowl, combine flour, baking soda, cream of tartar, salt, nutmeg, and sugar.
3. Cut in the butter until mixture resembles coarse crumbs. Stir in the currants. Add beaten eggs and buttermilk. Stir gently until the ingredients are combined.
4. On a well-floured surface, roll out the dough to ½-inch thickness. Cut out about 16 hearts with a heart-shaped cutter. Place hearts on a lightly greased cookie sheet.
5. Beat egg yolks and milk together. Brush mixture over the tops of the scones.
6. Bake until well risen and golden brown, 12 to 15 minutes.

Note: Scones may be prepared a day ahead and reheated in a 200-degree oven for about 5 minutes.

Yields about 16 scones.

Cinnamon Butter:

1 cup lightly salted
  butter, softened
¼ cup firmly packed light
  brown sugar
1 tbsp. ground cinnamon

1. In a small mixing bowl, mix together butter, brown sugar and cinnamon until thoroughly blended.
2. Serve immediately or cover and refrigerate.

Yields about 1 cup.

To Serve:
Remove Cinnamon Butter from refrigerator and allow it to soften at room temperature for about 20 minutes. Serve scones warm with Cinnamon Butter.

Heart Scones with Cinnamon Butter.

Butter Crescents

½ cup butter or margarine,
    softened
½ cup confectioners' sugar
2 cups all-purpose flour, sifted
1 tsp. vanilla
1 cup walnuts, finely ground

1. Preheat oven to 350 degrees.
2. Place butter or margarine in a medium-size mixing bowl. Stir in confectioners' sugar, flour, vanilla, and ground walnuts. Mix thoroughly.
3. Roll dough into small balls, about teaspoon size. Place balls on an ungreased baking sheet. Shape each ball into a crescent.
4. Bake for 13 minutes. Watch carefully, making sure that crescents do not brown.

Yields about 28 crescents.

President Ronald Reagan

President Ronald Reagan chose the Coronet Room, which is part of the Crown Room, to host an elegant luncheon for President Miguel de la Madrid of Mexico. Under the regal chandelier designed by Frank L. Baum, a sumptuous lunch of Chilled Avocado Soup and Hearts of Palm Salad followed by Médaillons of Alaskan Salmon accented with Parisienne Potatoes and a Lattice of Green Beans was served on silver trays. A refreshing dessert of Fresh Fruit Kirsch and Almond Petits Fours ended the minisummit luncheon.

To serve this luncheon, the White House had its own waiters working with the hotel staff.

MENU

Chilled Avocado Soup with Caviar Dot

Hearts of Palm Salad
Herb Vinaigrette Dressing

Médaillons of Alaskan Salmon
Dill Beurre Blanc Sauce

Parisienne Potatoes

Lattice of Green Beans
Gingered Baby Carrots

Fresh Fruit Kirsch

Almond Petits Fours

Prior to his presidency, Ronald Reagan was a frequent visitor during his time as governor of California. He is shown here with (left to right) daughter Patti, wife Nancy, and son Ron, Jr. in 1958.

Chilled Avocado Soup with Caviar Dot

2 large ripe avocados
1½ cups Chicken Stock
 (see recipe)
1 cup sour cream
¼ cup dry vermouth
1 tbsp. fresh lemon juice
1 tbsp. fresh lime juice
1 medium-size onion, chopped
1 tsp. salt
½ tsp. white pepper
½ tsp. garlic powder
4 cups iceberg lettuce, shredded
1 oz. black lumpfish caviar
1 oz. American red caviar
24 lemon leaves, washed and dried

1. Cut avocados in half lengthwise and remove pits. Carefully remove avocado from shells and dice. Leave enough avocado adhering to shell to form a cup. Cut a thin slice from the bottom of the shells if necessary to stabilize them.

2. In a blender or food processor, combine diced avocado, chicken stock, sour cream, vermouth, lemon juice, lime juice, and onion. Purée. Season with salt, pepper, and garlic powder. If soup is too thick, add additional stock.

3. Cover and refrigerate for about 3 hours.

To Assemble:

1. Place 1 cup shredded lettuce on each of four salad plates. Set avocado shells on top of lettuce and pour chilled soup into avocado shells.

2. Float a dot of black lumpfish caviar and a dot of American red caviar in center of soup.

3. Place 6 lemon leaves around each avocado shell.

Serves 4.

Hearts of Palm Salad with Herb Vinaigrette Dressing

Salad:
½ cup pine nuts
Salt
**12 radicchio leaves, washed
  and dried**
**8 butter lettuce leaves,
  washed and dried**
**1 16-oz. can hearts of palm,
  cut into 12 1-inch slices**
2 tomatoes, cut into 12 wedges

1. Preheat oven to 350 degrees.
2. Spread pine nuts on a nonstick cookie sheet, sprinkle lightly with salt. Bake for 3 minutes, watching carefully that they do not burn; then remove from oven and set aside.

Herb Vinaigrette:
¾ cup virgin olive oil
½ cup champagne vinegar
⅓ cup water
2 tbsp. fresh lemon juice
2 tsp. dried dill leaves
1 tsp. dried oregano
1 tsp. dried fennel
2 tsp. dried chives
¼ tsp. salt
⅛ tsp. white pepper

In a small bowl, whisk together all the ingredients.

Yields about 1⅓ cups.

To Assemble:
1. Arrange 3 radicchio leaves and 2 leaves of butter lettuce on each of four salad plates.
2. Arrange 3 slices of hearts of palm at the 6 o'clock position.
3. Arrange 3 tomato wedges on the right side of the layered lettuce. Sprinkle salads with pine nuts and top with Herb Vinaigrette.

Serves 4.

Médaillons of Alaskan Salmon Dill Beurre Blanc Sauce

Salmon:
**1¾ pounds fillet of salmon,
  bones removed**
1 tbsp. butter or margarine
Salt
White pepper
4 sprigs fresh dill (for garnish)

1. Cut salmon into 12 slices, ¾ inch thick.
2. In a large skillet, heat butter or margarine. Place salmon médaillons in skillet and cover with a tight lid. Cook over medium-low heat for approximately 3 minutes. Turn and cook 3 more minutes. Turn off heat, salt and pepper both sides, then allow médaillons to rest for 1 minute. Set aside and keep warm.

Dill Beurre Blanc Sauce:

6 shallots, peeled and chopped
1 cup white wine
1 cup Fish Stock
  (see recipe)
⅓ cup heavy cream
1 cup very cold butter,
  cut into small pieces
¼ tsp. salt
⅛ tsp. pepper
⅛ cup fresh dill,
  chopped

1. In a medium-size saucepan, combine shallots, wine, and stock. Cook over low heat until mixture is reduced by two-thirds. Add heavy cream and blend thoroughly.

2. Remove from heat and add butter, one piece at a time, stirring constantly until all the butter has been added.

3. Add salt, pepper, and fresh chopped dill. Stir well. Keep warm until served.

Note: Instructions for assembly with potatoes, green beans, and baby carrots follow recipe for Gingered Baby Carrots.

Serves 4.

Parisienne Potatoes

3 large russet potatoes
6 tbsp. clarified butter
  (see recipe)
Salt
White pepper

1. Peel potatoes, then scoop out balls from the potatoes with a melon-ball cutter. Dry potato balls well with a paper towel.

2. In a heavy skillet, heat butter over medium-high heat. Sauté the potatoes, shaking the skillet, until they are golden brown.

3. Sprinkle potatoes with salt and white pepper. Reduce heat to low and cook potatoes covered, shaking the skillet occasionally, so potatoes do not stick. Cook for about 12 to 15 minutes, or until potatoes are tender. Remove from skillet.

Serves 4.

Lattice of Green Beans

¾ lb. fresh green beans,
  ends removed
¼ cup virgin olive oil
2 large cloves garlic,
  peeled and minced
1 tsp. salt
1 tsp. lemon pepper
1 tsp. coriander

1. In a medium-size saucepan, steam beans for 7 minutes, or until they are crisp-tender, but still bright green. Rinse under cold water, drain, and set aside.

2. Heat oil in a saucepan or skillet. Add garlic, then cook over low heat until the garlic is tender, but not brown. Cool the oil briefly, then pour the oil and garlic mixture over the beans. Add salt, lemon pepper, and coriander. Allow the beans to absorb flavors for at least 1 hour.

3. Reheat before serving.

Note: Save any remaining green beans for a tossed salad the next day.

Serves 4.

Gingered Baby Carrots

12 baby carrots
¾ cup orange juice
1 teaspoon fresh ginger, minced
Water

1. Cut tops off baby carrots leaving ¼ inch of green stem. Scrape carrots.
2. In a medium-size saucepan, combine carrots, orange juice, ginger, and enough water to cover carrots. Boil until carrots are tender, approximately 12 to 15 minutes.
3. Drain and serve.

Note: Fresh minced ginger is available in 7½-ounce jars at Asian markets.

Serves 4.

To Assemble Plate:
1. Spoon 2 ounces of Dill Beurre Blanc Sauce on each of four dinner plates. Arrange 3 Médaillons of Alaskan King Salmon on top of sauce in a fan shape. Place dill sprig in the center of médaillons.
2. Arrange 3 Gingered Baby Carrots to the left of the salmon. Arrange Parisienne Potatoes at the 12 o'clock position on each plate.
3. Place green beans crisscrossed to the right of the salmon fillets. (See photograph at beginning of this chapter.)

Fresh Fruit Kirsch

1 orange
½ mango
1 fresh peach
½ fresh pineapple
1 red delicious apple,
    unpeeled
1 banana
⅔ cup grapes
1 star fruit, peeled
    and sliced
3 oz. kirsch

1. Peel orange and remove white membrane. Peel mango and peach. Core and remove rind from pineapple. Core apple. Cut fruit into bite-size pieces. Peel banana and slice. Transfer all fruit except star fruit to a medium-size mixing bowl and fold in grapes.
2. Divide fruit into four dessert bowls. Place star fruit slice on top of each portion. Refrigerate.
3. Pour kirsch over fruit and serve very cold.

Serves 4.

Almond Petits Fours

Almond Cake:
1¼ cup almond paste
¾ cups sugar
¾ cup unsalted butter
    (at room temperature),
    cut into small pieces
4 large eggs
2 oz. all-purpose flour
1 tsp. almond extract
Vegetable cooking oil spray
Flour (for dusting
    baking pan)
4 oz. raspberry jam

1. Preheat oven to 350 degrees.
2. In a large mixing bowl, combine almond paste and sugar; then blend with an electric mixer until thoroughly mixed.
3. Add 4 tablespoons butter, then add eggs one at a time and beat until mixture is smooth, about 4 minutes.
4. Add flour and almond extract. Continue to beat until mixture is smooth.
5. Spray a 15½ x 10 x ¾-inch baking pan with nonstick vegetable spray. Dust lightly with flour. Add batter and bake for 14 to 15 minutes, until golden brown.
6. Remove cake from oven, cool, and place on a cutting board. Cut cake in half horizontally. Spread jam over one layer of cake, then cover with second layer. Refrigerate layer cake for 3 hours.

Petits Fours Glaze:
8 cups confectioners' sugar
½ cup water
½ cup light corn syrup
2 tsp. almond extract

1. Mix all ingredients in top of double boiler until smooth.
2. Heat just until lukewarm, then remove from heat. Let glaze remain over hot water to prevent thickening. If necessary, add hot water, a few drops at a time, for desired consistency.

Decorator Frosting:
2 cups confectioners' sugar
2 to 3 tbsp. water
Red and yellow food coloring

1. In a small mixing bowl, combine confectioners' sugar and water. Blend thoroughly. If frosting is too stiff, add a few more drops of water. Divide frosting into two portions. Tint one-half of the frosting with red food coloring and tint the remaining frosting with yellow food coloring.
2. Transfer frosting into decorating bags with small-size tips.

To Assemble:
1. Remove layer cake from refrigerator and place on a cutting board. With a 1¾-inch round cutter, cut out twenty circles of cake.
2. Place cakes on wire racks over a jelly-roll pan. Pour glaze over tops and sides of cakes. Allow glaze to harden.
3. Pipe designs and borders on Petits Fours with tinted decorator frosting as you desire. Transfer to a serving platter.

Yields 20.

President
Carlos Salinas de Gortari

President Carlos Salinas de Gortari of Mexico visited with Governor Pete Wilson of California at the Hotel del Coronado in September of 1991. The Center for United States-Mexican Studies at the University of California at San Diego, which hosted the visit, chose the Crown Room for a luncheon of Smoked Carpaccio with Aioli Sauce, followed by a delicate salad of Baby Greens with Truffle Vinaigrette Dressing. Sautéed Fillet of Mahimahi topped with Poached Scallops was the entree. A composite of fresh Mixed Berries with Citrus-Yogurt Sauce concluded the luncheon.

MENU

Smoked Carpaccio with Aioli Sauce

Baby Greens with Truffle Vinaigrette Dressing

Fillet of Mahimahi Topped
with Poached Scallops
Tri-Pepper Wine Sauce

Pimiento-Chive Rice Pilaf

Yellow Crookneck Squash
filled with Broccoli Florets

Mixed Berries with Citrus-Yogurt Sauce

Smoked Carpaccio with Aioli Sauce

Carpaccio:
1 tbsp. butter or margarine
1 tbsp. liquid smoke
1 8-oz. filet mignon
Salt
Freshly ground pepper
1 oz. fresh Parmesan cheese,
  grated

1. In a medium-size skillet, melt butter or margarine. Spoon liquid smoke over filet mignon, then sear for 1 minute on each side. Lightly salt and pepper steak.
2. Cool steak and place in the freezer for about 10 minutes, or until firm enough to slice paper-thin.
3. Remove steak from freezer. Cut in paper-thin slices with an electric knife. Set aside.

Aioli Sauce:
3 garlic cloves, peeled and minced
½ tsp. salt
1 cup mayonnaise
1 tbsp. extra virgin olive oil
½ tsp. fresh lemon juice
Dash Tabasco

1. Mash garlic and salt in a small bowl using the back of a spoon, or in a mortar using a pestle.
2. Transfer garlic and salt mixture to a medium-size bowl. Whisk in mayonnaise, olive oil, lemon juice, and Tabasco. Refrigerate until cold.

Note: Aioli sauce may be prepared a week ahead of time if covered and kept refrigerated.

To Assemble:

1. Spoon 2 ounces of Aioli Sauce onto each of four salad plates.

2. Divide filet mignon slices into four portions. Arrange beef slices overlapping on top of the Aioli Sauce.

3. Sprinkle with additional freshly ground pepper and Parmesan cheese.

Serves 4.

Baby Greens with Truffle Vinaigrette Dressing

2 cups baby romaine
2 cups baby oak leaf lettuce
1 egg yolk
1 oz. balsamic vinegar
1 oz. brandy
1 oz. truffles, chopped with juice
½ tsp. Dijon-style mustard
½ tsp. fresh garlic, peeled
    and minced

1. Wash and dry lettuce, tear into bite-size pieces and mix together.

2. In a small mixing bowl, combine egg yolk, balsamic vinegar, brandy, chopped truffles with their juice, mustard, and garlic. Whisk until well blended.

3. Divide lettuce onto four salad plates. Sprinkle with dressing.

Serves 4.

Fillet of Mahimahi Topped with Poached Scallops and Tri-Pepper Wine Sauce

Fish:
4 4-oz. mahimahi fillets
½ cup all-purpose flour
2 tbsp. olive oil
1 clove garlic, peeled and minced
2 ti leaves, washed and dried

1. Preheat oven to 350 degrees.

2. Dredge mahimahi fillets in flour, set aside.

3. In a large skillet, heat oil until hot but not smoking. Add garlic and fillets. Sauté for 1 minute on each side.

4. Remove fillets from skillet and transfer to a greased 13 x 9 x 2-inch baking pan. Bake fillets at 350 degrees for about 10 minutes.

Poached Scallops:
2 tbsp. fresh lemon juice
2 tbsp. fresh lime juice
2 tsp. cilantro, chopped
2 tsp. salt
⅛ tsp. white pepper
8 large scallops (about ¼ lb.)
1 cup Fish Stock (see recipe)

1. In a medium-size mixing bowl, combine lemon juice, lime juice, cilantro, salt, and pepper. Add scallops and stir gently; then refrigerate for 30 minutes.

2. Remove scallops from refrigerator. Transfer to a saucepan. Add stock and bring to a simmer; then poach for about 5 to 7 minutes. Remove from poaching liquid.

Tri-Pepper Wine Sauce:

1 tbsp. olive oil
1 tsp. red bell pepper, chopped
1 tsp. yellow bell pepper, chopped
1 tsp. green bell pepper, chopped
2 tbsp. flour
½ cup chablis wine
1 cup Fish Stock (see recipe)
½ tsp. salt
⅛ tsp. white pepper

1. While fillets are baking, add olive oil and peppers to the same skillet used for sautéing the mahimahi. Sauté for 1 minute.

2. Add flour, wine, fish stock, salt, and pepper. Cook and stir until sauce is thickened. Set aside and keep warm.

Note: Instructions for assembling Fillet of Mahi Mahi topped with Poached Scallops and Tri-Pepper Wine Sauce plate follow the recipe for Yellow Crookneck Squash filled with Broccoli Florets.

Serves 4.

Pimiento-Chive Rice Pilaf

2 tbsp. unsalted butter
1 cup long-grain white rice
1½ cups Chicken Stock
  (see recipe)
1 tbsp. Tio Pepe sherry wine
2 tbsp. pimiento, drained and diced
1 tbsp. fresh chives, chopped
1 tsp. salt
¼ tsp. white pepper

1. In a medium-size saucepan, melt 1 tablespoon of butter over medium heat. Add rice and cook, stirring, until butter is absorbed.

2. Add stock and sherry, stir well, and increase heat to high. Bring rice to a boil; then reduce heat to low. When froth settles, stir and cover. Continue to cook for about 20 minutes until liquid is absorbed. Turn off heat and let rice set with cover tilted for 10 minutes.

3. With a spatula, fold in pimiento, chives, salt, and pepper. Serve immediately or mold into individual custard cups.

To Mold:

1. Grease custard cups. Add remaining tablespoon of soft butter to prepared rice and blend to melt.

2. Carefully spoon rice mixture into cups and pack down with the back of a spoon. Do not overpack. Cover cups with foil and place in a 350-degree oven for 15 minutes, or until heated through.

3. When ready to serve, remove foil and quickly turn over onto plate. Tap bottom of cups with spoon and rice will unmold easily.

Serves 4.

Yellow Crookneck Squash Filled with Broccoli Florets

8 yellow crookneck squash (about 2½ lb.)
1 pint water
1 tsp. onion powder
1 tsp. garlic salt
¼ tsp. white pepper
4 tbsp. butter or margarine, melted
12 broccoli florets

1. Carefully hollow out inside of crookneck squash. Cut a thin slice off the bottom of each squash, so it will stand upright. Place the squash in a medium-size saucepan; add water, onion powder, garlic salt, and pepper. Cook for 5 minutes.

2. Remove squash from water and rinse in cold water. Pour 2 tablespoons melted butter or margarine over squash.

3. Add broccoli florets to same seasoned cooking water; bring to a boil. Cook for 3 minutes, then remove from water and rinse in cold water.

4. Arrange florets into hollowed out squash. Pour remaining 2 tablespoons butter over florets and transfer to a 13 x 9 x 2-inch baking pan. Bake for 15 minutes in a 350-degree oven.

Serves 4.

To Assemble Plate:

1. Place ½ ti leaf on each of four dinner plates. Place a mahimahi fillet on top of each ti leaf. Place two scallop slices atop each fillet. Spoon Tri-Pepper Wine Sauce over scallops and mahimahi.

2. Arrange Pimiento Chive Rice Pilaf mold on the right side of dinner plate.

3. Place two Yellow Crookneck Squash filled with Broccoli Florets at the 6 o'clock position on each plate.

Mixed Berries with Citrus-Yogurt Sauce

½ cup strawberries
½ cup blueberries
½ cup boysenberries
½ cup raspberries
8 oz. yogurt
2 tbsp. orange juice
1 lemon
1 lime
1 orange

1. Wash and dry berries and carefully combine them in a medium-size mixing bowl.
2. In a small mixing bowl, combine yogurt and orange juice. Blend thoroughly.
3. With a potato peeler, peel two strips of outer rind from the lemon, lime, and orange. Cut strips into fine slivers, or use a zester to make citrus strips.

Note: The zest of citrus fruit is the outer colored layer of skin—not the white pith, which is bitter, or the actual flesh of the fruit.

To Assemble:
1. Divide the berries into four portions and place them in four stemware glasses.
2. Spoon orange-yogurt mixture over berries, and top each with lemon, lime, and orange zest.

Serves 4.

CHAPTER THREE

Cocktail Buffets

Irresistible tidbits of Jalapeño Cheese Straws and Smoked Trout and Dill Endive Spears are ideal to serve with cocktails or as a prelude to dinner. Before dinner tidbits allow you the opportunity to display your culinary talents while stimulating enthusiasm for the dinner to follow. Include an arrangement of three or four colorful, elegant hors d'oeuvres displayed on silver trays for a variety of bite-size enticements.

A cocktail buffet is one of the most popular and versatile ways to entertain. It can be simple yet sophisticated—a combination of old favorites and trendy new ideas. Guests look forward to cocktail buffets because they are able to help themselves to a variety of exotic and innovative creations. The work of the host and hostess is essentially over once the buffet table has been set, so they can enjoy the party with their special guests. At a cocktail buffet, you can offer your guests enough to eat to balance and complement their cocktails, making dinner unnecessary.

Plan your menu around a theme such as the Del's Valentine Buffet. Hearts are the main attraction, and you can accomplish many things with heart-shaped cookie cutters. They can be used to cut out cocktail bread for an attractive cheese board with cheeses that are also cut into heart shapes. Brie cheese infused with cognac can be easily shaped to resemble a heart. Heart-shaped petits fours

are an excellent way to sweeten your cocktail buffet.

For an upscale cocktail party, invite a small, select group of movie devotees for an 'Academy Award-Winning Buffet.' Set a table with a black tablecloth and gold runners down the center of the table. Place a black top hat in the center of the table, and set out various sizes and shapes of gold candles. The scene is set for dining on Nova Scotia Salmon Cheese Cake and Coconut Shrimp with Tomatillo Relish. You will win an Oscar from your guests for your performance as a chef, and you earn stardom as a creative host.

For an informal cocktail buffet, invite your sports enthusiast friends and score a touchdown with a cocktail buffet for Super Bowl Sunday. Your guests will get into the cheering spirit with hearty fare such as Stuffed Edam Cheese with Dill-Sesame Crackers and Winning Goal-Post Beef Dip. Your guests may not all be cheering for the same team, but you will definitely be voted most valuable host or hostess.

As you look over your social calendar and add up the parties that you have attended, it could be time to just "Rejoice and Reciprocate" with a versatile cocktail buffet. Sugar-Spiced Pork Loin, Petite Noodle Pudding, and Roquefort-Stuffed Shrimp provide your guests an opportunity for gastronomic exploration, while you entertain old and new friends.

Valentine of Hearts Cocktail Buffet for Twenty-Four

Every year, the Del invites couples from San Diego County who were married at the Del from six months to fifty years ago to participate in a romantic rendezvous at the hotel on February fourteenth, Valentine's Day. Many couples take advantage of this invitation to renew their marriage vows in the hotel's picturesque Garden Patio. This one-of-a-kind event features a four-foot-tall wedding cake and refreshments.

For more than a century, the Del's legendary romantic allure has attracted those in love. The Duke and Duchess of Windsor and Ronald and Nancy Reagan have been some famous romantic couples from the past. Today, romantics from near and far enjoy Valentine's Day at the Del.

An early photograph of the Garden Patio. The hotel was built around a rectangular garden about an acre in size, with a fountain in the center (which was replaced by the gazebo shown). It was illuminated by means of incandescent lights and planted with almond, fig, loquat, lime, olive, banana, guava, lemon, orange, and pomegranate trees as well as other tropical plants and flowers.

MENU

Grand Marnier Beef Tenderloin

Jumbo Shrimp with Chili Dipping Sauce

Orange-Glazed Heart Sausages

Piquant Veal Meatballs

Spinach Bars

Red-Skinned New Potatoes with
Three Caviars

Cheese Board of Assorted Hearts with
Cocktail Rye and Pumpernickel Hearts

Brie Infused with Cognac and
Apricot Preserves

Petits Fours Hearts

Valentine of Hearts Cocktail Buffet. Center: *Piquant Veal Meatballs.* Clockwise from lower left: *Brie Cheese Heart infused with Cognac and Apricot Preserves, Jumbo Shrimp with Chili Dipping Sauce, Petits Four Hearts, Orange-Glazed Heart Sausages.*

Grand Marnier Beef Tenderloin

2 4-lb. beef tenderloins
Lemon pepper
Onion salt
2 tbsp. butter or margarine
1 cup Grand Marnier liqueur
2 tbsp. minced onion

1. Trim any fat off tenderloins. Rub tenderloins with lemon pepper and onion salt until they are well coated.
2. In a large skillet, melt 1 tablespoon butter or margarine. Sear tenderloin for about 1 minute on each side. Transfer to a 13 x 9 x 2-inch glass baking pan. Melt remaining tablespoon of butter or margarine and repeat procedure with other tenderloin.
3. With a sharp paring knife, cut very slightly in to the tops of the tenderloins. Pour Grand Marnier over tops of tenderloins. Top with onion. Refrigerate, covered, and marinate overnight.
4. Preheat oven to 375 degrees.
5. Remove tenderloins from refrigerator and bring to room temperature. Bake for 45 minutes for medium rare.
6. Remove from oven and allow tenderloins to rest for 15 minutes. Slice paper thin and place on a platter.
7. Serve with assorted mustards and small buns that have been partially split.

Serves 24.

Jumbo Shrimp with Chili Dipping Sauce

Shrimp:
72 (about 6 lb.) large
  shrimp, shelled
4 bay leaves

1. In a dutch oven, bring 2 quarts of water to a boil. Add shrimp and bay leaves. Cook and stir constantly until just done, about 3 to 4 minutes. Do not overcook.
2. Drain shrimp and immerse in cold water, drain again. Peel and devein shrimp and remove tails. Transfer to a serving bowl and refrigerate for at least 3 hours.

Chili Dipping Sauce:
1½ cups mayonnaise
¾ cup bottled barbecue sauce
2 drops Tabasco

1. In a medium-size mixing bowl, combine all the ingredients. Blend thoroughly.
2. Transfer to a small dish and serve with jumbo shrimp.

Serves 24.

Orange-Glazed Heart Sausages

3 lb. summer beef sausage, smoked and fully cooked
1 cup brown sugar
1 tbsp. flour
1 tbsp. Dijon-style mustard
1 tbsp. prepared mustard
1 tbsp. vinegar
¼ cup orange juice concentrate, undiluted

1. Slice sausage into about fifty-six ¼-inch slices. Spread slices out on a cutting board. Using a 2-inch heart-shaped cookie cutter, cut each slice into a heart. Set aside in a large mixing bowl. (Use the sausage scraps to enhance a tossed green salad.)

2. In a medium-size saucepan, combine all ingredients except the sausage hearts. Simmer over low heat for 25 minutes, stirring occasionally. Pour sauce over sausage hearts; then use a rubber spatula to mix carefully and coat all of the hearts. Transfer to a serving bowl or to a chafing dish to keep warm.

Yields about 56 hearts.

Piquant Veal Meatballs

Meatballs:
2 lb. ground veal
1 cup dry bread crumbs
⅓ cup chopped fresh parsley
⅓ cup ketchup
½ cup finely minced onion
2 eggs, slightly beaten
2 cloves garlic, peeled and minced
2 tbsp. soy sauce
¼ tsp. thyme
½ tsp. salt
¼ tsp. black pepper

1. In a large mixing bowl, combine all the ingredients and mix well. Cover mixture and place in refrigerator for about 2 hours to allow seasonings to blend.

2. Remove mixture from refrigerator and shape into balls the size of large olives. (Meatballs may be frozen at this point for later use.) Place meatballs in a 13 x 9 x 2-inch baking pan. Set aside.

Piquant Sauce:
1 16-oz. can jellied cranberry sauce
1 12-oz. bottle chili sauce
⅓ cup ketchup
2½ tbsp. dark brown sugar
1 tbsp. lemon juice

1. Preheat oven to 350 degrees.

2. In a medium-size saucepan, combine all the ingredients. Simmer over low heat, stirring well until sauce is heated through. Pour sauce over meatballs.

3. Bake uncovered for 45 minutes. Transfer to a serving dish or chafing dish and serve hot with cocktail forks or frilly toothpicks.

Yields about 60 meatballs.

Spinach Bars

4 tbsp. butter or margarine
3 eggs, slightly beaten
1 cup flour
1 tsp. baking powder
1 cup milk
½ tsp. garlic powder
½ tsp. salt
1 tsp. oregano
1 small onion, finely chopped
8 oz. cheddar cheese, grated
8 oz. jack cheese, grated
2 10-oz. pkg. frozen chopped spinach, thawed and thoroughly drained

1. Preheat oven to 350 degrees.
2. In a 13 x 9 x 2-inch baking pan, melt butter or margarine. Set aside.
3. In a large mixing bowl, combine all the remaining ingredients. Spoon into baking pan. Bake for 35 minutes.
4. Cool slightly before cutting into squares. Serve at room temperature.

Note: Spinach bars may be prepared in advance and frozen. Place baked bars on a cookie sheet and freeze. Transfer frozen bars to plastic bags. Before serving, remove from bags, place on cookie sheet, heat in oven at 325 degrees for 12 minutes.

Yields 24 bars.

Red-Skinned New Potatoes with Three Caviars

60 (about 3 lb.) tiny red-skinned new potatoes
Vegetable oil
1½ cups sour cream
2 oz. salmon caviar, well chilled
2 oz. black lumpfish caviar, rinsed, drained, and well chilled
2 oz. golden whitefish caviar, well chilled
⅓ cup minced chives

1. Preheat oven to 375 degrees.
2. Wash and thoroughly dry potatoes. Coat them lightly with vegetable oil. Place potatoes on baking sheets and bake for about 40 minutes, or until cooked.
3. Cut a thin slice off the top side of each potato. With a small melon ball scoop, remove the center portion of the potato and discard. Leave enough of the potato adhering to the sides, so the potatoes will stand up. It may be necessary to cut a very thin slice off the bottom of some of the potatoes to stand them up.
4. Spoon sour cream into potato cavities. Dot some with salmon caviar and others with black and golden whitefish caviar. Top with sprinkled chives.

Serves 24.

Cheese Board of Assorted Hearts with Cocktail Rye and Pumpernickel Hearts

½ lb. jalapeño jack cheese
2 lb. Port Salut cheese
3 lb. cheddar and mozzarella mixed cheese
1 lb. gouda cheese
1 loaf sliced cocktail rye bread
1 loaf sliced cocktail pumpernickel bread
3 tbsp. butter or margarine, softened
1 bunch purple grapes, washed and dried and cut into clusters

1. Slice all cheeses into ¼-inch slices. With a 1½-inch heart cutter, cut out cheese hearts. Set aside.

2. Spread cocktail rye bread and cocktail pumpernickel bread out on a wooden cutting board. Lightly butter slices. With the same 1½-inch heart cutter, cut out heart shapes from the bread slices.

3. Arrange cheese hearts and breads, placing them side-by-side on a platter or heart-shaped cutting board. Garnish with grape clusters.

Serves 24.

Brie Infused with Cognac and Apricot Preserves

4 or 5 lb. brie cheese
12 to 14 lemon leaves, washed and dried
1 cup apricot preserves
¾ cup cognac
2 boxes heart-shaped water crackers or 2 baguettes, cut into ½-inch slices
8 strawberries (for garnish)

1. Remove rind from brie. With a paring knife, round off corners to resemble a heart.

2. Allow brie to come to room temperature (about 1 hour). Arrange lemon leaves around the rim of a serving platter. Place brie on platter. Pierce top with a fork about 3 or 4 times. Set aside.

3. In a medium-size saucepan, combine apricot preserves and cognac. Simmer over low heat, stirring the mixture until it is hot, but not boiling. Pour mixture over brie and allow it to seep through the tiny holes for about 1 hour.

4. Serve with heart-shaped water crackers or sliced baguettes. Garnish with strawberries.

Serves 24.

Petits Fours Hearts

Hearts:

1 pkg. (18¼ oz.) white cake mix with pudding (and required ingredients for preparation)
Vegetable cooking spray

1. Following the package directions, prepare cake mix and bake in a 15½ x 10 x ¾-inch jellyroll pan that has been sprayed with nonstick vegetable spray.
2. Cut cake into small hearts with a 2-inch heart-shaped cutter. Place cakes on wire racks over the jellyroll pan.

Red Heart Glaze:

8 cups confectioner's sugar
½ cup water
½ cup light corn syrup
2 tsp. vanilla extract
1 drop red food coloring

1. Mix all ingredients in the top of double boiler until smooth. Heat just until lukewarm; then remove from heat.
2. Let glaze remain over hot water to prevent thickening. If necessary, add hot water, a few drops at a time, for desired consistency. (Glaze may be reheated and used again.)

Valentine Frosting:

2 cups confectioners' sugar
2 to 3 tsp. water

1. In a small mixing bowl, combine confectioners' sugar and water. Blend thoroughly. If frosting is too stiff, add a few drops of water.
2. Place frosting in a pastry bag.

To Assemble:

1. Pour Red Heart Glaze over cakes to coat tops and sides.
2. Use a small star tip to decorate edges of petits fours, outlining them with tiny stars. With a 1-S pastry tip, you can write the first names of your guests on each heart.

Yields about 40 2-inch hearts.

Academy Award-Winning Buffet for Eighteen

An evening at home with the Oscars calls for a cocktail buffet filled with an assortment of trendy imaginative culinary treats. It is the cook's imagination and light-hearted approach that turns the occasion into a glorious and memorable party. When you send out invitations, ask your guests to dress in the style of the twenties, thirties, or forties. Have some posters or photographs of the movie stars displayed near your television screen. You are sure to win the nomination for best host or hostess for your role in this elegant cocktail buffet.

MENU

Smoked Trout and Dill Endive Spears

Steak Tartare

Miniature Crab Cakes
Spicy Remoulade Sauce

Vegetable Strudel with Wisconsin Muenster Cheese, Walnuts, and Tomato-Basil Relish

Coconut Shrimp with Tomatillo Relish

Nova Scotia Salmon Cheesecake

Minted Fruit Skewers

Lemon Bars

A false tower (center) *was built on the roof of the hotel for* The Stunt Man *(starring Peter O'Toole). It was later blown up for the 1979 movie.*

Smoked Trout and Dill Endive Spears

2 tsp. chopped fresh dill
2 tbsp. sour cream
1 tsp. fresh lemon juice
1 large shallot, minced
½ tsp. salt
¼ tsp. black pepper
36 Belgian endive leaves
 (about 4 large heads)
5 4-oz. smoked trout fillets,
 cut into 36 portions
½ red bell pepper, thinly sliced
 (for garnish)
6 sprigs fresh dill (for garnish)
1 2-oz. jar salmon
 caviar

1. In a medium-size mixing bowl, combine dill, sour cream, lemon juice, shallot, salt, and pepper. Place mixture in a pastry bag with a small 1-S pastry tip. Set aside.

2. On the base of each endive leaf, place one portion of trout and two strips of red bell pepper, then pipe about ¾ teaspoon of sour cream mixture on top of trout. Garnish with dill sprigs and a dot of salmon caviar.

Yields 36.

The television series "Simon & Simon" centered one of its stories around the hotel's haunted room. Pictured here are stars Gerald McRaney and Jameson Parker, with Jeannie Wilson, a regular on the early shows.

The television series "Hart to Hart" turned the Hotel del Coronado into a Caribbean resort. Pictured here are stars Stefanie Powers and Robert Wagner.

Steak Tartare

8 anchovy fillets
2 cloves garlic, peeled and minced
2 lb. lean ground sirloin or tenderloin
3 egg yolks
¼ tsp. freshly ground pepper
1 tsp. dry mustard
2 tbsp. Worcestershire sauce
4 tbsp. capers, drained
2 tbsp. cognac
2 tbsp. chopped parsley
Juice of 1½ lemons
1 loaf party pumpernickel bread

1. In a large mixing bowl, combine anchovy fillets and garlic. Mash with the back of a wooden spoon, then add all other ingredients except the pumpernickel bread. Mix thoroughly and form into a loaf or pack into a 5-cup mold that has been lined with plastic wrap. Refrigerate for 6 hours.

2. Remove from refrigerator. Unmold or place loaf on a serving platter surrounded with slices of pumpernickel bread.

Serves 18.

Miniature Crab Cakes with Spicy Remoulade Sauce

3 lb. cooked crabmeat, flaked and picked clean of shells
3 eggs, well beaten
¾ cup mayonnaise
3½ cups fine bread crumbs
¼ cup finely chopped parsley
1 cup finely chopped celery
1 tsp. cayenne pepper
1 tsp. dry mustard
1 medium onion, finely chopped
3 tbsp. finely chopped chives
3 tbsp. fresh lemon juice
1 tsp. salt
1 tsp. paprika
½ cup all-purpose flour
1 cup unsalted butter

1. In a mixing bowl, stir together crabmeat, eggs, mayonnaise, bread crumbs, parsley, celery, cayenne pepper, mustard, onion, chives, lemon juice, salt, and paprika until thoroughly blended.

2. With a tablespoon, shape the mixture into small round patties about ½ inch thick. Place them on a tray lined with waxed paper. Cover with additional wax paper and refrigerate for about 1 hour.

3. To cook the crab cakes, lightly dust them on both sides with flour. Melt the butter in a large skillet over medium heat. Fry the crab cakes in several batches until deep golden brown, 3 to 5 minutes on each side. Drain on paper towels and transfer to chafing dish.

Spicy Remoulade Sauce:

2 cups mayonnaise
½ cup ketchup
½ cup minced parsley
¼ cup minced onion
2 tbsp. prepared white
  horseradish
4 tsp. white vinegar
1 tsp. grated lemon peel
2 tsp. Tabasco sauce
2 tsp. paprika
2 tsp. finely chopped chives

1. In a medium-size mixing bowl, combine all ingredients and blend thoroughly. Chill.
2. Transfer to a serving bowl and serve with crab cakes.

Yields about 48 1-inch cakes.

Vegetable Strudel with Wisconsin Muenster Cheese, Walnuts, and Tomato-Basil Relish

12 Phyllo dough sheets
2 lb. medium-size fresh
  asparagus spears (tips only)
4 crookneck yellow squash
  (skin only), cut into
  julienne strips
2 large carrots, cut
  into julienne strips
2 cups bread crumbs panko
1½ cups finely chopped walnuts
1 lb. unsalted butter, melted
½ lb. Wisconsin Muenster
  cheese, sliced about
  ⅛ inch thick (18 slices)
60 walnut halves (for garnish)
60 fresh basil leaves (for garnish)
Parchment paper

Note: Phyllo dough may be found in the frozen section of local supermarkets. Panko bread crumbs are a Japanese variety and may be found in Asian markets. Strudels should be cut with electric knives.

1. Preheat oven to 350 degrees.
2. Defrost Phyllo dough according to package directions.
3. In a large saucepan, bring 2 quarts of water to a boil. Blanch carrots only for 1 minute. Drain and plunge carrots into cold water. Drain and set aside. Pat dry with paper towels. (Vegetables may be prepared a day in advance, covered, and refrigerated.)
4. In a small mixing bowl, combine bread crumbs and walnuts. Set aside.
5. Place a sheet of Phyllo on a sheet of parchment paper, brush Phyllo with melted butter, and lightly sprinkle bread crumb mixture on Phyllo sheet. Place a second sheet of Phyllo on top of the first one. Brush with melted butter and sprinkle with bread crumb mixture. Repeat procedure until you have four layers.
6. With the long side of the Phyllo toward you, arrange filling ingredients: Starting 1 inch from the bottom edge, lay three slices of cheese across the dough. Layer ⅓ cup of carrots, squash, and asparagus tips in the center of the cheese slices. Top with three more slices of cheese.
7. With the help of the parchment paper, lift edge closest to you and roll tightly, jellyroll fashion. Brush strudel lightly with butter and sprinkle lightly with bread crumb mixture. Lay seam side down on a nonstick cookie sheet.
8. Repeat procedure for second and third strudel.
9. Bake for 15 to 20 minutes until golden brown. Remove from oven and allow strudel to rest for 10 minutes before slicing. Slice off ends and cut each strudel into ten slices. Transfer slices to a serving platter and garnish with walnut halves and basil leaves.

Tomato-Basil Relish:

5 medium-size tomatoes (about 1¾ lb.), peeled and finely chopped
1 bunch scallions, finely chopped
2 cloves garlic, peeled and minced
2 tbsp. chopped fresh basil
1 tsp. sugar
Juice of 1 lemon
Salt and pepper to taste
2 basil leaves (for garnish)

Combine ingredients in a small bowl. Serve with strudel.

Yields 30 strudel slices.

Coconut Shrimp with Tomatillo Relish

Shrimp:

6 egg whites, slightly beaten
¾ cup Dijon-style mustard
1 tbsp. cornstarch
4 cups unsweetened flaked coconut
8 sprigs parsley, chopped
4 tbsp. cornmeal
25 large shrimp, shelled and cleaned
1 pt. Canola oil

1. In a small-size mixing bowl, thoroughly whisk together egg whites, mustard, and cornstarch until smooth. Set aside.

2. In a medium-size mixing bowl, combine coconut, parsley, and cornmeal. Set aside.

3. Split shrimp in half, dip into batter, then roll them in breading, coating shrimp evenly.

4. In a large skillet, heat the oil. Cook shrimp for about 2 minutes on each side until golden brown, then place cooked shrimp on a serving platter. Add additional oil if necessary, and repeat procedure until all shrimp are cooked.

Yields 50 pieces.

Tomatillo Relish:

1 shallot, finely chopped
1 clove garlic, peeled and minced
⅛ tsp. cayenne pepper
Juice of 1 orange
¼ cup chablis wine
1 mango, peeled, cubed, and divided in half
12 tomatillos, peeled, chopped, and divided in half
2 tsp. chopped cilantro
½ tsp. chopped mint

1. In a medium-size saucepan, combine shallot, garlic, cayenne pepper, orange juice, wine, half the mango, and half the tomatillos. Bring to a simmer, remove from heat, transfer to a food processor, and purée. When mixture is cool, stir in cilantro and mint.

2. Place remaining mango and tomatillos in a small serving dish. Pour puréed mixture over both. Serve with Coconut Shrimp.

Note: Tomatillos are a green vegetable (similar to a tomato) with a paper-thin husk. They are available at Latin-American markets, specialty food stores, and some supermarkets.

Nova Scotia Salmon Cheesecake

3 tbsp. fine bread crumbs

5 tbsp. freshly grated Parmesan cheese

3 tbsp. butter or margarine

⅔ cup minced onion

¼ cup finely chopped red bell pepper

⅛ cup finely chopped green bell pepper

⅛ cup finely chopped yellow bell pepper

3½ 8-oz. pkg. (28 oz.) cream cheese, softened

4 eggs

½ cup heavy cream

½ cup grated Jarlsburg cheese

5 oz. Nova Scotia salmon, chopped

⅛ tsp. Tabasco sauce

3 sprigs fresh dill (for garnish)

1. Preheat oven to 300 degrees.

2. Butter a 9-inch springform pan. Combine bread crumbs with 2 tablespoons Parmesan; then sprinkle bottom and sides of pan with mixture, shaking around pan to coat.

3. Melt butter or margarine in a small skillet, add onion and peppers and sauté until tender. Set aside.

4. Using an electric mixer, combine cream cheese, eggs, and cream until smooth. Add remaining 3 tablespoons Parmesan, Jarlsburg, and sautéed mixture. Mix on low speed until blended. Stir in salmon and add Tabasco.

5. Pour batter into prepared pan; set pan in slightly larger pan. Pour boiling water into larger pan until it comes up 2 inches on the sides of the springform pan.

6. Bake for 1 hour and 40 minutes, then turn off oven. Do not open oven door, but let cake sit in oven 1 hour more.

7. Lift cake pan out of larger pan to cool to room temperature on a wire rack. Refrigerate.

To serve:

1. Remove from refrigerator 1 hour before serving.

2. Loosen around edge of pan with knife; unmold. Garnish with fresh dill sprigs.

Serves 24.

Minted Fruit Skewers

1½ cups Gewürztraminer wine

2½ cups chopped fresh mint

2 tbsp. fresh lemon juice

2 tbsp. orange juice concentrate

9 cups seasonal fruits (bananas, nectarines, pineapple, plums, strawberries) cut into bite-size pieces

4 sprigs fresh mint (for garnish)

1. In a large mixing bowl, blend wine, mint, lemon juice, and orange juice concentrate.

2. Place fruit in marinade and refrigerate overnight.

3. Remove fruit from marinade and divide evenly among 18 8-inch bamboo skewers. Start and end with a strawberry. Transfer to a serving platter and garnish with fresh mint sprigs.

Serves 18.

Lemon Bars

1 cup butter or margarine, softened
½ cup confectioners' sugar
1 tsp. vanilla extract
2 cups flour
4 eggs
2 cups granulated sugar
Grated rind of 1 lemon
6 tbsp. fresh lemon juice
¼ cup confectioners' sugar (for topping)

1. Preheat oven to 350 degrees.

2. Grease a 13 x 9 x 2-inch baking pan.

3. In a mixing bowl, combine butter or margarine, confectioners' sugar, and vanilla extract; beat until fluffy. Gradually add flour, mixing until well combined. Spread evenly in prepared pan. Bake for 20 minutes, then remove from oven.

4. In a medium-size mixing bowl, combine eggs, sugar, lemon rind, and lemon juice; stir to blend all ingredients (do not beat). Pour lemon mixture over baked crust.

5. Return to oven and bake until topping is set and lightly browned, 18 to 22 minutes.

6. Sift additional confectioners' sugar over pastry to generously cover top. Cut into bars and remove from pan when cool. Serve on a platter.

Yields 36 bars.

Super Bowl Sunday Touchdown Buffet for Sixteen

One of America's greatest pastimes is following spectator sports. Age or gender is of no importance when the sports bug bites you. Sports fans sit in rain, sleet, or snow to watch their favorite teams perform.

Why not do it the easy way? Take this opportunity to invite some of your sports enthusiast friends over to view the winning team in the comfort of your home. Super Bowl Sunday is a perfect time for family and friends to spend a few hours cheering their favorite team.

Set out a bowl of Seasoned Popcorn Mix and Jalapeño Cheese Straws for easy munching. At half time, serve your hearty cocktail buffet with its variety and contrast of flavors.

MENU

Assorted Beer and Wine

Seasoned Popcorn Mix

Jalapeño Cheese Straws

Herb Dip with Rainbow of Crudités

Stuffed Edam Cheese
Dill-Sesame Crackers

Creamy Baked Crab Dip

Sesame Chicken Strips with Mustard
Dipping Sauce

Winning Goal-Post Beef Dip

Roquefort-Stuffed Shrimp

Sweet and Sour Cocktail Spareribs

Chocolate-Grape Bon Bons

Seasoned Popcorn Mix

8 cups popped popcorn
1 cup goldfish crackers
1½ cups miniature pretzels
½ cup peanuts
½ cup cashews
¼ cup butter or margarine
¼ tsp. fines herbes
¼ tsp. garlic powder
1½ tsp. Worcestershire sauce

1. Preheat oven to 250 degrees.
2. In a large mixing bowl, combine popcorn, crackers, pretzels, peanuts, and cashews. Set aside.
3. Melt butter or margarine in a 13 x 9 x 2-inch baking pan in the oven. Remove from oven; stir in fines herbes, garlic powder, and Worcestershire sauce. Drizzle butter or margarine mixture over popcorn mixture in bowl; stir to coat.
4. Place popcorn mixture in same baking pan. Bake for 1 hour, stirring every 15 minutes. Cool completely. Store in an airtight container.

Yields about 6 cups.

Jalapeño Cheese Straws

1 17¼-oz. pkg. frozen puff pastry
½ lb. Monterey Jack cheese
   with jalapeño peppers, grated
1 tsp. chili powder
1 tsp. salt
1 large egg, beaten

1. Thaw puff pastry according to package directions. Preheat oven to 375 degrees.
2. On a lightly floured surface, roll one sheet of puff pastry with a floured rolling pin (keeping other sheet refrigerated) into a 15-inch square; cut square in half. Sprinkle half of grated cheese onto half of puff pastry sheet; top with other half of pastry. Roll pastry into a 15 x 10-inch rectangle.
3. Sprinkle rectangle with ½ teaspoon chili powder and ½ teaspoon salt; press in gently with rolling pin. Turn rectangle over and brush with half of beaten egg. Cut rectangle crosswise into twenty 10 x ¾-inch strips.
4. Twist each pastry strip several times, then place them ½ inch apart on a large greased cookie sheet. Bake for 15 to 20 minutes, until cheese sticks are crisp and brown. Remove cheese sticks from cookie sheet and cool on wire rack.
5. Repeat procedure with remaining puff pastry sheet. Store in a loosely covered container.

Note: Frozen puff pastry is available in the frozen section of most local supermarkets.

Yields 40 cheese straws.

Herb Dip with Rainbow of Crudités

2 cloves garlic
½ cup watercress, coarsely
   chopped
½ cup shallots, coarsely
   chopped
¼ cup parsley, coarsely
   chopped
⅛ cup basil leaves, coarsely
   chopped
1 tsp. onion salt
1 2-oz. can anchovies, drained
Juice of 1 lemon
½ cup mayonnaise
1½ cups sour cream

1. In a blender, combine garlic, watercress, shallots, parsley, basil leaves, onion salt, anchovies, and lemon juice. Blend until mixture is smoothly puréed.
2. Stir in mayonnaise and sour cream. Transfer to a serving bowl. Cover and refrigerate for 24 hours.

Yields 2½ cups dip.

Crudités:
2 bunches radishes
1½ lb. carrots,
   cut into spears
1½ lb. pencil-thin
   asparagus, blanched
1 basket cherry tomatoes
1 lb. fresh mushrooms,
   sliced
1 head endive
1 bunch broccoli,
   blanched, drained,
   and cut into florets

1. Wash radishes and cut all the leaves to the same length. With a small paring knife, cut each radish into four petals from tip to leaf end, without cutting through the base. Place radishes in a bowl of water with ice cubes. When they open out like roses, drain and place them on the crudité platter.
2. Clean and prepare the remaining vegetables as directed. Arrange vegetables on a platter, grouping them together in a rainbow pattern.
3. Serve with dip.

Serves 16.

Stuffed Edam Cheese

1 4-lb. Edam cheese
2 tbsp. Worcestershire sauce
¼ cup Dijon-style mustard
¼ cup prepared mustard
¾ cup sour cream
1 tsp. cayenne pepper
3 tbsp. fines herbes

1. Remove cheese from refrigerator and allow it to reach room temperature.
2. Cut off top of cheese about 1 ½ inches down to form a lid. Set top aside.
3. Hollow out cheese, leaving about ¼ inch on the sides and bottom of cheese to form a shell. Place scooped out cheese and the remaining ingredients in a food processor. Process ingredients to a smooth paste.
4. Refill the cheese shell with processed paste. Set the lid to the side of stuffed cheese if you wish.
5. Transfer cheese to a serving platter and surround with Dill-Sesame Crackers (recipe follows) or crackers of your choice.

Serves 16 to 18.

Dill-Sesame Crackers

Ice water
36 saltine crackers
½ cup (1 stick) butter, melted
   (do not use margarine)
1 clove garlic, peeled and
   mashed
1 tsp. dried dill
2 tbsp. sesame seeds

1. Preheat oven to 400 degrees. Grease 2 cookie sheets.
2. Pour ice water in a shallow dish or pie plate. Place several crackers at a time into water in a single layer, pushing gently just below the surface. Let them stand for about 30 seconds. When corners soften, carefully remove crackers with a slotted spatula to prepared cookie sheets. Place crackers about ½ inch apart.
3. When cookie sheets are filled, tip to drain excess water.
4. In a small bowl, mix butter and garlic. With a pastry brush, very gently coat each cracker with garlic-butter mixture. Sprinkle crackers with dill and sesame seeds.
5. Bake at 400 degrees for 15 minutes, then at 300 degrees for 25 minutes. Cool on a rack, then store in a tightly covered container.

Yields 36 crackers.

Creamy Baked Crab Dip

2 8-oz. pkg. cream cheese
1 lb. fresh (or 3 6-oz. cans)
   crabmeat
4 tbsp. grated onion
1 tsp. prepared horseradish
6 tbsp. sour cream
1 tsp. salt
1 tsp. white pepper
1 tsp. Worcestershire sauce
2 tbsp. white wine
⅔ cup sliced toasted almonds

1. Preheat oven to 375 degrees.
2. In a large mixing bowl, combine all ingredients except almonds. Mix thoroughly, then transfer to a greased 10-inch glass pie pan. Place almonds on top and bake for 30 minutes.
3. Remove from oven and serve with crackers or party rye bread.

Serves 18.

Sesame Chicken Strips with Mustard Dipping Sauce

Chicken:
- **3 eggs, slightly beaten**
- **3 tbsp. cornstarch**
- **6 tsp. soy sauce**
- **3 lb. boneless, skinless chicken breasts, cut into strips**
- **¾ cup bread crumbs**
- **1½ tsp. garlic powder**
- **¼ cup plus 1 tbsp. butter or margarine, melted**
- **¾ cup sesame seeds**

1. Preheat oven to 400 degrees.
2. In a medium-size bowl, blend together eggs, cornstarch, and soy sauce. Add chicken strips and stir. Allow to stand for 10 minutes.
3. In a large bowl, combine bread crumbs and garlic powder. Roll chicken strips in mixture, coating well. Arrange chicken strips on a greased cookie sheet, then drizzle with melted butter and sprinkle with sesame seeds.
4. Bake uncovered for about 15 minutes, until chicken strips are tender. Transfer to a platter and serve at room temperature.

Mustard Dipping Sauce:
- **3 cups mayonnaise**
- **3 tbsp. Dijon-style mustard**
- **2 tsp. Worcestershire sauce**
- **2 drops Tabasco sauce**

1. Combine all ingredients in a medium-size bowl. Mix well.
2. Chill for 30 minutes, then transfer to a small serving bowl.

Serves 16.

Winning Goal-Post Beef Dip

- **2 lb. lean ground beef**
- **6 scallions (white part only), chopped**
- **2 cloves garlic, peeled and minced**
- **8 fresh tomatoes, peeled and diced**
- **2 6-oz. cans tomato paste**
- **4 jalapeño peppers, minced**
- **2 tbsp. Worcestershire sauce**
- **2 tsp. oregano**
- **4 tsp. chili powder**
- **2 tsp. salt**
- **½ tsp. ground black pepper**
- **1¼ cups white seedless raisins**

1. In a large nonstick skillet, brown ground beef with scallions and garlic. Add remaining ingredients and simmer over very low heat for 2 hours. Skim off any fat.
2. Serve hot in a chafing dish with blue corn tortilla chips.

Serves 16.

Roquefort-Stuffed Shrimp

1 3-oz. pkg. cream cheese
1 lb. large shrimp, shelled,
  cooked, and cleaned
¼ cup Roquefort cheese
3 tbsp. white wine
⅛ tsp. garlic salt
½ cup finely chopped parsley
1 head purple cabbage

1. Remove cream cheese from the refrigerator and bring to room temperature.
2. Split each shrimp halfway through from the top, then chill.
3. In a medium-size mixing bowl, blend cream cheese with Roquefort cheese and wine. Add garlic salt and mix thoroughly.
4. Stuff shrimp with mixture and roll stuffed side in chopped parsley. Refrigerate until served.

To Serve:
1. Cut bottom off cabbage, so it stands up.
2. Place a toothpick in each shrimp and stick as many shrimp as possible in the cabbage. Excess shrimp may be placed around the base of the cabbage.

Yields approximately 20 shrimp.

Sweet and Sour Cocktail Spareribs

Ribs:
8 qt. water
2 onions (about 1½ lb.),
  cut in half
4 cloves garlic, peeled and cut
  in half
2 tsp. salt
2 tsp. garlic salt
1 tsp. garlic powder
1 tsp. ground black pepper
4 lb. pork spareribs

1. In a dutch oven, bring water to a boil. Add onions, garlic, salt, garlic salt, garlic powder, and pepper. Add ribs and simmer uncovered for 25 minutes.
2. Drain ribs thoroughly, then transfer to a baking pan that has been lined with foil. Arrange ribs rounded side down. Set aside.

Note: Have the butcher split each rack of ribs lengthwise through the bones into 2-inch wide pieces.

Sweet and Sour Sauce:

1½ cups hoisin sauce

1½ cups port wine

1 cup rice vinegar

3 tbsp. sesame oil

⅓ cup dark soy sauce

¼ cup sugar

5 tbsp. minced cilantro

1 tsp. minced ginger root

3 tbsp. cornstarch dissolved
   in 3 tbsp. water

1. In a medium-size saucepan, combine all ingredients except the cornstarch mixture and bring to a boil.

2. Add cornstarch and cook for 2 minutes, stirring continuously.

To Serve:

1. Pour Sweet and Sour Sauce over ribs, coating them thoroughly.

2. Refrigerate for 24 hours, basting occasionally.

3. When ready to serve, preheat oven to 400 degrees. Bake ribs for 25 minutes, basting with remaining sauce until ribs are a glossy dark brown. Transfer to a serving platter or chafing dishes.

Serves 16.

Chocolate-Grape Bon Bons

1 cup semisweet chocolate
   baking chips

2 tbsp. butter or margarine

2 doz. green or black
   seedless grapes,
   rinsed and patted dry

3 tbsp. minced crystallized
   ginger

1. Combine chocolate and shortening in the top of a double boiler. Place over simmering water. Stir until chocolate is melted and smooth, about 2 minutes.

2. Cover a 12 x 15-inch cookie sheet with waxed paper. Drop 1-teaspoon portions of melted chocolate about 1½ inches apart. Set a grape in the center of each portion. Sprinkle ginger on chocolate.

3. Chill until firm, at least 20 minutes. Cover when chocolate is firm. When ready to serve, remove bon bons from cookie sheet and transfer to doily-lined serving plate.

Note: Chocolate-Grape Bon Bons may be prepared a day in advance.

Yields 24 bon bons.

Rejoice and Reciprocate Cocktail Buffet for Twelve

Cocktail buffets are increasing in popularity as a means to entertain friends. Buffets are a vital part of the cooking scene and an enjoyable way to serve guests. This trend offers many advantages. Besides being able to accommodate more people than a sit-down dinner, buffets allow guests to choose from an assortment of delightful frivolities. Guests also tend to be more adventuresome in seeking to satisfy their curiosity about various dishes. With a friendly group of people, your warm welcome, and this versatile cocktail buffet, you will have the ingredients for a party that will earn you a reputation as the best host or hostess in town.

MENU

Sugar-Spiced Pork Loin
Mustard-Jalapeño Sauce
Cheddar Biscuits

Petite Noodle Puddings

Grilled Swordfish and Salmon Canapés
Red Pepper Rouille Relish

Ham Pinwheels on English Cucumber Slices

Chile-Cheese Cups

Shrimp Mini Quiche

Asparagus Bundles

Boursin Pecan-Stuffed Figs

Pecan Pie Bars

Sugar-Spiced Pork Loin with Mustard Jalapeño Sauce

Pork loin:
2 tbsp. minced garlic, peeled
2 tbsp. kosher salt
1½ tsp. freshly ground black pepper
⅓ cup firmly packed brown sugar
1 tbsp. cinnamon
1 tbsp. dry mustard
½ tsp. cayenne pepper
1 tsp. thyme
¾ cup olive oil
2 boneless pork loins (2 ½lb. each)

1. Preheat oven to 400 degrees.
2. In a small mixing bowl, combine all the ingredients except the olive oil and pork loins. Set aside.
3. Rub olive oil into pork loins. In a large nonstick skillet, sear outside of pork loins. Transfer to a roasting pan, then pat sugar-spice mixture on both pork loins and bake for 60 minutes.
4. Remove from oven, let cool to room temperature. Slice thin and serve with Mustard-Jalapeño Sauce and Cheddar Biscuits (recipes follow).

Note: Leftovers are great for sandwiches the next day.

Serves 12.

Mustard Jalapeño Sauce:

**4 oz. dried apricots,
chopped**

**1 16-oz. can apricot
halves, drained**

¾ cup bourbon whiskey

**¼ cup Dijon-style
mustard**

½ tsp. ground cumin

**1 4-oz. can green chiles,
diced**

**¼ tsp. dried red
pepper flakes**

Juice of 1 lime

1. In a medium-size saucepan, combine all ingredients except the green chiles, red pepper flakes, and lime juice. Bring to a boil, then reduce heat and simmer uncovered for 30 minutes.

2. Transfer mixture to a blender and purée coarsely. Remove mixture to a bowl and stir in green chiles, red pepper flakes, and lime juice.

Yields about 2 cups.

Cheddar Biscuits

**2 cups unbleached
all-purpose flour**

**1½ cups shredded
sharp cheddar cheese**

2 tsp. baking powder

½ tsp. baking soda

**7 tbsp. unsalted butter,
chilled and cut into
pieces**

¾ cup buttermilk

½ tsp. sugar

½ tsp. salt

1 egg yolk

1. Preheat oven to 425 degrees.

2. Lightly grease a large, heavy cookie sheet.

3. In a medium-size bowl, combine flour, ½ cup cheese, baking powder, and baking soda. Cut in butter until mixture resembles a grainy meal.

4. In a small bowl, combine ⅔ cup buttermilk with sugar and salt. Stir to dissolve. Whisk in yolk and add to flour mixture. Stir until dough gathers into a ball, adding more buttermilk, 1 teaspoon at a time, if necessary to bind dough.

5. Knead down on a lightly floured surface until just smooth, about 30 seconds. Flatten dough with hands to a thickness of ½ inch. Cut out rounds using 2-inch biscuit or cookie cutter. (Do not twist cutter while cutting through dough, or biscuits will rise unevenly.)

6. Transfer rounds to prepared cookie sheet. Reduce oven temperature to 400 degrees and bake for 10 minutes. Sprinkle biscuits with remaining cup of cheese. Bake until cheese melts and biscuits are golden brown, about 20 minutes. Cool on a rack and serve warm.

Note: Cheddar biscuits may be prepared the day before. To warm, place biscuits on a cookie sheet and heat in a 300-degree oven for 5 minutes. Recipe may be doubled.

Yields 18 biscuits.

Petite Noodle Puddings

1 16-oz. pkg. thin
  noodles
½ cup (1 stick)
  butter or margarine
6 eggs
4 cups milk
½ cup (1 stick)
  butter or margarine,
  softened at room
  temperature
1 cup sugar
2 tsp. cinnamon
1 8-oz. pkg. cream cheese

1. Preheat oven to 325 degrees.

2. Cook noodles according to package directions. Place cooked noodles in a colander, rinse in cold water, and set aside.

3. In a 10 x 15 x 2-inch glass baking pan, melt ½ cup butter or margarine. Set aside.

4. Separate eggs, beat whites until stiff, then set aside. In a large mixing bowl, combine milk, ½ cup softened butter or margarine, and egg yolks. Fold in drained noodles and add beaten egg whites to mixture.

5. Place in prepared glass baking pan. Sprinkle top with sugar and cinnamon. Dot with cream cheese and bake for 45 minutes to 1 hour. Remove from oven and cut into 48 small squares. Serve at room temperature.

Note: Petite Noodle Puddings may be prepared ahead of time and frozen.

Yields 48 puddings.

Grilled Swordfish and Salmon Canapés with Red Pepper Rouille Relish

Canapés:
¼ tsp. fresh lemon juice
¼ cup olive oil
1 tsp. salt
¼ tsp. pepper
1½ lb. fresh swordfish,
  cut into 36 portions
½ lb. smoked salmon,
  cut into 36 strips
18 cocktail-size slices
  pumpernickel bread, cut
  diagonally into halves
36 chives
2 tsp. black lumpfish
  caviar, drained and
  rinsed

1. Preheat broiler to 475 degrees.

2. In a small mixing bowl, combine lemon juice, olive oil, salt, and pepper. Set aside.

3. Place swordfish cubes in a baking pan. Pour lemon-oil mixture over swordfish. Broil for about 1½ minutes on each side.

4. Remove from broiler and wrap salmon strips around swordfish cubes. Set aside.

Red Pepper Rouille Relish:

¼ cup pimiento

1 tbsp. garlic, peeled and chopped

2 tsp. fresh lemon juice

1 tsp. chopped anchovy

1 egg yolk

¼ cup olive oil

½ tsp. salt

¼ tsp. black pepper

1. In a food processor, combine pimiento, garlic, lemon juice, and anchovy. Process for 30 seconds.

2. Slowly add egg yolk and oil. Process for 1 minute. Add salt and black pepper and transfer to a small dish.

To Assemble:

1. Spread Red Pepper Rouille Relish on pumpernickel triangles.

2. Place swordfish and salmon canapés on pumpernickel triangles. Garnish with 1 chive doubled over and tucked into salmon canapé.

3. Top with a dot of caviar.

Yields 36 canapés.

Seafood Canapés containing Smoked Trout and Dill Endive Spears, Coconut Shrimp with Tomatillo Relish, and Grilled Swordfish and Salmon Canapés.

Ham Pinwheels on English Cucumber Slices

1 8-oz. pkg. cream cheese

1 tbsp. milk

2 tbsp. finely minced onion

2 tbsp. sweet pickle relish

6 drops Tabasco sauce

⅛ tsp. dry mustard

5 slices boiled ham

2 English cucumbers

1. Soften cream cheese at room temperature; then beat with milk until light and fluffy. Stir in onion, relish, Tabasco sauce, and mustard.

2. Divide mixture into five portions. Lay out ham slices and blot them to remove any moisture. Spread one portion of cheese mixture on each ham slice. Roll each up tightly from long side. Wrap in wax paper or plastic wrap and chill overnight.

3. When ready to serve, score cucumbers with a fork and slice into ¼-inch slices. Remove ham rolls from refrigerator and cut into ½-inch-thick slices. Place ham rolls on cucumber slices.

Yields about 2½ dozen.

Chile-Cheese Cups

8 oz. grated cheddar cheese

8 oz. grated Monterey Jack cheese

1 cup sour cream

¼ cup chopped and drained pitted black olives

¼ cup chopped and drained stuffed green olives

⅔ cup diced canned green chiles

½ cup minced scallions (white part only)

1 tsp. cumin

1 tsp. garlic powder

1 tsp. dried oregano

Vegetable oil

60 won ton wrappers

1. Preheat oven to 350 degrees.

2. In a large bowl, combine all ingredients except oil and won ton wrappers. Taste and adjust the seasonings.

3. Brush wrappers lightly with oil on both sides.

4. To prepare won ton cups, oil a minimuffin tin and place 1 wrapper in each cup. Brush each wrapper with oil.

5. Bake at 350 degrees until crisp, about 10 to 15 minutes; then remove the cups from the muffin tin, and place them on a cookie sheet. Repeat procedure with remaining won tons, then increase oven temperature to 375 degrees.

6. Fill cups with the cheese mixture and bake at 375 degrees for about 10 minutes, or until filling is hot and bubbly.

Yields about 60 cups.

Shrimp Mini Quiche

Quiche Shells:

3 oz. cream cheese, softened

¼ lb. butter or margarine, softened

1½ cups all-purpose flour

1. Preheat oven to 400 degrees.

2. Combine cream cheese and butter or margarine, beating until smooth.

3. Add flour and mix well. Shape dough into thirty 1-inch balls.

4. Place dough balls in lightly greased minimuffin tins; then shape them into shells. Prick bottoms and sides of pastry shells with fork.

5. Bake for 5 minutes. Let cool in pan on wire rack. Repeat procedure with remaining batter.

Shrimp Filling:

30 small cooked (bay) shrimp
1 extra-large egg,
  beaten
½ cup heavy cream
1½ tbsp. brandy
½ tsp. salt
½ tsp. pepper
1½ tsp. fresh chopped
  dill (or 1 tsp. dried)
1⅔ oz. Gruyère cheese

1. Preheat oven to 350 degrees.
2. Transfer quiche shells to a cookie sheet. Place one shrimp in each shell.
3. In a small mixing bowl, combine egg, cream, brandy, salt, pepper, and dill. Divide mixture evenly among shells, about 1 tablespoon each.
4. Slice cheese into thirty small triangles and place one on each quiche.
5. Bake for 20 minutes, or until set. Cool.

Note: These mini quiche can be made in advance. Cool them, then freeze in foil. To reheat, place frozen mini quiche on a cookie sheet. Bake at 375 degrees for 7 to 10 minutes.

Yields 30 quiche.

Asparagus Bundles

25 fresh asparagus spears
1 cup butter or
  margarine
4 egg yolks
1 tbsp. chopped fresh mint
1½ tbsp. lemon juice to taste
25 slices (or 1½ loaves)
  thin-sliced white bread

1. Preheat broiler.
2. Snap off and discard tough stalk ends of asparagus. Wash stalks in cold water, then cook for about 6 to 7 minutes in boiling water. Drain, rinse with cold water, then set asparagus aside.
3. In a small saucepan, melt butter or margarine, keep very hot. Process egg yolks until frothy in a food processor fitted with a metal blade. With motor running, gradually add hot melted butter in a thin stream; process until blended. Transfer to a bowl, cover, and refrigerate until mixture is thickened. Stir in mint and lemon juice.
4. Trim crusts from bread slices and spread bread with sauce. Cut each asparagus spear in half; place 2 halves on each bread slice. Bring the two opposite corners to center of each slice and fasten with a wooden pick. Dot with more sauce, arrange asparagus bundles on a baking sheet, and broil until crisp and golden. Transfer to a serving platter.

Yields 25 bundles.

Boursin Pecan-Stuffed Figs

12 purple figs
6 tbsp. finely chopped pecans
3 tbsp. virgin olive oil
3 tbsp. chablis wine
3 tbsp. white wine vinegar
3 tsp. finely chopped parsley
⅛ tsp. dry mustard
½ tsp. freshly ground black
   pepper
2 5-oz. pkg. Boursin cheese

1. With a sharp paring knife, slice tops off figs and reserve them. With a small spoon, hollow out figs, leaving shells intact. Transfer pulp to a bowl and mix with pecans. Set aside.
2. In a small mixing bowl, whisk together olive oil, wine, and vinegar. Add parsley, mustard, and pepper; then add Boursin cheese and fig-pecan mixture. Blend thoroughly.
3. Spoon mixture into figs. Replace tops of figs and arrange on a serving platter.

Serves 12.

Pecan Pie Bars

Crust:
1 cup sifted all-purpose flour
½ cup rolled oats
¼ cup brown sugar, packed
½ cup (1 stick) butter or margarine

1. Preheat oven to 350 degrees.
2. In a medium-size mixing bowl, combine flour, oats, and brown sugar. Cut in butter with pastry blender until mixture resembles coarse crumbs.
3. Press mixture into greased 9 x 9 x 2-inch pan; then bake for about 15 minutes. Remove from oven and set aside.

Filling:
3 eggs
¾ cup light corn
   syrup
1 cup coarsely chopped pecans
1 tsp. vanilla extract
¼ tsp. salt
½ cup brown sugar, packed
1 tbsp. flour

1. In a medium-size mixing bowl, beat eggs slightly. Add remaining ingredients and blend well.
2. Pour mixture over partially baked crust. Return to oven and bake at 350 degrees for about 25 minutes.
3. Cool to room temperature. Cut into bars.

Yields about 3 dozen bars.

CHAPTER FOUR

Brunches for Festive Occasions

No meal presents more opportunities for surprise than brunch. There are no hard and fast rules for the menu. Brunch is a popular style of casual California entertaining. With a leisurely approach and the inclusion of easy-to-prepare foods, brunch becomes the host's response to the hurried pace of modern American life—a time to wind down from a hectic week and enjoy family and friends in a relaxing atmosphere. Brunch is becoming one of America's favorite meals and one of the most versatile forms of entertaining. Because of its informality, it is a flexible and relatively inexpensive way to entertain groups of friends. Spontaneity is an important ingredient, so let your imagination take charge, be innovative, and have fun.

Advance preparation lightens the work on the day of your brunch. The preparation of Marinated Fillet of Sole begins twenty-four hours before your New Year's Day party. Spicy Ham and Cheddar Pudding is prepared the night before your Mother's Day brunch, as is Raspberry-Lemonade Mold and chilled Poached Salmon with Creamed Cucumber Sauce for your Easter celebration. Get in the habit of baking muffins and croissants a week in advance. Wrap them carefully and store them in the freezer.

Pecan-Cinnamon Bundt Cake and Lemon-Topped Poppy Seed Brunch Cake may be baked ahead of time, with the lemon topping poured over the cake the morning it is served.

New Year's Day Brunch for Twelve dazzles with ritzy accents of frozen vodka encased in ice and flowers and assorted caviars. Easter Brunch for Eight features Peppered Baby Lamb Chops as well as Rosemary-Topped Potato and Onion Pie. Cheddar Baked Eggs are in the oven while you enjoy Chilled Venetian Bellini cocktails. Mother's Day for Six includes elegant platters of French cheeses and smoked fish with the Del's Signature Chocolate Mousse for dessert. The Award-Winning Sunday Brunch concludes the chapter with the chef's own recipes of Tomato Cups Florentine filled with Scrambled Eggs and Cheddar Cheese and Canadian Bacon and Apple Wedges with Red Onion Marmalade. By organizing and preparing in advance, you can be free to enjoy your guests and sip on Smashing Citrus Cocktails or fresh orange juice served in a scooped-out orange shell.

Your brunch, just like the Del's, will stay with your guests as a happy memory of carefree pleasure.

Following page: *A Sampling of the Award-Winning Sunday Brunch.* Clockwise from bottom: *Tomato Cups Florentine filled with Scrambled Eggs and Cheddar Cheese, American Fried Potatoes, Canadian Bacon and Apple Wedges with Red Onion Marmalade; Trout and Salmon Platter; Cranberry-Orange Muffins, Lemon-Blueberry Muffins, Banana-Raisin Muffins; and Smashing Citrus Cocktail.*

New Year's Day Brunch for Twelve

New Year's Day is the beginning of a new year and the appropriate time to reflect and reminisce with twelve close friends. For an unusual New Year's Day celebration, when you feel like "putting on the Ritz," start with American caviar and a bottle of your favorite vodka encased in ice and flowers. Plan the first meal of the new year to be generous and soothing, with an array of familiar comfort foods. Combine the elegant touch with traditional dishes such as Southern Biscuit Muffins and Hoppin' John Salad—the southern fare that brings good luck to all your New Year's Day guests.

Advance preparation of honeydew melon marinated overnight in port wine and fillet of sole bathed in white wine for two days allows you to enjoy your friends in a relaxed and congenial atmosphere. Your guests will be delighted to be included in this very special get-together for the morning after, leaving everyone with warm memories of their first day of the new year.

MENU

Festive Frozen Vodka with
Fresh Orange Juice

American Caviar Sampler

Melon Slices in Port Wine with
Coconut Banana Bites

Marinated Fillet of Sole with
Horseradish Apple Cream

New Year's Day Hoppin' John Salad

Baked Zippy Deviled Eggs

Glazed Bacon with Brown Sugar and Walnuts

Southern Biscuit Muffins

Lemon-Topped Poppy Seed Brunch Cake

Pineapple-Apricot Cheesecake Bars

Festive Frozen Vodka with Fresh Orange Juice

1 liter vodka
1 ½-gallon milk carton, empty
Distilled water
Flowers and leaves
1 cloth napkin
1 shallow crystal or glass bowl
½ gallon freshly squeezed orange juice

1. Place the bottle of vodka in the empty ½-gallon milk carton.
2. Fill the carton with distilled water. Stuff a few leaves and flowers, such as roses or carnations, into the water along the sides of the carton.
3. Freeze the carton, with bottle and flowers upright, in the freezer overnight, or until a solid block of ice has formed.
4. Remove from freezer and let set at room temperature for about 20 to 30 minutes.
5. Cut the carton away and return the block of ice with vodka to the freezer until ready to serve.

6. Place a folded napkin in a shallow crystal or glass bowl to catch the melting ice.

7. To serve, remove the cap from the vodka and pour to your heart's delight. Set out pitchers of orange juice for those who choose to start the New Year with a mellow screwdriver. Have the shot glasses available for the more daring and those who feel no pain from the night before.

Serves 12.

American Caviar Sampler

3 oz. salmon caviar
3 oz. golden whitefish caviar
3 oz. black lumpfish caviar
  (or caviar of your choice)
2 eggs, hard cooked
4 scallions, peeled and finely chopped
3 lemons, cut into wedges
5 slices white bread, crusts removed, toasted, and cut into points

1. Arrange caviars in glass dishes on a serving platter.

2. Separate yolks and egg whites. Grate both and place in small serving dishes.

3. Place scallions in a small serving dish.

4. Arrange egg yolks, egg whites, scallions, lemon wedges, and toast points on the platter, surrounding the caviar.

Serves 12.

Melon Slices in Port Wine with Coconut Banana Bites

Melon Slices:
2 honeydew melons, rinds removed
2 cups port wine
4 sprigs mint

1. Cut a plug 1-inch in diameter in each melon. Pour 1 cup of wine into each melon, then reinsert plugs.

2. Refrigerate overnight.

3. Before serving, drain wine, cut melons into slices, and remove seeds. Arrange slices on a large platter and garnish with mint.

Coconut Banana Bites:
1 cup sour cream
2 tbsp. confectioners' sugar
2 cups flaked coconut
6 bananas, cut into 1-inch slices

1. Preheat oven to 350 degrees.

2. In a medium-size mixing bowl, blend together sour cream and confectioners' sugar.

3. Toast coconut in oven until lightly golden, about 5 minutes; cool. Dip each piece of banana into sour cream mixture, then roll in coconut.

4. Place in a single layer on a waxed paper-lined cookie sheet and refrigerate for 24 hours. When ready to serve, add bananas to melon platter.

Serves 12.

Marinated Fillet of Sole with Horseradish Apple Cream

Fillets:

3 cups chablis wine
½ cup fresh lemon juice
3 tsp. salt
3 tsp. black peppercorns
**8 fresh sage leaves
   (or sprinkle dried)**
8 bay leaves
3 lb. fresh sole fillets

1. In a medium-size saucepan, bring wine, lemon juice, salt, peppercorns, sage, and bay leaves to a boil. Remove from heat; let cool.

2. Rinse fillets in cold water; drain well and place in a 13 x 9 x 2-inch baking pan. Pour cooled wine mixture over fillets. Cover and allow to marinate in refrigerator for 24 hours.

3. Preheat oven to 375 degrees.

4. Remove fillets from refrigerator. Lift fillets out of marinade; set aside. Discard half the marinade; heat the remaining marinade in a saucepan. Bring to a boil. Place fillets in 13 x 9 x 2-inch baking pan; pour marinade over them. Bake for about 4 minutes. Remove fillets from oven and transfer to a serving platter. Repeat process until all fillets have been baked.

5. Chill cooked fillets in refrigerator and serve with Horseradish Apple Cream (recipe follows).

Horseradish Apple Cream:

3 Jonathan apples
6 tbsp. creamed horseradish
3 cups heavy cream
2 tbsp. sugar

1. Peel, quarter, core, and finely shred apples. Place in a small bowl with horseradish.

2. Whip cream with sugar until stiff. Fold into horseradish and apple mixture.

Serves 12.

New Year's Day Hoppin' John Salad

2 cups dried black-eyed peas,
  picked over and rinsed
1 medium onion, coarsely chopped
2 bay leaves
1 tsp. salt
½ cup diced smoked ham
4 scallions (white and green parts),
  chopped
1 small red bell pepper, cored,
  seeded, and chopped
½ cup olive oil
½ cup vegetable oil
½ cup red wine vinegar
2 large garlic cloves,
  peeled and finely chopped
¼ tsp. cayenne pepper
1 cup raw long-grain white rice,
  cooked

1. Place the black-eyed peas in a large kettle with water to cover. Place over medium-high heat and bring to a boil. Reduce heat and simmer for 2 minutes. Remove kettle from heat, cover, and let stand for one hour.

2. Drain the peas, rinse, and return to the pot. Cover with fresh water and add the onion, bay leaves, and salt. Return the kettle to the stove and bring the mixture to a boil. Reduce heat and simmer the peas for one hour, or until tender but not mushy. Drain the peas, remove the bay leaves, and cool.

3. Place the peas, ham, scallions, and pepper in a large bowl.

4. To prepare the dressing, combine the oils, vinegar, garlic, and cayenne in a jar; cover and shake well to mix. Pour the dressing over the peas and toss well to mix all ingredients.

5. Cover the bowl and allow the mixture to marinate overnight. A few hours before serving, remove the mixture from the refrigerator and bring to room temperature. Add the rice, toss the salad again, and chill until serving time.

Serves 12.

Baked Zippy Deviled Eggs

Eggs:
12 eggs, hard-cooked
½ cup mayonnaise
1 tbsp. grated onion
½ tsp. dry mustard
⅛ tsp. curry powder
8 slices bacon, cooked,
  drained, and crumbled
2 cups Cream Sauce (recipe
  follows)
1 4-oz. can sliced mushrooms,
  drained
1½ cups grated sharp
  cheddar cheese

1. Peel eggs, cut in half lengthwise, and remove yolks. Place yolks in a medium-size mixing bowl; then add mayonnaise, onion, mustard, curry powder, and crumbled bacon. Blend until smooth.

2. Stuff the 24 egg white halves with mixture. Place eggs in greased 13 x 9 x 2-inch baking dish.

3. Cover eggs with Cream Sauce. Sprinkle mushrooms over Cream Sauce. Top with grated cheese. Bake at 350 degrees for 30 minutes.

THE HOTEL DEL CORONADO COOKBOOK

Cream Sauce:

4 tbsp. butter
4 tbsp. all-purpose flour
2 cups hot milk
¼ tsp. salt
¼ tsp. paprika

1. Melt butter over low heat; then stir in flour until smooth. Slowly stir in milk, salt, and paprika.
2. Cook and stir sauce with whisk until smooth and boiling.

Serves 12.

Glazed Bacon with Brown Sugar and Walnuts

3 lb. sliced bacon
¾ cup dark brown sugar, firmly packed
3 tsp. all-purpose flour
1½ cups chopped walnuts

1. Preheat oven to 350 degrees.
2. Arrange bacon slices close together, but not overlapping, on a broiler rack in a roasting pan.
3. In a medium-size mixing bowl, combine brown sugar, flour, and walnuts; then sprinkle evenly over bacon.
4. Bake until crisp and brown, about 30 minutes. Drain on paper towels, transfer to chafing dish, and serve warm.

Serves 12.

Southern Biscuit Muffins

5 cups all-purpose flour
½ cup sugar
3 tbsp. baking powder
1½ cups cold butter
2 cups plus 4 tbsp. cold milk

1. Preheat oven to 400 degrees.
2. Grease two 12-cup muffin tins.
3. In a large bowl, combine flour, sugar, and baking powder. Cut in butter until mixture resembles coarse crumbs. Stir in milk just until flour mixture is moistened.
4. Spoon batter into muffin tins. Bake for 20 minutes or until golden. Remove from pans. Cool on wire rack. Serve with whipped butter and boysenberry preserves.

Yields 24 muffins.

Lemon-Topped Poppy Seed Brunch Cake

Cake:

¾ cup butter or margarine, softened
1½ cups sugar
6 egg yolks
3 cups cake flour
3¼ tsp. baking powder
¾ cup poppy seeds
1 cup milk
6 egg whites

1. Preheat oven to 350 degrees.

2. In a large mixing bowl, combine butter or margarine and ¾ cup sugar. With an electric mixer, blend for 2 minutes at medium speed. Add egg yolks, one at a time, beating at medium speed for 2 minutes after each addition. Continue procedure until all egg yolks have been added. Set aside.

3. In a large mixing bowl, sift together cake flour, baking powder, and poppy seeds. Add milk, and blend on low speed for 2 minutes. Add to egg mixture, then blend for 2 more minutes on medium speed.

4. In a medium-size mixing bowl, combine egg whites and remaining ¾ cup sugar; whip at high speed for 5 to 6 minutes. Fold into cake batter. Pour batter into a buttered bundt cake pan.

5. Bake for 30 to 35 minutes, or until cake tester inserted in center comes out clean. Cool in pan for 15 minutes, then invert on a serving platter.

Lemon Topping:

½ cup granulated sugar
⅓ cup fresh lemon juice

1. Combine ingredients in the top of a double boiler. Cook and stir over low heat for 5 to 6 minutes.

2. Remove from heat and pour over poppy seed brunch cake. Cool for 4 minutes.

Lemon Icing:

4 cups confectioners' sugar
¼ cup fresh lemon juice
¼ cup water
1 or 2 drops yellow food coloring

Blend the ingredients together and pour over cooled cake.

Serves 12.

Pineapple-Apricot Cheesecake Bars

⅓ cup plus 1 tbsp.
  butter, softened
⅓ cup plus 1 tbsp. brown sugar
1¼ cups flour
¾ cup chopped walnuts
¼ cup sugar
1 3-oz. package cream cheese
1 egg
2 tbsp. milk
1 tbsp. lemon juice
1 tsp. vanilla extract
¾ cup pineapple-apricot jam

1. Preheat oven to 350 degrees.

2. Cream butter with brown sugar; stir in flour and nuts. Reserve 1 cup of crumb mixture for topping and press the remainder into the foil-lined bottom of an 8 x 8-inch baking pan.

3. Bake for 15 minutes, until slightly browned. Cool.

4. Blend together sugar and cream cheese. Add egg, milk, lemon juice, and vanilla; beat well.

5. Spread crust with jam, then top with cream cheese mixture, spreading evenly. Sprinkle with crumb mixture, press lightly. Bake for 30 minutes, then cool and cut into bars.

Yields 12 to 16 bars.

Easter Brunch for Eight

An Easter Sunday brunch is the perfect way to celebrate spring renewal. Set a lively colorful table with yellow linen. To create a maypole effect for your centerpiece, fill a vase with spring flowers such as daffodils, tie pastel ribbons around the vase, and attach them to individual bud vases, one per place setting. Carry out the Easter theme on your buffet table with small baskets of dyed Easter eggs (later to be hidden for a kiddies' Easter egg hunt).

At the Del, Easter is celebrated with two lavish brunches that accommodate the more than four thousand guests who make reservations well in advance. In the garden patio, the antics of Harvey, the live six-foot-four-inch costumed Easter bunny who hops along handing out Easter baskets to all the excited children, are always a special attraction.

With a little preplanning, cooking a festive celebration need not be an exhausting task on Easter morning. Preparation of Grand Marnier Fruit Bowl, Raspberry Lemonade Mold, and Poached

Menu for Easter Sunday, April 17, 1938.

Salmon with Creamed Cucumber Sauce
the day before leaves only the Cheddar Baked
Eggs, Rosemary-Topped Potato and Onion
Pie, and Peppered Baby Lamb Chops to be
prepared on Easter morning. Bake and
freeze the muffins and Sour Cream Coffee
Cake a week in advance, and you will
be able to enjoy a warm, festive Easter.

MENU

Chilled Venetian Bellinis

Grand Marnier Fruit Bowl

Raspberry Lemonade Mold

Poached Salmon with Creamed
Cucumber Sauce

Cheddar Baked Eggs

Rosemary-Topped Potato and Onion Pie

Peppered Baby Lamb Chops with Mint Sauce

Herbed Whole Wheat Muffins with
Whipped Cinnamon Butter

Glazed Hot Cross Muffins

Sour Cream Coffee Cake with
Chocolate and Walnuts

Chilled Venetian Bellinis

6 cups canned peach nectar, chilled

3 bottles Asti Spumante wine, chilled

1. Empty peach nectar into a large glass pitcher.
2. Pour 1 ounce peach nectar into each of eight wine glasses. Slowly add the Asti Spumante to fill the glasses; mix gently. Serve immediately.

Serves 8.

Grand Marnier Fruit Bowl

1 6-oz. can frozen orange juice concentrate, thawed
½ cup Grand Marnier liqueur
2 pt. fresh strawberries
8 fresh peaches
2 tbsp. sugar

1. Stir together orange juice concentrate and Grand Marnier.
2. Wash and hull strawberries, leaving them whole. Peel, pit, and slice peaches.
3. Place fruit in crystal or glass bowl, sprinkle with sugar. Pour orange juice mixture over fruit. Stir gently to combine.
4. Cover and refrigerate overnight, stirring once or twice.

Serves 8.

Raspberry Lemonade Mold

1 10-oz. package frozen
  raspberries, thawed
1 6-oz. package
  raspberry gelatin
1½ cups boiling water
1 pt. vanilla ice cream, softened
1 6-oz. can frozen pink lemonade
  concentrate, thawed
¼ cup pecans, chopped

1. Drain raspberries and reserve syrup. In a medium-size bowl, dissolve gelatin in boiling water. Stir in softened ice cream. Add reserved raspberry syrup and lemonade concentrate; blend until smooth.

2. Chill until partially set. Watch carefully because gelatin sets up quickly. Fold in raspberries and pecans, then pour into a 5-cup mold and chill overnight.

3. Run a knife around the edges of the mold, dip mold in warm water, then invert onto a serving platter.

Serves 8.

Poached Salmon with Creamed Cucumber Sauce

Salmon:
6 cups Fish Stock
  (see recipe)
3 cups French Colombard wine
10 peppercorns
2 carrots, coarsely chopped
1 large onion, coarsely chopped
1 bay leaf
1 tsp. ground coriander
½ tsp. dried thyme
8 6-oz. salmon fillets, skinned
½ cup vegetable oil
4 tbsp. fresh lemon juice
Salt and freshly ground
  black pepper
1 tbsp. dried dill weed
2 heads romaine lettuce, washed
  and patted dry
2 tbsp. chives, chopped

1. Combine stock, wine, peppercorns, carrots, onion, bay leaf, coriander, and thyme in large saucepan. Bring to boil over medium-high heat, skimming foam as it accumulates. Cover partially, reduce heat, and simmer for about 30 minutes.

2. Strain stock through a colander into a large skillet. Place over medium heat and bring to gentle simmer. Reduce heat to low, add salmon, and poach until almost cooked through, about 6 minutes.

3. Remove from heat, let fish cool in stock. Drain fillets well. Arrange in a single layer in shallow baking pans. Sprinkle with oil, lemon juice, salt, pepper, and dried dill. Cover and refrigerate overnight.

Creamed Cucumber Sauce:

1 large cucumber
¼ cup light cream
1 tbsp. lime juice
10 watercress leaves, blanched
½ cup heavy cream
1 tsp. salt
3 drops Tabasco sauce
1 tsp. grated lime rind
**8 tbsp. chopped chives
  (for garnish)**

1. Peel the cucumber and cut it into small pieces. Discard any large seeds. Drop pieces into a blender or food processor; add light cream, lime juice, and watercress leaves. Blend until cucumber is puréed and mixture is a pale green.

2. Whip the heavy cream, then fold purée into whipped cream. Add salt and Tabasco sauce, then stir in the lime rind.

Yields about 2 cups.

To Assemble:

1. Cut romaine into thin strips. Arrange strips on a large serving platter.

2. Drain salmon and pat dry with paper towels. Lay salmon fillets over romaine, sprinkle lightly with salt and pepper, then spoon Creamed Cucumber Sauce over fillets and garnish with chopped chives.

Serves 8.

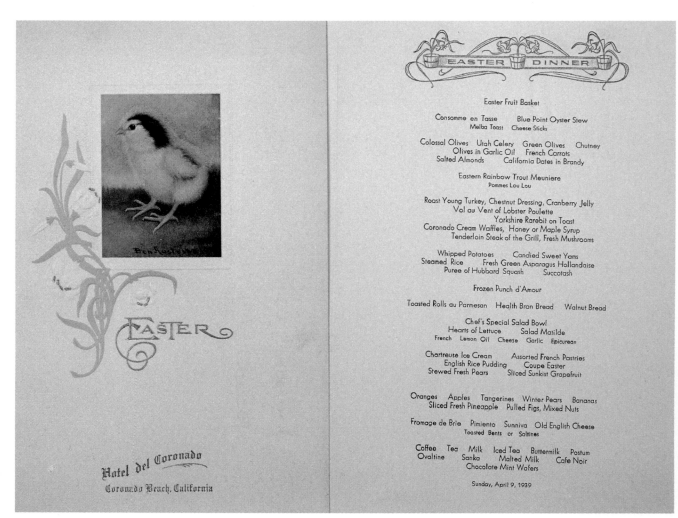

Menu for Easter Sunday, April 9, 1939.

THE HOTEL DEL CORONADO COOKBOOK

Cheddar Baked Eggs

2 tbsp. butter
6 scallions (white part only), thinly sliced
12 eggs, beaten
1⅓ cups milk
¾ tsp. salt
½ tsp. white pepper
4 cups grated cheddar cheese

1. Preheat oven to 350 degrees.
2. Melt butter in a skillet over medium-low heat. Sauté scallions in butter until soft.
3. Beat eggs in a large mixing bowl. Add milk, salt, pepper, scallions, and all but ½ cup of cheese.
4. Pour mixture into a greased 2-quart rectangular casserole.
5. Bake uncovered at 350 degrees for 30 minutes, or until mixture is set. Remove from oven and sprinkle with remaining cheese. Return to oven and continue to bake until cheese melts.

Serves 8.

Rosemary-Topped Potato and Onion Pie

8 tbsp. olive oil
3 medium white onions, thinly sliced
1 cup water
4 tsp. salt
1 tsp. freshly ground black pepper
4 medium russet potatoes (about 2¼ lb.), peeled
16 black olives, pitted
8 sprigs fresh rosemary
2 sprigs fresh rosemary (for garnish)

1. Preheat oven to 350 degrees.
2. Heat 4 tablespoons of olive oil in a skillet. Add onions and sauté for 5 minutes. Add water, half the salt, and half the pepper. Cover, reduce heat, and simmer. Continue cooking, stirring occasionally, until the onions caramelize, 10 to 15 minutes. Remove from heat and set aside.
3. Coarsely shred the potatoes and toss in a bowl with the remaining salt and pepper. Set aside.
4. Heat 2 tablespoons of the olive oil over moderate heat in a skillet with a 6-inch diameter bottom. Spread half the potatoes evenly in the pan and cook until the bottom is light brown, about 5 minutes. Carefully flip the pancake and cook for 2 minutes more. Transfer potato pancake, lighter side up, to a baking sheet. Set aside.
5. Repeat the above process with the remaining oil and potatoes.
6. Spread the tops of the pancakes with the cooked onions. Arrange olives and rosemary on top.
7. Bake for 20 minutes. Transfer to a serving platter and cut into wedges. Decorate platter with fresh rosemary sprigs. Serve warm.

Serves 8.

Peppered Baby Lamb Chops with Mint Sauce

Mint Sauce:

4 tbsp. finely chopped fresh mint
1 tbsp. rice wine vinegar
1 tbsp. lime juice
1 tsp. finely chopped fresh thyme
1 tsp. finely chopped
fresh shallots
1 tsp. chili sauce
¼ tsp. salt
1 egg yolk
6 tbsp. olive oil
3 tbsp. hazelnut oil

1. Place all ingredients except the oils in a food processor or a blender and process until smoothly combined.
2. With the machine running, slowly pour the oils into the processor to build a thick mixture. Set aside.

Note: Rice wine vinegar may be found in Asian markets.

Lamb Chops:

8 baby loin lamb chops
8 small slivers Parmesan cheese
1½ tbsp. finely cracked black
peppercorns
1½ tbsp. finely cracked white
peppercorns
8 tbsp. Dijon-style mustard
4 tbsp. olive oil
4 tbsp. diced tomato
(for garnish)
12 small mint sprigs (for garnish)

1. With a small, sharp knife, carefully cut a narrow slit in the side of each lamb chop near the bone. Insert a sliver of Parmesan cheese into each chop.
2. In a small mixing bowl, blend the black and white peppercorns into the mustard. Dip both sides of each chop in the mixture to coat them lightly.
3. Heat 2 tablespoons of the olive oil in a medium-size skillet over high heat, until it begins to smoke. Place four chops in the skillet and sauté them for 3 minutes; then turn and sauté for 2 minutes on the other side. Remove the chops and set them aside. Add the remaining 2 tablespoons of olive oil, heat it, and cook remaining chops.
4. Place the Mint Sauce on a serving platter and arrange the chops on top of sauce. Garnish platter with diced tomato and mint sprigs.

Serves 8.

Herbed Whole Wheat Muffins with Whipped Cinnamon Butter

Muffins:
1 cup all-purpose flour
1 cup whole wheat flour
⅓ cup sugar
2 tsp. baking powder
½ tsp. baking soda
½ tsp. salt
½ tsp. dried basil leaves
¼ tsp. dried marjoram leaves
¼ tsp. dried oregano leaves
⅛ tsp. dried thyme leaves
1 cup buttermilk
2 tbsp. butter, melted
1 egg, beaten
2 tbsp. wheat germ

1. Preheat oven to 400 degrees.
2. Grease a 12-cup muffin tin. In a large bowl, combine flours, sugar, baking powder, baking soda, salt, and herbs.
3. In a small bowl, combine buttermilk, butter, and egg; then stir into flour mixture just until moistened.
4. Spoon into muffin tin and sprinkle wheat germ on top. Bake for 15 to 20 minutes, or until lightly browned and a cake tester inserted in center comes out clean. Remove from pan.
5. Serve with Whipped Cinnamon Butter (recipe follows).

Yields 12 muffins.

Whipped Cinnamon Butter:
1 cup (2 sticks) butter, softened
2 tsp. cinnamon

1. Whip butter until fluffy. Fold in cinnamon and blend thoroughly.
2. Place butter mixture in a serving dish.

Yields 1 cup.

Glazed Hot Cross Muffins

Muffins:
2 cups all-purpose flour
¾ cup sugar
2 tsp. baking powder
½ tsp. salt
¼ tsp. ground cinnamon
½ tsp. allspice
1 cup milk
½ cup lightly salted butter or margarine, melted and cooled
1 egg, lightly beaten
1 tsp. vanilla extract
½ tsp. grated orange peel
¼ tsp. grated lemon peel
1 cup currants

1. Preheat oven to 375 degrees.
2. Grease a 12-cup muffin tin. In a large mixing bowl, stir together flour, sugar, baking powder, salt, cinnamon, and allspice.
3. In a small bowl, stir together milk, butter or margarine, egg, vanilla, orange peel, and lemon peel.
4. Make a well in center of dry ingredients; then add milk mixture and stir just to combine. Stir in currants.
5. Spoon batter into prepared muffin tin. Bake for 15 to 20 minutes, or until a cake tester inserted in center of one muffin comes out clean.
6. Remove muffin tin to wire rack. Cool 5 minutes before removing muffins from cups. Let muffins cool on rack.

Glaze:

½ **cup plus 1 tbsp.**
    confectioners' sugar
2 **tbsp. freshly squeezed**
    lemon juice

1. Combine confectioners' sugar and lemon juice.
2. Drizzle glaze over each muffin to form a cross. Serve warm, or store completely cooled muffins in an airtight container at room temperature. Muffins freeze well.

Yields 12 muffins.

Sour Cream Coffee Cake with Chocolate and Walnuts

2 **cups plus 2 tbsp. all-purpose**
    flour
¾ **cup plus 2 tbsp. sugar**
8 **oz. (2 sticks) unsalted butter,**
    at room temperature
2 **tsp. baking powder**
1 **tsp. baking soda**
¼ **tsp. salt**
3 **eggs**
1 **cup sour cream**
2 **tsp. vanilla extract**
1 **cup chopped walnuts**
4 **oz. bittersweet chocolate,**
    broken into small pieces

1. Preheat oven to 350 degrees.
2. Butter a 9-inch round cake pan. Dust pan with 2 tablespoons each of the flour and sugar. Tap out the excess.
3. In a medium-size mixing bowl, beat butter with the remaining ¾ cup sugar at high speed until light and creamy, about 7 minutes.
4. In another bowl, combine the remaining 2 cups flour with baking powder, baking soda, and salt. Sift twice. Add ½ cup of the flour mixture to the mixing bowl and blend into butter mixture on low speed. Beat in 1 egg. Continue to blend in flour mixture, ½ cup at a time, alternately with the remaining 2 eggs. Beat in remaining flour mixture along with sour cream and vanilla extract.
5. Using a spatula, thoroughly fold in chopped walnuts and chocolate pieces. Pour batter into the prepared baking pan, spreading with a spatula to smooth the surface.
6. Bake for 45 to 55 minutes, until the cake begins to shrink from the sides of the pan, the surface cracks slightly, and a cake tester inserted in center comes out clean. Let cake cool in pan for 10 minutes, then unmold and transfer to a wire rack. Let stand for at least 2 hours, until completely cool, before serving.

Note: Coffee cake may be prepared up to a week in advance. Cool, wrap well, and freeze. Defrost in the wrapping overnight.

Serves 12.

Mother's Day Brunch for Six

We owe special thanks to President Woodrow Wilson, who in 1914 set aside the second Sunday in May as a national holiday to honor America's mothers.

Let's pamper Mother and a few of her special friends with a labor-of-love brunch for six. This is the perfect time to set the table with a feminine touch. Pastel linen, napkins tied with ribbons, and a bouquet of carnations (the traditional Mother's Day flower) for the centerpiece will show your love and affection. Express your feelings through this get-together when presents alone do not seem to say all that you feel.

French cheeses and smoked whitefish are selected to provide an elegant touch—the accent is on foods that are not part of Mother's usual daily diet. No bacon and eggs over easy today—it's Spicy Ham and Cheddar Pudding, Mushroom-Sausage Strudel, and other delicacies followed by The Del's Signature Chocolate Mousse for this festive occasion. This brunch is intended to make Mother feel catered to and cared for by a loving cook.

MENU

Mimosa Cocktails

Citrus-Honey Compote

Smoked Fish Platter

French Cheese Platter

Spicy Ham and Cheddar Pudding

Mushroom-Sausage Strudel

Minicroissants with Strawberry Butter

Pecan-Cinnamon Bundt Cake

The Del's Signature Chocolate Mousse

Esther Williams and her two sons pose for a photograph during the Centennial weekend. They were frequent visitors when the boys were children.

Mimosa Cocktails

6 cups freshly squeezed orange juice

2 (750-ml) bottles chilled brut champagne

1 basket strawberries, washed and air dried

1. Fill six champagne glasses ⅔ full with orange juice. Slowly add champagne to fill the glasses, stir gently.

2. Garnish with a strawberry.

Yields 12 servings.

Citrus-Honey Compote

1 cup water
½ cup honey
Zest and juice of 1 lemon
3 pink grapefruits, peeled,
  sliced, and seeded
3 navel oranges, peeled, sliced,
  and seeded

1. In a small saucepan, bring the water, honey, and lemon zest to a boil over medium heat. Reduce the heat to low and simmer uncovered for 5 minutes. Let cool to room temperature.

2. In a large bowl, combine grapefruit, orange, lemon juice, and honey mixture. Cover and refrigerate overnight.

3. Serve in a glass bowl. Set bowl on a pedestal cake plate to elevate.

Note: Whenever your menu calls for a buffet, you should elevate some of the items and use platters of various sizes to add interest to your buffet table.

Serves 6.

Smoked Fish Platter

1 bunch radishes (about 8 oz.),
  trimmed
1 large carrot
2 tbsp. chopped parsley
1 tbsp. lemon juice
¼ tsp. sugar
¼ tsp. salt
⅛ tsp. freshly ground black
  pepper
1 bunch romaine, washed and air
  dried
½ lb. smoked sablefish
½ lb. smoked whitefish
1 bunch parsley (for garnish)

1. Trim radishes. Wash under cold running water and pat dry with paper towels. Using small holes of grater, grate radishes into a medium-size bowl (or grate them in a food processor fitted with shredding disk). You should have about 1½ cups.

2. Peel and trim carrot. Grate as you did the radishes.

3. Place shredded vegetables in coarse-mesh sieve and, using back of spoon, press to extract juices. Transfer vegetables to medium-size bowl. Add parsley, lemon juice, sugar, and salt and pepper to taste. Toss, cover, and refrigerate.

4. When ready to serve, toss once more and set bowl of shredded vegetables in the center of a platter. Cover platter with romaine.

5. Cut sablefish and whitefish into serving portions and arrange on romaine. Garnish with parsley.

Note: Smoked fish may be found in specialty markets, some delis, or local supermarkets.

Serves 6.

French Cheese Platter

1 head Salad Savoy lettuce
½ lb. Camembert cheese
½ lb. goat cheese
½ lb. gourmandise cheese
½ lb. rondelle cheese
Water crackers
2 bunches champagne grapes
  or Tokay grapes (for garnish)

1. Wash and air dry lettuce; arrange leaves on a platter.
2. Arrange assorted cheeses on lettuce leaves. Garnish with grapes and serve with water crackers.

Serves 6.

Spicy Ham and Cheddar Pudding

1½ tbsp. bacon fat
1 medium-size Spanish onion,
  coarsely chopped
½ lb. cooked ham (about 1¼
  cups), coarsely chopped
1 4-oz. can diced green chiles,
  drained
½ tsp. chili powder
½ tsp. dried oregano, crumbled
½ lb. sharp cheddar cheese,
  grated
16 thin (3-inch-square)
  slices whole wheat bread,
  crusts removed
4 eggs
2 cups milk

1. Melt bacon fat in a skillet over medium heat. Add onion and sauté, stirring frequently until softened, about 5 minutes. Add ham, chiles, chili powder, oregano, and half of the grated cheese. Stir until mixed.
2. Cut each bread slice in thirds. Arrange a third of the slices in a single layer in a greased 9 x 9-inch baking pan. Spoon on half of the cooked onion in an even layer.
3. Layer another third of the bread, and spoon on the remaining half of the filling. Top with the remaining bread.
4. In a large bowl, beat eggs lightly; then slowly beat in milk. Pour egg mixture over bread; sprinkle with remaining half of the cheese. Cover and refrigerate overnight.
5. Preheat oven to 325 degrees. Bake uncovered, until the center is puffed and golden brown, about 50 to 60 minutes.

Serves 6.

Mushroom-Sausage Strudel

2 lb. mild Italian sausage
2 lb. fresh mushrooms, minced
¼ cup minced shallots
6 tbsp. butter
Salt and freshly ground pepper
   to taste
16 oz. cream cheese
8 sheets Phyllo pastry
¾ cup butter, melted
1 cup seasoned bread crumbs

1. Remove sausage from its casing. Sauté in a small skillet until it is no longer pink and crumbles into small pieces. Drain and set aside.

2. Sauté mushrooms and shallots in 6 tablespoons of butter over medium heat, stirring frequently. Cook until pieces separate and liquid has evaporated. Add salt and pepper. Combine mushroom mixture with sausage and cream cheese, blending thoroughly.

3. Spread a sheet of Phyllo pastry on a lightly dampened towel. Quickly brush with melted butter and sprinkle with a few bread crumbs. Top with second sheet and repeat procedure. Top again with third sheet and repeat procedure. Top with fourth sheet, brush with melted butter, but omit crumbs. Spoon half the mushroom-sausage mixture along the narrow edge of the Phyllo pastry, leaving a 2-inch border at the sides. Fold in sides, using the towel to assist in rolling up Phyllo pastry.

4. Preheat oven to 400 degrees.

5. Place strudel on a nonstick cookie sheet, brush with melted butter. Repeat procedure using the remaining sheets of Phyllo and mushroom-sausage mixture. Bake until brown, about 20 minutes, then cut and serve.

Note: Phyllo pastry may be found in the frozen section of local supermarkets.

Serves 8 to 10.

Minicroissants with Strawberry Butter

Croissants:
1 8-oz. package refrigerated
   crescent dinner rolls
2 tbsp. butter, softened
2 egg yolks beaten with 2
   tsp. water (egg wash)

1. Preheat oven to 375 degrees. Separate dough into eight scored triangles. Cut each in half, making sixteen triangles.

2. Spread lightly with softened butter. Starting at wide end, roll up. Place point side down on ungreased cookie sheets; curve to shape crescents.

3. Brush tops of rolls lightly with egg wash. Bake for 10 to 12 minutes.

Note: Croissants may be prepared in advance. After baking, wrap well in foil and freeze. To serve, defrost at room temperature for 2 to 3 hours. Keep wrapped. Heat at 300 degrees for 5 to 7 minutes before serving. Serve warm.

Yields 16 minicroissants.

Strawberry Butter:

1 cup butter
1 cup strawberry jam

1. Whip butter until fluffy.
2. Add strawberry jam to whipped butter; mix until well blended.

Pecan-Cinnamon Bundt Cake

1½ cups chopped pecans
¾ cup brown sugar, packed
1 tbsp. ground cinnamon
2 cups unbleached all-purpose flour
1 cup whole wheat pastry flour
1 tbsp. baking powder
1 tsp. baking soda
½ tsp. salt
1 cup (2 sticks) unsalted butter, softened
1¼ cups granulated sugar
1½ cups sour cream
3 eggs
1½ tsp. grated lemon zest
Confectioners' sugar

1. Preheat oven to 350 degrees.

2. To prepare the filling, combine pecans, brown sugar, and cinnamon in a bowl, stir to mix well. Set aside.

3. Sift together the flours, baking powder, baking soda, and salt in a large bowl.

4. In a separate bowl, cream butter, sugar, and sour cream until light and fluffy. Add eggs, one at a time, beating well after each addition. Stir in the lemon zest. Add the dry ingredients and beat just until smooth.

5. Pour about half the batter into a nonstick bundt pan. Sprinkle the filling evenly around the center of the batter, preventing the filling from touching the sides of the pan. Cover with the remaining batter. Bake for 45 to 55 minutes, or until a cake tester inserted in center comes out clean.

6. Cool in the pan for 10 minutes before inverting onto a cake plate. Dust with confectioners' sugar before serving.

Serves 8 to 12.

The Del's Signature Chocolate Mousse

Mousse:

**6 1-oz. squares semisweet
   chocolate**
4 eggs, separated
2 tbsp. Irish cream liqueur
3 tbsp. sugar

1. Melt chocolate in the top of a double boiler over barely simmering water. Remove from heat and cool chocolate to lukewarm. Beat in egg yolks, one at a time, beating well after each addition; then beat in liqueur.

2. Beat egg whites in a bowl until foamy. Gradually beat in sugar until the meringue forms stiff peaks. Stir one third of the meringue into the chocolate mixture. Gently fold the chocolate mixture into the remaining meringue until no white streaks remain.

Whipped Cream Garnish:

⅔ cup heavy cream
½ tsp. vanilla extract
2 tbsp. confectioners' sugar

Whip cream with vanilla extract and sugar until mixture forms stiff peaks.

Chocolate Curls:

**1 4 to 6 oz. bar of semi-sweet
   chocolate, chilled**

Scrape long side of bar with a potato peeler to make chocolate curls.

To Assemble:
1. Place mousse in a glass bowl.
2. Top mousse with Whipped Cream Garnish and Chocolate Curls.

Serves 6.

The Award-Winning Sunday Brunch for Eight

For the past fifteen years, the Del's Sunday Brunch has been named the number one brunch by readers of *San Diego Magazine.* After a morning golf game or church, fourteen hundred guests make brunch in the Crown Room their Sunday tradition. Sipping on Smashing Citrus Cocktails, they relax as they are entertained by a harpist, who sits on a richly covered velvet chair positioned in the loft, a space that was once reserved for special dignitaries.

Tricolor Pasta Salad and the Del's very own version of Waldorf salad are lavishly displayed with platters of smoked trout and salmon. The recipes are scaled down in this chapter to serve eight people. Colorful Tomato Cups Florentine filled with Scrambled Eggs and Cheddar Cheese, American Fried Potatoes, as well as Canadian Bacon and Apple Wedges with Red Onion Marmalade are sure to produce an award-winning brunch for you and your guests.

THE HOTEL DEL CORONADO COOKBOOK

MENU

Smashing Citrus Cocktails

The Del's Own Waldorf Salad

Seasonal Fresh Fruit Platter

Trout and Salmon Platter

Tricolor Pasta Salad

Tomato Cups Florentine Filled with
Scrambled Eggs and Cheddar Cheese

American Fried Potatoes

Canadian Bacon and Apple Wedges
with Red Onion Marmalade

Banana-Raisin Muffins with
Whipped Almond Butter

Lemon-Blueberry Muffins

Cranberry-Orange Muffins

Pear Upside-Down Cake

Hotel del Coronado

CORONADO BEACH, CALIFORNIA

E. S. BABCOCK, MANAGER

❧ Breakfast ❧

Fruit in Season

Strawberries with Cream   Baked Apples, with Cream
Green Figs, with Cream   Lemon Blend
Cantaloupe   Sliced Tomatoes
Stewed Prunes   Orange Marmalade   Raspberry Jam

Grape Nuts   Cracked Wheat

Fish Balls   Salt Mackerel, Boiled or Broiled
Codfish with Cream   Smoked Salmon
Finnan Haddie, del Coronado

Broiled Dove   Fried Spring Chicken

OYSTERS: Fancy Roast, or Broiled

Clam Broth   Clam Stew   Oyster Stew

Eggs as Ordered

Omelettes: Plain, with Cheese or Rum
Scrambled Eggs: Plain, with Ham or Parsley
Shirred Eggs: Plain, Spanish Style or à la Turque
Fried Eggs: with Hazelnut Butter or Bacon

Sirloin Steak, with Fried Onions   Pork Chops
Lamb Chops, with French Peas   English Mutton Chops
Fried Veal Cutlets, breaded, Tomato Sauce
Breakfast Bacon   Grilled Ham   Corned Beef Hash
Country Sausage
Calf's Liver   Fried Tripe   Fried Mush
Mutton Kidneys sauté, with Mushrooms

Potatoes—Baked, Saratoga, Lyonnaise

Toast   Cream Toast
French Rolls   Albany Rolls   Corn Bread   Graham Rolls
Wheat Muffins
Griddle Cakes   Waffles
Maple Syrup   Strained Honey
Coffee   Hot Milk   Chocolate   Cocoa
Black, English Breakfast and Green Tea

Guests will please exercise a little patience, as all dishes on this card are cooked to order.

MEAL HOURS—Breakfast, 6:00 to 10:00 Luncheon, 12:30 to 2:00 Dinner, 6:00 to 8:00
Sunday Breakfast, 7:00 to 10:00
Nurses and Children, Breakfast, 6:00 to 9:00 Lunch, 12:00 to 1:30 Dinner, 5:30 to 7:00

SUNDAY, SEPTEMBER 2, 1900

Breakfast menu for Sunday, September 2, 1900. Guests are asked to "please exercise a little patience, as all dishes on this card are cooked to order."

Smashing Citrus Cocktails

8 large oranges
6 cups chilled orange juice
8 oz. vodka
8 tsp. Grand Marnier liqueur
2 tsp. grenadine
**8 strawberries, washed and dried
(for garnish)**

1. Cut a ½-inch slice off tops of oranges, scoop out pulp and discard. Cut a very thin slice off bottom of each orange, so it will stand upright.

2. In a pitcher, combine orange juice, vodka, Grand Marnier, and grenadine. Stir until well blended.

3. Pour into orange shells. Garnish with strawberries and serve with short straws.

Serves 8.

The Del's Own Waldorf Salad

4 tbsp. lemon juice
8 Red Delicious apples, unpeeled, cored, and chopped
6 stalks celery, diced
¾ cup walnuts, chopped
¾ cup raisins, chopped
¼ cup sour cream
¼ cup mayonnaise
½ cup heavy cream, whipped
12 walnut halves (for garnish)
6 red apple wedges (for garnish)

1. Sprinkle lemon juice over the apples to prevent them from turning dark in color.
2. In a large mixing bowl, combine the apples, celery, walnuts, and raisins. In a small mixing bowl, mix together the sour cream, mayonnaise, and whipped cream.
3. Carefully fold the sour cream mixture into the apple mixture.
4. Transfer to a large glass bowl. (A footed trifle bowl works well.) Decorate the top with walnut halves and apple wedges.

Serves 8.

Seasonal Fresh Fruit Platter

2 oranges
1 cantaloupe
1 honeydew melon
⅓ of a whole watermelon
1 pineapple
1 small head Salad Savoy or radicchio (for garnish)
1 small bunch seedless black grapes
1 small bunch Thompson seedless grapes
2 cups strawberries

1. Wash all the fruit. Peel and slice oranges. Cut away rind of melons and pineapple and cut into ½-inch slices.
2. Wash and dry Salad Savoy or radicchio. Separate leaves and place on a large serving platter.
3. Arrange fruit in rows on the platter, keeping all of one kind in a row. Cut bunches of grapes into small clusters and place them at the ends of the platter. Arrange strawberries over the top of the sliced fruit to add color.

Serves 8.

Trout and Salmon Platter

1 head romaine lettuce, washed and dried
12 oz. smoked trout fillets, cut into 1½-inch strips
12 oz. smoked salmon, cut into 1½-inch strips
½ lemon, cut into slices (for garnish)

1. Cut romaine into four wedges, then place them on a platter. Lay the trout strips and salmon strips alternately over the romaine wedges. They can overlap—the romaine wedges assist in making an attractive presentation.
2. Garnish with lemon slices.

Note: Smoked trout may be found in specialty markets or in some local supermarkets.

Serves 8.

Tricolor Pasta Salad

1 lb. rainbow pasta
1 medium-size carrot, sliced
1 medium-size zucchini, sliced
3 yellow crookneck squash
   (about 1½ lb.), chopped
1 red bell pepper, cored,
   seeded, and chopped
1 green bell pepper, cored,
   seeded, and chopped
1 yellow bell pepper, cored,
   seeded, and chopped
2 tsp. salt
1 tbsp. onion powder
½ tsp. white pepper
1 tsp. oregano
½ tsp. Tabasco sauce
2 tbsp. grated Parmesan cheese
½ cup vegetable oil
¼ cup vinegar

1. In a 4-quart saucepan, cook pasta in boiling water according to the directions on the package. Drain thoroughly, rinse pasta in cold water, and set aside.

2. In a large mixing bowl, combine the remaining ingredients. Fold into the pasta and refrigerate.

3. To serve, transfer pasta to a glass bowl, so the rainbow colors of the pasta show through.

Serves 8.

Tomato Cups Florentine Filled with Scrambled Eggs and Cheddar Cheese

4 medium-size tomatoes, cut in
   half
1 bunch fresh spinach, cleaned
   and stems removed
2 tbsp. butter
6 eggs, beaten
¼ tsp. salt
⅛ tsp. white pepper
¾ cup grated cheddar cheese

1. Gently scoop out a third of the pulp from the tomato halves. Set tomatoes in a greased 13 x 9 x 2-inch baking pan. Set aside.

2. Remove spinach stems and wash spinach thoroughly.

3. Fill a 2-quart saucepan ¾ full of water and bring to a rapid boil. Submerge spinach for 30 seconds in boiling water; remove and drain. Rinse spinach in cold water. Drain and pat dry with paper towels.

4. Line each tomato cavity with spinach leaves.

5. In a medium-size skillet, melt the butter. Add beaten eggs, salt, pepper, and cheddar cheese. Scramble lightly. Remove from heat and fill tomato cups with scrambled egg mixture. Transfer to a serving platter.

Serves 8.

American Fried Potatoes

4 8-oz. russet potatoes
½ cup butter or margarine
½ tsp. salt
¼ tsp. white pepper
2 sprigs parsley washed and dried
  (for garnish)

1. Place potatoes in a 2-quart saucepan. Cover with water and bring to a boil. Cook until tender, about 25 minutes. Drain and allow to cool.

2. Remove skins from potatoes, then cut into ¼-inch slices. Cover potatoes and refrigerate. (This recipe may be prepared the day before up to this point.)

3. In a large skillet, melt half of the butter or margarine. Add half the potato slices (do not overlap); then fry on each side for about 1½ minutes, until golden brown. Season with half the salt and pepper. Repeat the process with the remaining potato slices.

4. Transfer to serving platter; keep warm in oven until serving time. Garnish with parsley.

Serves 8.

Canadian Bacon and Apple Wedges with Red Onion Marmalade

Canadian Bacon:
3 tbsp. butter or margarine
16 ⅛-inch thick slices
  Canadian bacon
3 scallions (green part only),
  minced (for garnish)

1. In a large skillet, melt butter or margarine.

2. Add bacon, and sauté for about 1 minute on each side, until heated. Remove bacon from skillet and set aside.

Apple Wedges:
½ cup butter or margarine
4 Red Delicious apples, washed,
  cored, and sliced
  into 24 wedges
½ cup brown sugar
2 tbsp. cinnamon
½ cup unsweetened apple juice

1. Melt butter or margarine in a large skillet.

2. Add apple wedges and sauté for 2 minutes. Sprinkle brown sugar, cinnamon, and apple juice over apple wedges. Continue to cook and stir for about five minutes, until apples are tender. Remove from heat and set aside.

Red Onion Marmalade:
½ cup butter or margarine
3 medium-size red onions,
  thinly sliced
½ cup brown sugar
½ cup water

1. In a large skillet, melt butter or margarine, add onion slices, and sauté for 3 minutes.

2. Add brown sugar and water. Continue cooking until onions are soft and tender and caramelized with sugar. Simmer for 5 minutes. Place in an ovenproof dish. Set aside.

To Assemble:

1. Place Canadian bacon slices in the center of a large oval serving platter.

2. Arrange 12 apple wedges on each side of the Canadian bacon. Sprinkle minced scallion tops over bacon.

3. Spoon onion marmalade over apple wedges.

Serves 8.

Banana-Raisin Muffins with Whipped Almond Butter

Muffins:

1⅔ cups all-purpose flour
¼ cup sugar
2 tsp. baking powder
½ tsp. salt
½ cup plus 4 tbsp. sliced almonds
2⅔ cups flaked coconut
½ cup raisins
2 small bananas, chopped (about 1⅓ cups)
1 egg
½ cup milk
¼ cup plus 2 tsp. firmly packed brown sugar
7 tbsp. butter, melted
¼ tsp. cinnamon

1. Preheat oven to 375 degrees.

2. Grease a twelve-cup muffin tin. In a large mixing bowl, combine flour, sugar, baking powder, and salt. Mix in ½ cup almonds, 1 cup coconut, and raisins. Blend in bananas.

3. In a small mixing bowl, beat egg, milk, ¼ cup brown sugar, and 3 tablespoons butter. Add to flour mixture and mix until moistened.

4. In a small mixing bowl, mix together remaining coconut, 4 tablespoons almonds, 4 tablespoons butter, 2 teaspoons brown sugar, and cinnamon. Spoon topping evenly over each muffin.

5. Bake for about 25 minutes, or until a cake tester inserted in center of one muffin comes out clean. If muffins brown too quickly, cover with foil.

Yields 24 muffins.

Almond Butter:

1 cup finely chopped almonds
2 cups butter
4 cups confectioners' sugar
4 tsp. almond extract

1. Preheat oven to 350 degrees.

2. Spread almonds on a nonstick cookie sheet, then bake for about 5 minutes.

3. Whip butter until fluffy, add confectioners' sugar, almond extract, and chopped almonds. Mix until well blended. Place in a small serving dish near muffins.

Yields about 2¼ cups.

Lemon-Blueberry Muffins

2 cups all-purpose flour
⅔ cup plus 1 tbsp. sugar
1 tsp. baking powder
1 tsp. baking soda
½ tsp. salt
1 8-oz. container lemon yogurt (about 1 cup)
¼ cup lightly salted butter or margarine, melted and cooled
1 egg, lightly beaten
1 to 2 tsp. grated lemon peel
1 tsp. vanilla extract
2 cups fresh or frozen (thawed and drained) blueberries

1. Preheat oven to 350 degrees.

2. Grease a twelve-cup muffin tin. In a large mixing bowl, stir together flour, ⅔ cup sugar, baking powder, baking soda, and salt.

3. In a small mixing bowl, stir together yogurt, butter, egg, lemon peel, and vanilla extract until blended. Make a well in center of dry ingredients, add yogurt mixture, and stir just to combine. Stir in blueberries.

4. Spoon batter into prepared muffin tin and sprinkle with the remaining tablespoon of sugar.

5. Bake for 20 to 25 minutes, or until a cake tester inserted in center of one muffin comes out clean.

6. Remove muffin tins to wire rack. Cool for 5 minutes before removing muffins from cups. Let muffins cool on rack. Serve warm, or cool completely and store in an airtight container at room temperature. Muffins freeze well.

Yields 12 muffins.

Cranberry-Orange Muffins

2 cups all-purpose flour
½ cup firmly packed light brown sugar
½ cup vacuum-packed wheat germ with brown sugar and honey
2 tsp. baking powder
½ tsp. baking soda
½ tsp. salt
1 cup fresh or frozen (thawed and drained) cranberries
⅓ cup sugar
¾ cup orange juice
⅓ cup vegetable oil
1 egg, lightly beaten
1½ tsp. grated orange peel
1 tsp. vanilla extract
½ cup chopped pecans

1. Preheat oven to 400 degrees.

2. Grease a twelve-cup muffin tin. In a large mixing bowl, stir together flour, brown sugar, wheat germ, baking powder, baking soda, and salt. In a small mixing bowl, stir together cranberries and sugar; let stand 2 minutes.

3. In a medium-size mixing bowl, stir together orange juice, oil, egg, orange peel, and vanilla extract until blended. Make a well in center of dry ingredients; then add cranberry mixture and orange juice mixture and stir just to combine. Stir in pecans.

4. Spoon batter into prepared muffin tin. Bake for 15 to 20 minutes, or until a cake tester inserted in center of one muffin comes out clean.

5. Remove muffin tins to a wire rack. Cool for 5 minutes before removing muffins from cups. Finish cooling on rack. Serve warm, or cool completely and store in an airtight container at room temperature. Muffins freeze well.

Yields 12 muffins.

Pear Upside-Down Cake

⅓ cup plus 3 tbsp.
   unsalted butter, at room
   temperature
¾ cup brown sugar
¼ tsp. nutmeg
2 pears, peeled, cored, halved,
   and sliced
1½ cups cake flour
1 tsp. baking powder
¼ tsp. baking soda
¼ tsp. salt
½ cup granulated sugar
½ tsp. vanilla
1 large egg
½ cup buttermilk

1. Preheat oven to 350 degrees.
2. Lightly grease an 8-inch round cake pan. Set aside.
3. Melt 3 tablespoons butter in a small saucepan. Stir in brown sugar and nutmeg. Remove from heat and pour into prepared cake pan. Allow mixture to cool.
4. Sift together cake flour, baking powder, baking soda, and salt. Set aside.
5. In a medium-size mixing bowl, combine granulated sugar, ⅓ cup butter, vanilla, and egg. Blend on low speed with an electric mixer for 2 minutes.
6. Add sifted ingredients and mix on low speed for 2 minutes. Add buttermilk and blend on low speed for 1 more minute, or until all ingredients are thoroughly blended together. Set aside.
7. Arrange pear slices over cooled topping in cake pan. Pour cake batter over pears and bake for 20 to 25 minutes, or until a cake tester inserted in the center comes out clean.
8. Remove cake from oven. Cool on rack for 2 minutes. Run a knife around the inside edge of pan, cover cake with a serving plate, and invert the cake onto plate, fruit side up. Cool slightly before serving. Serve warm.

Serves 8.

CHAPTER FIVE

Tying the Knot at the Del

Fine food is carefully selected to complement the time of day and the location, making a wedding or reception at the Del an occasion to be remembered. To introduce the families of the bride and groom to one another, a rehearsal dinner is the perfect setting for Champagne Cocktails accompanied by fresh Mushrooms Stuffed with Escargot, followed by a first course of Scallops Mediterranean with Jade Sauce and a delicate salad of Gathered Greens with Sherry Vinaigrette Dressing. Breast of Duck with Kumquat Sauce serves as the entree, concluding with Hearts of Bavarian Cream with Caramel Sauce and Candied Orange Peel.

If the ceremony is taking place in the morning around ten o'clock, a breakfast starting with Crème de Cassis Mimosas and Fresh Citrus Frappé followed by Smoked Salmon Pinwheels on Brioche Toast and fresh strawberries hollowed out and filled with Boursin cheese is an elegant choice.

For an afternoon wedding, an outdoor seated luncheon served under a white tent is appropriate. A menu of Chilled Melon Soup in Cantaloupe Shell followed by Classic Lobster Salad and Triple-Dipped Strawberries leaves the wedding couple with fond memories.

The Del's Strawberries and Cream Wedding Cake, topped with roses and Dendrobium orchids from the bridal bouquet. In the background is the Garden Patio Gazebo, located in the courtyard of the Hotel del Coronado.

A late afternoon or dinner reception may be highlighted by a buffet filled with the wedding couple's favorite fare and a festival of hors d'oeuvres followed by Ballotine of Chicken with Pistachios and Kumquats, Vol-au-Vent Hearts filled with Shrimp Newburg, and Petite Beef Wellingtons. The culmination of the reception, of course, is the Del's Strawberries and Cream Wedding Cake, crowned with an assortment of flowers to match the bridal bouquet.

At the Del, all this is expected to magically take place without a hitch. For example, consider the case of the "Wedding Cake Meltdown." For this particular wedding, the bride ordered the cake from a bakery in Los Angeles, 145 miles from the hotel. The cake was a four-tiered masterpiece. The driver arrived with the cake three hours before the ceremony, assembled his work of art in a prominent location in front of a bay window in the assigned banquet room, and departed. That day, the sun chose to shine brightly through the bay window into the banquet room. By the time the banquet captain in charge of the wedding preparations arrived to ensure that the room was ready, the bride and groom ornament had slid to the floor and the cake was in an advanced stage of meltdown. Within minutes, the Del's pastry chef arrived and wheeled the cake to his walk-in freezer. Pastry tube in hand, he rescued the cake from its imminent collapse and returned it intact in time for the wedding. With a little magic, everything took place without a hitch, just as expected.

Wherever you decide to tie the knot, this exciting occasion is one that can be remembered forever with an elegant array of sumptuous delicacies.

Rehearsal Dinner for Twelve

Formal weddings are making a comeback, and more of them taking place at home. A wedding with attendants requires a rehearsal, so all the participants feel at ease and know their roles in the big event. What better way to acquaint the immediate wedding party than to follow the rehearsal with an elegant dinner that sets the mood for the wedding.

MENU

Champagne Cocktails

Spiced Cashews and Pecans

Mushrooms Stuffed with Escargot

Gathered Greens
Sherry Vinaigrette Dressing

Scallops Mediterranean
Jade Sauce

Rose Bouquet Sorbet

Breast of Duck with Kumquat Sauce

Almond Wild Rice

Baby Corn Wrapped in Zucchini Strips

Hearts of Bavarian Cream with
Caramel Sauce and Candied Orange Peel

Champagne Cocktails

24 sugar cubes
Angostura bitters
2 750-ml bottles chilled champagne
24 lemon twists

1. Place sugar cubes in a small bowl. Pour enough bitters over sugar cubes to saturate them.
2. Place a sugar cube in each of twelve glasses. Fill with champagne and top with a lemon twist.

Yields about 24 5-ounce servings.

Spiced Cashews and Pecans

4 tbsp. butter or margarine
2 cups cashews
2 cups pecans
2 tsp. garlic salt
½ tsp. cayenne pepper

1. Preheat oven to 300 degrees.
2. Melt butter or margarine in a shallow baking pan in the oven. Remove pan from oven and stir in cashews and pecans. Return pan to oven and bake for 25 minutes, stirring frequently.
3. In a small bowl, combine garlic salt and cayenne pepper.
4. Remove cashews and pecans from the oven and stir in seasonings. Cool and store in an airtight container.

Yields 4 cups.

Mushrooms Stuffed with Escargot

24 large mushroom caps, approximately 2 inches in diameter
1 cup (2 sticks) sweet butter
¼ cup minced shallots
4 large cloves garlic, finely minced
¼ cup finely minced fresh parsley
½ tsp. Dijon-style mustard
¼ tsp. nutmeg
½ tsp. salt
¼ tsp. white pepper
2 4½-oz. cans snails, rinsed and drained

1. Preheat oven to 375 degrees.
2. With a sharp knife, hollow out a depression on the inside of each mushroom cap. Set aside.
3. In a mixing bowl, combine ¾ cup butter, shallots, garlic, parsley, mustard, nutmeg, salt, and pepper. Beat with an electric mixer. Set aside.
4. In a large skillet, melt remaining ¼ cup butter. Add half the mushroom caps and sauté for 5 minutes. Transfer caps to a 13 x 9 x 2-inch baking pan and repeat procedure with the remaining half of the mushrooms.
5. With a melon ball cutter, scoop butter-shallot mixture into mushroom caps, then top with escargot and a dot of the butter-shallot mixture.
6. Place mushrooms in oven and bake for 15 minutes. Remove from oven and transfer stuffed mushrooms to serving platter.

Yields 24.

Gathered Greens with Sherry Vinaigrette Dressing

Greens:
1 head curly endive
1 head radicchio
1 head red leaf lettuce
2 bunches arugula
2 heads butter lettuce

1. Wash and dry lettuce greens; tear into bite-size pieces.
2. Place greens in a large mixing bowl and toss with Sherry Vinaigrette Dressing (recipe follows).

Serves 12.

Sherry Vinaigrette Dressing:

⅔ cup sherry wine
⅓ cup minced shallots
⅓ cup minced fresh chives
2 tsp. dried black peppercorns, coarsely chopped
2 cups Canola oil

1. In a large mixing bowl, whisk together sherry wine, shallots, chives, and peppercorns. Slowly whisk in oil.

2. Transfer to a jar, cover, and store in refrigerator.

Yields 2 ⅔ cups.

Scallops Mediterranean with Jade Sauce

Jade Sauce:

2 tbsp. butter or margarine
1 medium-size onion, chopped
1 qt. heavy cream
2 tbsp. chicken base
4 tbsp. Pesto Sauce (recipe follows)
½ cup chopped fresh spinach leaves
¼ cup chopped fresh parsley
4 tbsp. cornstarch dissolved in 4 tbsp. water
Salt and white pepper to taste

1. In a medium-size saucepan, melt butter or margarine, add onion, and sauté for 3 minutes. Add cream, chicken base, pesto sauce, spinach, and parsley. Bring to a simmer and cook for 10 minutes, stirring occasionally. Stir cornstarch into cooked sauce; sauce should be of medium consistency.

2. Remove sauce from stove, transfer to a blender, and purée. Add salt and pepper to taste. Strain sauce into a glass bowl. Fill an 8 x 8-inch ovenproof casserole ¾ full of boiling water. Set bowl of sauce in the water to keep it warm.

Pesto Sauce:

1 tbsp. vegetable oil
2 tbsp. pine nuts
1 bunch (about 2 cups) fresh basil, coarsely chopped
¼ cup coarsely chopped parsley
2 large cloves garlic, peeled
¼ cup olive oil
¼ tsp. white pepper
½ tsp. salt
⅓ cup freshly grated Parmesan cheese

1. In a small skillet, heat vegetable oil. Add pine nuts and cook until lightly toasted, about 3 minutes, stirring constantly. Remove from stove and set aside.

2. Wash and dry basil leaves and parsley. Set aside. In a food processor or blender, process garlic cloves until finely chopped. Add basil, parsley, olive oil, pepper, and salt. Process until mixture is thick and creamy.

3. Transfer to a bowl, stir in Parmesan cheese, cover, and refrigerate until ready to use.

Note: Leftover Pesto Sauce may be served over cooked pasta.

Yields about ⅔ cup.

Scallops Mediterranean:
1 cup olive oil
3 tbsp. minced garlic
2 cups all-purpose flour
**36 large sea scallops (about
1¼ lb.)**
1 cup chardonnay wine
½ cup fresh lemon juice
12 large scallions (for garnish)

1. Preheat oven to 375 degrees.
2. In a large skillet, heat a third of the olive oil and stir in a third of the garlic. Cook until garlic is lightly browned.
3. Place flour in a medium-size mixing bowl. Dredge scallops in flour, a few at a time. Place a third of them in skillet and brown for about 1 minute on each side. Transfer scallops and garlic to a 13 x 9 x 2-inch baking pan. Continue this process using the remaining oil and garlic until the scallops have all been browned.
4. Pour wine and lemon juice over scallops and place in oven. Bake for about 7 minutes, or until scallops are cooked. Remove from oven.

To Assemble:
1. Spoon Jade Sauce onto the center of each of twelve medium-size plates.
2. Place three scallops on top of sauce on each plate. Garnish with a Scallion Brush on the side of the plate (see index for instructions on making Scallion Brushes).

Serves 12.

Rose Bouquet Sorbet

Sorbet:
1 cup sugar
1¼ cups bottled water
**1¾ cups Sugar Syrup (recipe
follows)**
**2 cups fragrant red rose
petals**
**2 cups fragrant pink rose
petals**
Juice of 1 lemon
Juice of 2 limes
2 drops red food coloring

1. In a medium-size saucepan, combine sugar and water.
2. Cook over high heat, stirring with a wooden spoon, until all the sugar is dissolved. Continue to cook until the syrup comes to a boil, then immediately remove syrup from heat and cool.
3. In a large jar, combine the sugar syrup with the rose petals. Cover jar and allow mixture to stand overnight at room temperature.
4. Strain syrup into a medium-size mixing bowl. Stir in lemon juice, lime juice, and food coloring.
5. Transfer rose syrup to an ice-cream maker and freeze according to the manufacturer's directions.

Yields about 1 quart.

Crystallized Rose Petals:

6 to 8 roses
2 egg whites
1 tsp. water
¼ cup sugar

1. Pick rose petals from just-opened roses early in the morning. Carefully wash petals and pat dry with paper towels. Lay petals on a cookie sheet that has been lined with waxed paper.

2. In a small mixing bowl, beat egg whites and water until stiff. Brush each petal with egg white mixture. Sprinkle petals with sugar, then air dry.

To serve:

1. Place a small scoop of sorbet into each of twelve glass or crystal stemware dishes.

2. Place dessert dishes on a small plate and decorate plate with crystallized rose petals.

Breast of Duck with Kumquat Sauce

Duck:

6 tbsp. kosher salt
4 tbsp. freshly ground black pepper
⅛ cup plus 2 tbsp. dried thyme
¼ cup minced garlic
12 10-oz. duck breasts, boned, halved, and excess skin trimmed
1 cup white wine
2 qt. Chicken Stock (see recipe)
6 bay leaves
2 tbsp. clarified butter (see recipe)

1. In a medium-size mixing bowl, combine salt, pepper, thyme, and garlic.

2. Coat breasts with seasoning mixture. Place duck breasts into two 13 x 9 x 2-inch baking pans. Pour ½ cup of wine into each pan. Cover and refrigerate overnight.

3. Remove duck breasts from the refrigerator. Set aside. Place stock and bay leaves in a dutch oven. Bring to a boil, then lower heat to a simmer. Add twelve duck half-breasts, cover, and cook on low heat for 35 minutes. Remove cooked half-breasts from stock and place on a platter. Repeat process with remaining half-breasts. Remove from heat.

4. Heat 1 tablespoon of clarified butter in a large skillet. Add one half of the duck breasts, fat side down, and brown for about 2 minutes on each side until crisp and thoroughly heated. Remove from skillet, transfer to a large baking pan, and keep warm in a 200-degree oven. Repeat process with remaining duck breasts.

Kumquat Sauce:

1 qt. fresh kumquats
¼ cup vinegar
1 cup sugar
1 cup orange juice
¼ cup fresh lemon juice
½ tsp. crushed black peppercorns
1 bay leaf
1 small sprig thyme (or ¼ tsp. dried)
1 small leek, cleaned and thinly sliced
2 cups Brown Stock (see recipe)
¼ cup tomato paste
1 oz. Grand Marnier liqueur

1. Peel half the kumquats, removing all pulp from the peels. Reserve pulp. Cut peels in fine julienne slivers, place in a small saucepan, and cover with boiling water for 1 minute. Drain and reserve peels.

2. In a medium-size saucepan, combine vinegar and sugar, then cook over medium heat until mixture begins to caramelize. Add orange and lemon juices and reserved kumquat pulp, then cook until liquid reduces down to about one-fourth.

3. Add kumquat peel, peppercorns, bay leaf, thyme, and leek. Simmer until golden brown.

4. Add Brown Stock and tomato paste. Simmer, stirring occasionally, for 1 hour.

5. Before serving, add Grand Marnier.

Note: Kumquats are available in 9-ounce jars at Asian markets. Kumquat Sauce may also be served with baked chicken.

Yields about 2¼ cups.

To Serve:

1. Remove breasts from oven and place on a wooden cutting board. With a sharp knife, cut each breast at a 45-degree angle into slices about ¼ inch thick. Fan the duck slices on the right side of twelve dinner plates.

2. Spoon Kumquat Sauce over duck slices. Place Almond Rice and Baby Corn Wrapped in Zucchini Strips (recipes follow) on the left side of the plate. Serve extra Kumquat Sauce in a sauce boat.

Serves 12.

Almond Wild Rice

¼ cup vegetable oil
1 cup slivered almonds
2 medium onions (about ½ lb.),
  coarsely chopped
1 tbsp. finely chopped shallot
¼ cup finely chopped green
  bell pepper
2 cloves garlic, peeled and
  finely chopped
2 cups uncooked wild rice,
  rinsed three times in
  cold water and drained
¼ tsp. freshly ground black
  pepper
¼ tsp. ground red pepper
½ tsp. cinnamon
½ tsp. nutmeg
¼ tsp. cumin
4½ cups chicken broth, heated

1. Preheat oven to 325 degrees.
2. Heat vegetable oil in a large saucepan, add almonds, and stir until almonds are light brown. Remove almonds, drain on paper towels. Set aside.
3. Add onions, shallot, green pepper, and garlic to saucepan. Cook and stir until tender, but not brown. Add wild rice, black pepper, red pepper, cinnamon, nutmeg, and cumin. Cook and stir for about 6 minutes, then stir in chicken broth.
4. Transfer to a 4-quart casserole and bake, covered, in the center of oven for 1 hour and 15 minutes, or until rice is tender and liquid has been absorbed. Stir rice after it has been baking for 35 minutes.

Serves 12.

Baby Corn Wrapped in Zucchini Strips

1 15-oz. can baby corn
3 large zucchini (about 1 lb.)
¼ cup butter or margarine, melted
Salt
White pepper

1. Preheat oven to 325 degrees.
2. Remove twenty-four baby corn from liquid and pat dry.
3. Wash zucchini and cut off ends. In a medium-size saucepan, bring 1 quart of salted water to a boil. Blanch zucchini for 1 minute. Remove zucchini and place in ice water for a few seconds. Drain and slice zucchini lengthwise into twenty-four ⅛-inch strips. Wrap strips around corn.
4. Place wrapped corn seam side down in a greased 13 x 9 x 2-inch baking pan. Pour butter or margarine over corn and season with salt and pepper. Bake for 10 minutes, or until corn is heated through.

Serves 12 (2 per person).

Hearts of Bavarian Cream with Caramel Sauce and Candied Orange Peel

Hearts:
5 egg yolks
¾ cup sugar
¼ cup plus 1 tbsp.
  half-and-half cream
1½ tsp. unflavored gelatin
Juice of 1 orange
Zest of 1 orange

1. In a medium-size mixing bowl, combine egg yolks and sugar. Beat for 4 minutes with an electric mixer on high speed until mixture is light and fluffy. Set aside.
2. In a medium-sized saucepan, combine half-and-half and gelatin. Bring to a boil, stirring until gelatin is dissolved, then remove from heat and cool to 96 degrees (as measured by a cooking thermometer).
3. Fold juice and zest into whipped egg mixture. Add cooled gelatin and stir mixture until thoroughly blended.
4. Transfer to a nonstick 13 x 9 x 2-inch baking pan, and refrigerate overnight.

Caramel Sauce:
3 cups dark brown
  sugar
1 cup corn syrup
¼ cup butter or margarine,
  softened
5 oz. condensed milk

1. In a medium-sized saucepan, combine brown sugar, corn syrup, and butter or margarine. Bring to a boil and cook for 3 minutes.
2. Remove from heat, add condensed milk, and beat with an electric mixer until smooth.

Note: Cover and store leftover sauce in refrigerator to serve over ice cream.

Yields about 4 cups.

Candied Orange Peel:
3 oranges
1 cup sugar
1½ cups water
Superfine sugar

1. Using a zester or sharp paring knife, remove long strips of peel from oranges. Set aside.
2. In a medium-sized saucepan, bring sugar and water to a boil and cook for 3 to 4 minutes. Add orange peels and reduce heat. Simmer for 45 minutes, or until skin is transparent.
3. Cool peels on a wire rack set over a cookie sheet. Coat thickly with superfine sugar. Dry on rack for forty-eight hours, then refrigerate in an airtight container.

To Assemble:
1. When ready to serve, remove pan from refrigerator. With a 2½-inch heart-shaped cutter, cut out twelve Bavarian hearts.
2. Spoon 2 tablespoons of caramel sauce on each of twelve plates, add a heart, and top with candied orange peels.

Wedding Breakfast
for Eighteen

A morning wedding followed by a wedding breakfast allows the bridal couple to celebrate their vows and embark on their honeymoon early in the day. This artfully teamed menu allows most preparation to be done the day before, so the bridal couple can relax and enjoy the festivities as they begin life together as husband and wife.

MENU

Crème de Cassis Mimosas

Fresh Citrus Frappé

Smoked Salmon Pinwheels
Julienne of Leeks
Sauce Soubise

Brioche Toast

Boursin-Stuffed Strawberries

Apple Strudel with Whipped Sour Cream

The "bridal chamber" in 1889. It was described in a brochure as: "furnished in solid natural mahogany, the prevailing colors of upholstery and tapestry being pale blue and cream. The draperies are pale blue silk, fringed and fastened with old gold and blue."

Crème de Cassis Mimosas

3 750-ml bottles
  chilled champagne
1 qt. freshly squeezed
  orange juice
½ cup crème de
  cassis liqueur
2 oranges, halved
  and sliced
1 basket boysenberries,
  washed and air dried

1. Fill eighteen champagne flute glasses half full with champagne. Add orange juice until three-fourths full.

2. Top with a splash of crème de cassis. Garnish with a half-slice of orange and a boysenberry on a cocktail pick.

Note: Frozen boysenberries may be used if fresh berries are unavailable.

Yields about 36 4-oz. servings.

Fresh Citrus Frappé

Frappé:
1 qt. Tangerine Ice
  (recipe follows)
9 lemons, washed and dried
54 lemon leaves, washed and
  dried
4 grapefruit, peeled, pith
  removed, and separated into
  sections
4 oranges, peeled, pith removed,
  and separated into sections

1. Cut lemons in half lengthwise. Remove pulp with a serrated knife, leaving shell intact (discard pulp). Cut a thin sliver off bottom of lemon shells to stabilize them.

2. Arrange three lemon leaves on each of eighteen small dessert plates. Place lemon shell on leaves. Fill lemon cavity with Tangerine Ice. Arrange grapefruit and orange segments alternately around the base of the lemon half.

Serves 18.

Tangerine Ice:
¾ cup granulated sugar
½ cup water
3 cups fresh tangerine juice
1 tbsp. fresh lemon juice
1 tbsp. fresh lime juice

1. In a large saucepan, combine sugar and water and cook over low heat, stirring until sugar is dissolved. Cool syrup.

2. Blend in tangerine juice, lemon juice, and lime juice. Refrigerate until well chilled, about 1½ hours. Transfer mixture to an ice cream maker and freeze according to manufacturer's directions.

3. Store in a covered plastic container in freezer until ready to serve. Allow mixture to soften slightly before serving.

Yields about 1 quart.

Note: If tangerines are unavailable, oranges may be substituted.

Smoked Salmon Pinwheels, Julienne of Leeks, and Sauce Soubise

Sauce Soubise:

2 tbsp. butter or margarine, melted
2 cups diced onions
1 qt. heavy cream
2 tbsp. chicken base
6 tbsp. cornstarch dissolved in 6 tbsp. water

1. In a medium-size saucepan, heat butter or margarine. Add onions and sauté for 3 minutes, being careful not to brown onions. Add heavy cream and chicken base, then simmer for 10 minutes, stirring occasionally. Stir cornstarch into cream mixture. Sauce should be a medium-thick consistency. Remove from stove.

2. Pour mixture into a blender and purée. Strain sauce into the top of a double boiler. Keep warm over low heat.

Yields about 1 quart.

Julienne of Leeks:

1 bunch leeks (about 1¼ lb.)
¼ cup butter or margarine
4 tbsp. water
Salt
White pepper

1. Trim the root ends of the leeks, being careful to keep the leaves attached. Remove any wilted leaves, then cut off tops so leeks are 6 to 7 inches long. Wash thoroughly under cold water.

2. Cut leeks into strips, julienne-style. Melt butter or margarine in a large skillet. Add leeks and water and stir fry until leeks are tender. Add salt and pepper to taste. Set aside.

Salmon Pinwheels:

2 doz. large eggs
2 tsp. salt
1 tsp. white pepper
1½ lb. smoked salmon, minced
1 cup finely chopped scallions (white and green parts)
1 cup (2 sticks) butter or margarine, melted
Parchment paper

1. In a large mixing bowl, combine eggs, salt, and pepper. Beat until all yolks are broken. Stir in smoked salmon and scallions.

2. In a 10-inch nonstick skillet, heat 2 tablespoons of butter or margarine over medium heat until it begins to foam. Add two 4-ounce ladles of egg mixture. Slide skillet back and forth to keep omelette from sticking. As the bottom begins to set, slip a thin spatula under eggs, tilting the pan and lifting cooked portion to allow uncooked egg mixture to flow under it to the center of skillet. Cook slowly until egg mixture is firm.

3. Remove omelette from skillet onto a sheet of parchment paper, being careful not to break omelette. Omelette should be approximately ¼ inch thick.

4. Quickly roll omelette jellyroll-style, using the parchment paper to assist in rolling. Seam of roll should be at the bottom of the omelette. Transfer to a nonstick cookie sheet and keep warm in a 200-degree oven while repeating process six more times.

5. Remove salmon rolls from oven and slice each roll into nine slices about ¾ inch thick. Do not use the ends.

Serves 18 (3 per person).

To Assemble Plate:

1. Place one slice of Brioche Toast (recipe follows) cut in half diagonally in the center of each of eighteen dinner plates. Divide the leeks and place on top of Brioche Toast.

2. Arrange three Salmon Pinwheel slices on top of leeks, then spoon Sauce Soubise onto lower part of the plate. Garnish with two Boursin-Stuffed Strawberries (recipe follows).

Brioche Toast

1½ cups milk
1 yeast cake
8½ cups (2 ½ lb.) all-purpose flour
8 large eggs
½ cup granulated sugar
2½ tbsp. salt
1 lb. (4 sticks) plus 6 tbsp. unsalted butter, at room temperature, cut into ½-inch pieces
2 large egg yolks
½ tsp. heavy cream
Parchment paper

1. In a small saucepan, heat milk to 115 degrees (as measured by a cooking thermometer). Pour the milk into a large mixing bowl, add the yeast, and whisk until the yeast dissolves. Whisk in 1½ cups of flour.

2. Pour the remaining flour on top of the yeast mixture and, without stirring, leave the bowl uncovered in a warm place until the yeast mixture just begins to show through the top of the flour, anywhere from 10 to 30 minutes, depending on the temperature and humidity.

3. Place eggs in the bowl of an electric mixer fitted with a dough hook (or in a processor with a metal blade), and mix briefly until smooth. Add the yeast-flour mixture, sugar, and salt; then mix on slow speed (or pulse) just until combined. Increase the speed to medium (or process continuously) and mix just until the dough forms a ball that pulls away from the sides of the bowl. Add the butter and continue mixing until it is completely incorporated and the dough reforms a ball or climbs up the dough hook or blade.

4. Cover the bottom of a small sheet cake pan with parchment paper. Empty the dough into the pan and spread it out. Cover with another sheet of parchment paper and leave the dough in the refrigerator overnight.

5. Butter the insides of two 8½ x 4½ x 2½-inch ovenproof glass loaf pans. Divide the dough in two halves, roll into log shapes and fit into each pan. Leave the loaves in a warm place until the dough rises to the tops of the pans, 45 minutes to 1 hour.

6. Preheat oven to 375 degrees.

7. When the loaves have risen, beat together the egg yolks and cream. Brush mixture over the top of the loaves. Bake until the loaves are a golden brown, about 30 minutes. Unmold onto a wire rack to cool before slicing.

8. Slice each loaf into nine ½-inch slices. Lay slices on a cookie sheet and toast in 350-degree oven on both sides.

Yields 2 loaves.

Boursin-Stuffed Strawberries

36 medium-size strawberries
5 oz. Boursin cheese, at room temperature
¼ tsp. heavy cream
3 ½ oz. lumpfish caviar, rinsed and drained

1. Wash strawberries and thoroughly pat dry with paper towels. With a sharp paring knife, remove a thin slice off the bottom of the strawberries to form a base. With a small melon ball scoop, remove inside portion of the strawberries, leaving a small indentation.

2. Place Boursin cheese in a small bowl, add cream, and mix with a wooden spoon to thoroughly blend. Transfer cheese mix to a pastry bag with a small star tip. Pipe cheese into the cavity of each strawberry. Top with a small dollop of caviar.

Yields 36 stuffed strawberries.

Apple Strudel with Whipped Sour Cream

24 Phyllo dough sheets
2 21-oz. cans apple pie filling
½ cup raisins
½ cup chopped pecans
2 tbsp. cinnamon
1 cup unsalted butter, melted
¼ cup confectioners' sugar
Parchment Paper

1. Defrost Phyllo dough according to package directions.

2. In a medium-size mixing bowl, combine 1 can of apple pie filling with one half of the raisins, pecans, and cinnamon. Blend mixture together. Set aside.

3. Preheat oven to 375 degrees.

4. On a work surface, place an 18-inch piece of parchment paper with the long side facing you. Cover it with a sheet of Phyllo dough. Brush Phyllo dough lightly with butter. Layer and repeat process with the eleven remaining sheets of Phyllo, brushing each sheet lightly with butter.

5. Place the apple mixture evenly along the long side of Phyllo facing you, leaving a 2-inch border at each end. With the help of the parchment paper, lift the edge closest to you and roll up tightly, as you would a jellyroll. With the seam side down, fold the ends under to enclose the filling.

6. Brush strudel lightly with butter. Place seam side down on a nonstick cookie sheet.

7. For the second strudel, repeat the same process using the remaining twelve sheets of Phyllo dough.

8. Bake for 20 minutes or until golden. Remove from oven and cool. Transfer strudels carefully with a spatula to serving platters and sprinkle with confectioners' sugar. Slice strudels diagonally and serve warm with whipped sour cream (recipe follows).

Note: Phyllo dough may be found in the frozen section of local supermarkets. Strudels may be made a day in advance and kept covered loosely at room temperature. Reheat strudels in a preheated 400-degree oven for 15 minutes before serving.

Yields 2 strudels.

Whipped Sour Cream:

1 cup well-chilled heavy cream
¼ cup sour cream
¼ cup confectioners' sugar
1 tsp. vanilla extract

1. Place a small mixing bowl and beaters in the refrigerator for about 1 hour.

2. Remove bowl and beaters from refrigerator. Combine ingredients in the chilled bowl and beat until the mixture forms soft peaks. Transfer to a serving bowl.

Wedding Luncheon for Sixteen

An outdoor garden setting forms the backdrop for a ceremony that will long be remembered by the betrothed couple as well as their invited guests. If your patio lacks shade trees, a white tent will make a lovely substitute.

MENU

Fruited Champagne Punch

Golden Caviar Canapés

Chilled Melon Soup in Cantaloupe Shell

Roquefort and Pecan-Coated Grapes

Classic Lobster Salad

Swiss Cheese Puffs

Triple-Dipped Strawberries

Fruited Champagne Punch

1 cup sugar
1 cup water
1 fifth Jamaican rum, chilled
1 fifth bourbon, chilled
1 fifth cognac, chilled
1 pt. Grand Marnier liqueur, chilled
1 qt. strong tea
⅛ tsp. orange bitters
1 20-oz. can pineapple chunks, undrained
2 750-ml bottles champagne, chilled

1. Dissolve sugar in water; add rum, bourbon, cognac, and Grand Marnier and blend thoroughly.

2. Mix together tea, bitters, and undrained pineapple. Add to liquor and sugar-water mixture; mix well. Pour into chilled punch bowl.

3. Just before serving, add chilled champagne. Serve in champagne flutes or wine glasses.

Yields about 40 servings.

Golden Caviar Canapés

1 English cucumber
½ cup sour cream
¼ cup golden whitefish caviar
2 sprigs dill (for garnish)

1. Peel the cucumber and trim the ends. Score the flesh with the tines of a fork, so there will be a design when the cucumber is sliced horizontally. Cut cucumber into slices about ⅛ inch thick.

2. Place ½ teaspoon sour cream in the center of each cucumber slice and top with ¼ teaspoon of caviar. Garnish with a tiny sprig of dill tucked into the sour cream.

3. Arrange canapés on a platter and serve.

Yields 32 to 40 canapés.

Chilled Melon Soup in Cantaloupe Shell

8 medium-size cantaloupes
2 cups orange juice
4 cups plain yogurt
½ cup honey
¼ cup pickled ginger, minced
Fresh mint leaves (for garnish)

Note: Pickled ginger is available at Asian markets.

1. Cut cantaloupes in half, remove seeds. Scoop out cantaloupe flesh and reserve. Leave a small amount of cantaloupe flesh intact to form a bowl. Lay cantaloupe shells on two cookie sheets, cover with waxed paper, and refrigerate.

2. In a food processor or blender, combine half the cantaloupe flesh with one half the orange juice, yogurt, honey, and ginger. Purée, then repeat process with remaining half of the ingredients. Pour purée into a large mixing bowl and chill.

3. Line each of sixteen soup bowls with a cloth napkin. Place a cantaloupe shell into each bowl. Spoon soup into each shell. Garnish with fresh mint leaves.

Serves 16.

Roquefort and Pecan-Coated Grapes

1 10-oz. pkg. pecans
1 8-oz. pkg. cream cheese
⅛ lb. Roquefort cheese
2 tbsp. heavy cream
1 lb. red seedless grapes, washed
  and dried

1. Preheat oven to 350 degrees.

2. Spread pecans on a nonstick cookie sheet. Bake for 10 minutes, or until toasted. Chop nuts coarsely in food processor or by hand. Spread on a platter.

3. In a medium-size bowl, combine cream cheese, Roquefort cheese, and cream. With an electric mixer, beat until smooth. Drop grapes into the cheese mixture and gently stir by hand to coat them.

4. Roll grapes in the toasted pecans and transfer to a cookie sheet that has been lined with waxed paper. Chill until ready to serve, then transfer to a serving platter.

Note: Any leftover cheese mixture may be frozen and reused.

Yields about 50 grapes.

Classic Lobster Salad

8 8- to 10-oz. California lobster
  tails, cooked (reserve shells)
1½ cups chopped celery
½ cup chopped scallions (green
  and white parts)
1 cup Thousand Island Dressing
  (recipe follows)
½ tsp. salt
½ tsp. white pepper

1. Cut lobster shells in half lengthwise and remove meat from shells. Chop and place meat in a large mixing bowl. Fold in celery, scallions, and Thousand Island Dressing. Add salt and pepper.

2. Cover and refrigerate for at least two hours or overnight.

Thousand Island Dressing:
1 cup mayonnaise
1 hard-cooked egg, finely
  chopped
4 oz. chili sauce
3 oz. dill relish
1 tbsp. minced onions

Combine all ingredients in a medium-size mixing bowl. Stir until thoroughly blended. Cover and refrigerate.

For Garnish:

64 snow peas (about ¾ lb.)
48 baby carrots (about 2 lb.)
6 medium-size tomatoes, cut into 48 wedges
6 lemons, cut into wedges
16 large pitted black olives, sliced
1 head iceberg lettuce, finely shredded

1. In a medium-size saucepan, bring 2 quarts of water to a boil. Add snow peas and blanch for 30 seconds. Remove from boiling water and rinse in cold water immediately. Drain, cool, and refrigerate.

2. In the same saucepan, add enough water to make 2 quarts. Add carrots, cover, and cook for 20 minutes or until tender. Drain and refrigerate.

To Assemble:

1. Divide shredded lettuce and place onto sixteen large salad plates. Place a half lobster shell on the lettuce on each plate. Fill shells with lobster salad, allowing some to extend out of shell.

2. Garnish with three tomato wedges and two lemon wedges on one side of plate. Lay four snow peas and three baby carrots alternately on the other side of plate. Add four black olive slices on top of snow peas.

Note: To serve Classic Lobster Salad without the shell, serve open-faced piled high on a large croissant that has been sliced in half.

Serves 16.

Swiss Cheese Puffs

1 cup water
½ cup butter or margarine
½ cup all-purpose flour
½ cup whole wheat flour
¼ tsp. salt
½ tsp. sugar
4 large eggs
1 tsp. dry mustard
⅛ tsp. cayenne pepper
⅔ cup grated Swiss cheese

1. Preheat oven to 375 degrees.

2. In medium-size saucepan, boil water with butter or margarine until butter melts. Stir flour in all at once and beat with a wooden spoon until it forms a thick, glossy dough that leaves the sides of the pan. Add salt and sugar.

3. Remove saucepan from the heat and beat in the eggs, one at a time. Add the mustard, cayenne pepper, and grated cheese; blend well.

4. Drop by teaspoonfuls onto a greased cookie sheet. Bake for 30 minutes, or until puffed and golden brown. Serve warm with sweet butter.

Yields about 28 puffs.

Triple-Dipped Strawberries

**36 large strawberries with
    long stems**
18 oz. dark chocolate
18 oz. white chocolate
9 oz. milk chocolate

1. Wash strawberries and thoroughly pat dry with paper towels.

2. Melt the dark chocolate in the top of a double boiler over low heat. Holding the strawberry by the stem, dip it into the melted chocolate, turning the berry around, so the chocolate covers it completely on all sides. Leave the upper quarter of the berry uncovered (the part nearest the stem).

3. Place dipped strawberries on a tray that has been lined with waxed paper. Refrigerate for about 15 to 20 minutes until chocolate has hardened.

4. Wash and dry the top of the double boiler. Melt the white chocolate in the top of the double boiler over low heat. Remove strawberries from the refrigerator. Dip them so a small portion of the dark chocolate is showing. Refrigerate for 15 to 20 minutes until chocolate is hardened.

5. Wash and dry the top of the double boiler. Melt the milk chocolate in the top of the double boiler over low heat. Remove strawberries from the refrigerator. Dip the ends of the strawberries in milk chocolate. Return strawberries to the refrigerator for 15 to 20 minutes. When ready to serve, remove strawberries from the refrigerator and place them on a serving platter by gently running a spatula under them.

Yields 36 strawberries.

*Triple Dipped Strawberries in Dark,
White, and Milk Chocolate.*

Wedding Reception for Twenty-Four

A buffet table laden with an assortment of palatable enticements is planned here to serve twenty-four guests. Quantities can easily be doubled for a larger reception. The cake-cutting ceremony is the highpoint of a wedding reception. At a recent reception at the Del, the bride and groom's favorite fare was strawberries. The bride opted not only for Strawberries Romanoff for her wedding reception, but also chose The Del's Strawberries and Cream Wedding Cake, which was crowned with Dendrobium orchids and roses to match her bridal bouquet. A drum roll was played as the wedding cake was wheeled out, and photographers hurried to capture the bride and groom on film as they carved and shared their first piece of strawberry-layered wedding cake.

MENU

Citrus-Wine Sangria

Bleu Cheese-Stuffed Celery

Eggs à la Russe

Artichoke Bottoms Stuffed with Ratatouille

Petit Beef Wellingtons
Bordelaise Sauce

Vol-au-Vent Hearts Filled with
Shrimp Newburg

Ballotine of Chicken
with Pistachios and Kumquats
Cumberland Sauce

Swiss Fondue

Strawberries Romanoff

The Del's Strawberries and
Cream Wedding Cake

Citrus-Wine Sangria

1 gal. chilled chablis wine
6 6-oz. cans frozen lemon-limeade concentrate, thawed
2 6-oz. cans frozen orange juice concentrate, thawed
4 cups cold water
Fruited Ice Ring (recipe follows)

1. In a large bowl, stir together wine, lemon-limeade concentrate, orange juice concentrate, and water.
2. Serve in a punch bowl with Fruited Ice Ring (recipe follows).

Fruited Ice Ring:
2 qt. water
1 lemon (unpeeled), washed and sliced
1 orange (unpeeled), washed and sliced
1 lime (unpeeled), washed and sliced
8 lemon leaves, washed and dried
Ring mold, 9½ inches in diameter

1. Place 2 cups water in the bottom of ring mold. Place mold in freezer.
2. Pour remainder of water into a large saucepan and bring to a boil. Allow water to cool. Set aside.
3. Remove mold from freezer. Arrange lemon, orange, and lime slices and leaves alternately on top of the frozen water. Carefully pour remaining water over fruit and leaves. Return mold to freezer and freeze overnight.

To Serve:

1. Remove ice ring mold from freezer. Place mold in a bowl of hot water for about 1 minute, or until mold loosens. Immediately unmold into a punch bowl, fruit side up.
2. Pour Citrus-Wine Sangria around mold.

Yields about 50 half-cup servings.

Bleu Cheese-Stuffed Celery

½ cup sliced almonds, toasted
1 bunch celery
5 8-oz. pkg. cream cheese, room temperature
8 oz. bleu cheese, crumbled

1. Preheat oven to 350 degrees.
2. Spread almonds on a nonstick cookie sheet and bake for 5 to 7 minutes until lightly brown.
3. Separate celery into stalks; wash and pat dry with paper towels. Trim ends, discard leaves, and cut celery diagonally into about forty-eight pieces, each about 2 inches long. Place on a serving platter. Set aside.
4. Place cream cheese in a medium-size bowl and mix with a wooden spoon. Add bleu cheese and continue to mix until cheese mixture is well blended.
5. Transfer cheese mixture to a pastry bag. Using a small star tip, pipe cheese into celery. Top with toasted almonds. Serve chilled.

Yields 48 pieces.

Eggs à La Russe

30 hard-cooked eggs, cooled and peeled
½ cup mayonnaise
2 tbsp. Dijon-style mustard
⅛ tsp. Tabasco sauce
1 tsp. Worcestershire sauce
1 tsp. salt
½ tsp. white pepper
1 3½-oz. jar red lumpfish caviar
1 3½-oz. jar black lumpfish caviar, rinsed and drained

1. Cut twenty-four of the eggs in half lengthwise. Remove yolks and place in a medium-size mixing bowl. Place egg whites on a serving platter. Mash the egg yolks and the remaining six eggs. Add mayonnaise, mustard, Tabasco sauce, Worcestershire sauce, salt, and pepper. Mix thoroughly.
2. Transfer mixture to a pastry bag. Using a small star tip, pipe egg mixture into cavity of egg whites.
3. Top each stuffed egg with a dot each of red and black caviar.

Yields 48 eggs.

Arthichoke Bottoms Stuffed with Ratatouille

4 14-oz. cans artichoke bottoms
4 tbsp. olive oil
½ cup minced onions
1 tsp. minced fresh garlic
1 cup finely chopped fresh
  mushrooms
½ cup finely chopped red bell
  pepper
1 cup finely chopped unpeeled
  zucchini
1 cup finely chopped unpeeled
  eggplant
1 cup finely chopped yellow
  squash
1 cup finely chopped tomatoes
2 tbsp. finely chopped fresh
  oregano
2 tbsp. finely chopped fresh
  basil
1 cup white wine
1 tsp. salt
1 tsp. white pepper

1. Drain artichoke bottoms. With a sharp paring knife, remove a sliver off the bottom of artichokes to form a base. Place artichoke bottoms on a serving platter. Set aside.

2. In a large skillet, heat olive oil, add onions and garlic, and sauté for 1 minute. Add remainder of the ingredients except wine, salt, and pepper. Cook for 5 minutes, add wine, and cook for 5 minutes more. Vegetables should be *al dente*. Stir in salt and pepper.

3. Fill artichoke bottoms with ratatouille mixture and refrigerate until serving time.

Yields approximately 2½ to 3 dozen.

Petite Beef Wellingtons with Bordelaise Sauce

Beef Wellingtons:
6 lb. beef tenderloin
Salt
Coarsely ground black pepper
2 tbsp. butter or margarine
1 sheet frozen puff pastry
  (17¼-oz. pkg.)
1 14-oz. can pâté de foie gras
  (goose liver)
Duxelle Mushrooms
  (recipe follows)
2 eggs beaten with 2 tsp. water
  (egg wash)
Parchment paper

1. Preheat oven to 375 degrees.

2. Thaw a sheet of puff pastry for 20 minutes.

3. Trim tenderloin, remove all silver skin and side strip muscle.

4. Cut tenderloin lengthwise into four equal strips; sprinkle with salt and pepper. In a large skillet, melt butter or margarine, then sear tenderloins on each side. Remove from heat and set aside.

5. Unfold pastry sheet on a lightly floured cutting board. Roll out pastry to 14 x 11 inches; then cut lengthwise into four equal strips.

6. Spread pâté de foie gras lightly down the center of each pastry strip. Spoon the Duxelle Mushroom mixture on top of the pâté. Top each with a strip of tenderloin. Brush ends of pastry with egg wash and fold over tenderloin. Fold sides of pastry up over tenderloin, enclosing meat completely.

7. Line a cookie sheet with parchment paper. Transfer Wellingtons to the cookie sheet, seam side down.

8. Brush egg wash over each Wellington, then bake for 15 to 20 minutes, or until pastry is golden brown. Remove from oven and allow Wellingtons to rest for 30 minutes. Slice each Wellington into about twelve ¼-inch slices. Serve with Bordelaise Sauce (recipe follows).

Note: Frozen puff pastry sheets may be found in the frozen section of local supermarkets.

Yields about 48 slices.

Duxelle Mushrooms:

4 tbsp. butter or margarine
2 cups minced onion
2 lb. mushrooms, minced
1 tsp. dried thyme
1 tsp. dried oregano
1 tsp. dried basil
1 cup chablis wine
½ cup brandy

1. In a large skillet, melt butter or margarine. Add onions and sauté for 3 minutes. Add mushrooms, thyme, oregano, and basil and cook for 2 more minutes.

2. Add wine and brandy; continue cooking until liquid is absorbed, approximately 8 minutes. Allow mixture to cool.

Bordelaise Sauce:

2 tsp. butter or margarine
3 scallions (white part only), chopped
¾ cup cabernet sauvignon wine
2 cups Brown Stock (see recipe)
1 tsp. dried thyme
1 tsp. dried tarragon
½ tsp. salt
¼ tsp. pepper
2 tbsp. butter or margarine, cut into small pieces
1 tbsp. lemon juice
1 tbsp. chopped fresh parsley

1. In a medium-size saucepan, melt 2 teaspoons butter or margarine. Add scallions and sauté without browning for about 2 minutes. Add wine, cook, and stir until reduced by half.

2. Add stock, thyme, and tarragon; simmer for 5 minutes. Season with salt and pepper.

3. Whisk in 2 tablespoons butter or margarine pieces until sauce is smooth. Strain sauce through a sieve. Keep warm in the top of a double boiler over low heat.

4. At serving time, blend in lemon juice and parsley and transfer to a serving bowl.

Note: Leftover sauce is excellent with steaks or roast beef.

Yields about 3 cups.

Vol-Au-Vent Hearts Filled with Shrimp Newburg

Shrimp Newburg:

8 oz. (2 sticks) butter or margarine
1 cup finely chopped onions
4½ lb. medium-size shrimp, shelled, deveined, and coarsely chopped
2 cups sliced fresh mushrooms
¼ cup paprika
¼ cup fresh lemon juice
3 oz. sherry wine
1 gallon Medium Cream Sauce (recipe follows)
Salt
Pepper

1. In a stock pot, melt butter or margarine. Add onions and cook for 5 minutes. Add shrimp and cook for 5 more minutes, stirring constantly.
2. Add mushrooms, paprika, lemon juice, and wine. Continue cooking for another 5 minutes. Pour in cream sauce and blend. Bring to a boil, then add salt and pepper to taste.
3. Keep warm in the top of a double boiler until ready to use.

Note: Newburg may be prepared a day in advance if kept covered and refrigerated. To serve, allow Newburg to reach room temperature; then bring to simmer and serve. Leftover Newburg is excellent served over steamed rice.

Serves 24.

Medium Cream Sauce:

8 oz. (2 sticks) butter or margarine
1 cup all-purpose flour
1 gal. milk
1 tbsp. salt

1. Melt butter or margarine in a large saucepan. Stir in flour to make a roux. Simmer mixture, stirring constantly, for 8 to 10 minutes. Do not allow roux to brown.
2. In a separate large saucepan, combine milk and salt. Bring to a boil. Gradually whisk milk into roux. Continue to whisk until sauce is thickened and smooth. Bring to a boil, then immediately reduce heat to a simmer. Cook and stir for 5 minutes, then strain sauce into a mixing bowl and set aside.

Yields 1 gallon.

Vol-Au-Vents:

1 (17¼-oz.) pkg. frozen puff pastry
4 eggs lightly beaten with 4 tsp. water (egg wash)
2 tsp. butter or margarine, melted
Parchment paper

1. Preheat oven to 375 degrees.
2. Thaw puff pastry sheets on floured board for 20 minutes. Brush top of one sheet lightly with water, then place remaining sheet directly on top and roll out lightly with a rolling pin. Puff pastry must always be rolled from the outer edges to ensure that the dough bakes evenly.
3. Rub a 3-inch heart-shaped cutter in flour to coat edges. Cut pastry into twenty-four hearts. Place hearts on a cookie sheet that has been lined with a sheet of parchment paper. Brush hearts with egg wash.

4. Mark center of each heart with a 2-inch heart-shaped cutter without cutting through pastry. Allow hearts to stand for 30 minutes.

5. Lightly brush remaining sheet of parchment with melted butter or margarine. Place on top of hearts and bake for 20 or 25 minutes.

6. Remove from oven, cool slightly. Lift off tops with the point of a paring knife, then scoop out any undercooked interior and fill with Shrimp Newburg.

7. To serve, place hearts in a chafing dish.

Note: Puff pastry may be found in the frozen section of local supermarkets. Vol-au-Vent shells keep up to ten days in an airtight container, or they may be frozen and kept for up to eight weeks. When ready to use, remove from freezer, bring to room temperature, and heat in a 275-degree oven for 3 to 5 minutes.

Yields 24 hearts.

Ballotine of Chicken with Pistachios, Kumquats, and Cumberland Sauce

12 8-oz. boneless chicken breasts
1 cup pistachio nuts, minced
2 cups kumquats, drained and chopped
½ cup orange marmalade

1. Lay chicken breasts on a cutting board, skin side down. Pound each breast lightly with a mallet. Chicken breasts should be about ¼ inch thick. Set aside.

2. In a large mixing bowl, combine nuts, kumquats, and marmalade. Spoon mixture over chicken breasts, coating evenly. Roll up coated breasts tightly, jellyroll-style. Wrap in foil and seal ends.

3. In a dutch oven, bring 1 gallon of water to a boil. Place chicken breasts into boiling water and poach for 30 minutes. Remove from dutch oven, but do not remove foil. Allow breasts to cool at room temperature, then refrigerate for 6 hours.

4. Remove breasts from refrigerator, remove foil, and place breasts on a cutting board. Slice each roll into five or six slices that are ¼ inch thick. Transfer to a serving platter and serve with Cumberland Sauce (recipe follows).

Yields about 60 to 72 slices.

Cumberland Sauce:

2 cups fresh currants, crushed
¾ cup apple jelly
2 oranges
2 lemons
2 tsp. salted butter
2 small onions, peeled and
  chopped
2 tsp. mustard seeds, crushed
6 peppercorns, crushed
2 pinches ground ginger
2 tbsp. Worcestershire sauce
½ tsp. salt
¼ tsp. cayenne pepper

1. Sprinkle the currants with apple jelly. Set aside.

2. Cut a 2-inch strip of peel from the oranges and lemons. Remove the white pith, then cut the strips into very fine pieces. Set aside. Squeeze the fruit, reserving the juice.

3. Melt the butter in a saucepan, then sauté the onions until transparent. Add the reserved citrus juices, currants, mustard seeds, and peppercorns. Add ginger, Worcestershire sauce, salt, and cayenne pepper. Bring to a boil and cook for 5 minutes. Stir in the orange and lemon strips. Let the sauce cool before transferring to a small bowl to serve.

Note: Kumquats may be found in jars at Asian markets.

Swiss Fondue

2 cloves garlic, peeled
1½ cups dry white wine
3 lb. Swiss cheese, grated
3 lb. Gruyère cheese, grated
½ cup cornstarch
½ cup Kirsch liqueur
¼ tsp. ground nutmeg
Salt and pepper to taste
2 French baguettes, cut in
  half lengthwise, then cut
  into ½-inch squares

1. Rub the inside of a medium-size saucepan with garlic. Discard garlic. Add white wine and warm over low heat. Add Swiss and Gruyère cheeses, stirring constantly.

2. In a small mixing bowl, combine cornstarch with Kirsch. Add to the cheese mixture. Add ground nutmeg and salt and pepper to taste.

3. Transfer into two fondue pots. Serve with French baguette squares.

Serves 24.

Strawberries Romanoff

3 lb. medium-size strawberries
2 cups Grand Marnier liqueur
1 qt. sour cream
1 lb. light brown sugar
Mint leaves, washed and dried
  (for garnish)

1. Rinse and hull strawberries; dry thoroughly and place in a large, shallow casserole. Pour 1½ cups Grand Marnier over strawberries. Cover and refrigerate for 1 hour. Turn strawberries every 20 minutes.

2. In a large mixing bowl, combine remaining ½ cup of Grand Marnier with sour cream and brown sugar. Whip lightly until mixture is well blended. Cover and refrigerate for 1 hour.

3. Transfer Grand Marnier-sour cream mixture to a glass serving bowl. Place the bowl in the center of a large platter. Remove refrigerated strawberries from the marinade with a slotted spoon; arrange on platter around the dipping mixture. Garnish with mint leaves and serve chilled.

Serves 24.

The Del's Strawberries and Cream Wedding Cake

Equipment Required:

2 12-inch cake pans
2 8-inch cake pans
2 6-inch cake pans
2 14-inch cardboard cake circles, taped together and covered with aluminum foil and a doily
1 12-inch cardboard cake circle
1 8-inch cardboard cake circle
1 6-inch cardboard cake circle
1 8-inch plastic plate
1 6-inch plastic plate
8 9-inch plastic pillars
Parchment paper, cut into circles to fit each cake pan
Pink roses, Dendrobium orchids, or flowers matching the bridal bouquet and greenery

Preparation Guide:

1. Bake cakes and freeze one week before the wedding.
2. Prepare chocolate shavings and curls three days in advance and freeze.
3. Prepare strawberries the day before. Cover and refrigerate.
4. Fill and frost cakes the day before.
5. Assemble cake and decorate with flowers two hours before it is to be served.

Note: Because the quantities needed for the Del's Strawberries and Cream Wedding Cake serve fifty people, this recipe allows for the ingredients to be processed in two batches and combined.

Cakes:

Vegetable cooking spray
2¾ cups unsalted butter, at room temperature, cut into small pieces
8 cups granulated sugar
2 cups milk
¼ cup vanilla extract
¾ cup honey
3 tbsp. salt
3 tbsp. baking powder
9¼ cups cake flour
19 large eggs, at room temperature

1. Preheat oven to 350 degrees.
2. Coat cake pans with nonstick vegetable spray. Place parchment circles in each pan and spray lightly again.
3. In a large mixing bowl, combine butter and sugar. Using an electric mixer with a paddle attachment, blend ingredients on medium speed for 7 minutes, or until light and fluffy. Add 1 cup of milk, vanilla extract, and honey. Continue to beat on medium speed for 3 minutes. Transfer one half of mixture to a large mixing bowl. Set aside.
4. To the remaining half of the mixture, add half the salt, half the baking powder, and half the flour, ¼ cup at a time. Beat for 4 minutes on medium speed after each addition, scraping down the side of bowl with a spatula. Set aside.
5. In a separate large mixing bowl, whisk together eggs and remaining cup of milk. Add one half of the beaten egg mixture, 1 cup at a time, to the half batch of batter. Beat for 4 minutes on medium speed after each addition.
6. Transfer batter to a large mixing bowl. Set aside.
7. Repeat process with the remaining half of mixture in Step 3 until all the flour and egg mixture has been used up.

8. Combine the two batches of batter and blend together with a large wooden spoon.

9. Fill 12-inch cake pans with 6 cups of batter in each pan. Fill 8-inch cake pans with 3 cups of batter in each pan. Fill 6-inch cake pans with 1½ cups of batter in each pan. Bake 12-inch cakes for 38 to 40 minutes; 8-inch cakes, 28 to 30 minutes; and 6-inch cakes, 25 to 27 minutes. Cakes are done when a cake tester or toothpick inserted in the center of each cake comes out clean.

10. Remove cakes from oven, and allow them to cool for 10 minutes. Remove cakes from pans and cool thoroughly on wire racks, right side up. Remove parchment paper. Carefully slice off the raised center of cakes with a serrated knife to create a flat surface. Brush away any crumbs.

11. Wrap cakes thoroughly in plastic wrap and freeze.

Chocolate Shavings:
2½ lb. block white chocolate

1. Place chocolate on a cutting board. Scrape a large knife over chocolate toward you to make shavings and curls.

2. Place shavings on a cookie sheet and freeze. When chocolate is frozen, transfer to plastic bags and return to the freezer. Chocolate should not be defrosted before it is applied to the cakes.

To Fill and Frost Layers:
2 qt. nondairy whipped topping, defrosted
10 cups diced fresh strawberries

1. Remove cakes from freezer. Cut each cake in half horizontally, making two layers. Set layers aside.

2. Place 1 quart of whipped topping in a mixing bowl, beat on medium speed for 10 minutes, then on high speed for 5 minutes or until stiff. Transfer topping to a bowl and refrigerate. Repeat process with remaining quart of whipped topping.

3. Place 3 tablespoons of whipped topping on the center of the 12-inch cake circle. Spread topping around a little to prevent cake from shifting. Place one 12-inch cake layer on circle. With a spatula, spread 2 cups of whipped topping over the layer; then sprinkle with 1 cup of strawberries. Repeat procedure twice, then top with remaining layer. Frost top and sides of cake with 7 cups of whipped topping. Pat 3 cups of shaved chocolate onto sides of cake and sprinkle over top of cake. Set aside.

4. Place 2 tablespoons of whipped topping on the center of the 8-inch cake circle. Spread topping a little to prevent cake from shifting. Place one 8-inch cake layer on circle. With a spatula, spread 1 cup of whipped topping over the layer; sprinkle with ¾ cup strawberries. Repeat procedure twice, then top with remaining layer.

Frost top and sides of cake with 3½ cups of whipped topping. Pat 2 cups of shaved chocolate onto sides and sprinkle over top of cake. Set aside.

5. Place 1 tablespoon of whipped topping on the center of the 6-inch cake circle. Place one 6-inch cake layer on cake circle. With a spatula, spread ¾ cup whipped topping over the layer; sprinkle with ½ cup of strawberries. Repeat procedure twice. Top with remaining layer. Frost top and sides of cake with 1½ cups of whipped topping. Pat 1½ cups of shaved chocolate onto sides of cake. Sprinkle any remaining shaved chocolate over top of cake. Set aside. Any leftover chocolate may be sprinkled over all cakes.

To Assemble:

1. Place the 12-inch cake on the 14-inch cake circle. Assemble pillars and plastic plates according to package directions.

2. Gently press 8-inch plastic plate with pillars attached into the center of the 12-inch cake. Place 8-inch cake on the plastic plate. Repeat procedure with 6-inch plastic plate and pillars, adding the 6-inch cake.

3. Decorate top of cake with pink roses, Dendrobium orchids, or flowers matching the bridal bouquet and greenery. Cascade flowers down the sides of the 8-inch and 12-inch cakes. Decorate base of cake and cake table with additional flowers and greenery.

4. After the cake cutting ceremony, remove the 6-inch cake, wrap thoroughly, and freeze for one-year anniversary celebration.

Serves 50.

Newlyweds pose for a wedding picture in the Garden Patio of the Del.

CHAPTER SIX
Holiday Specialties

We all love holidays—they give us reason to abandon routine, to gather our close friends and families together, and to create unforgettable memories. The Del provides the setting. The holiday season at the Del takes on an air of Old World elegance and fairy tale splendor with opulent decorations and traditional dishes that we have come to expect, such as Herb-Roasted Turkey with Corn Bread, Pecan, and Oyster Dressing and Old-Fashioned Giblet Gravy. Some nontraditional dishes, such as cranberries simmered in cabernet sauvignon wine, and Corn Soufflés with Basil Cream are also on the menu. The year's holidays culminate in a mad rush of Thanksgiving, Christmas, and New Year's celebrations, which are the main themes of this chapter.

Since 1904, the lighting of the Hotel del Coronado's Christmas tree has announced the beginning of the holiday season. During the first week of December, a celebrity is invited to the Del to pull the switch that lights up the historic thirty-foot Christmas tree in the lobby. In 1904, that celebrity was Thomas Edison himself. The tree is magnificent—a tree for the imagination, suggesting 'once upon a time.' It is about fantasies and gentle dreams and how we all want holidays to be, with happy families, laughing children, and all-embracing love. The lobby is a cornucopia of old-fashioned colors, spicy scents, and winking lights—all wrapped in a cozy quilt of nostalgia.

New Year's Eve is the final holiday celebration of the year. The Del is braced for a mad rush to welcome the new year in grand style. A prominent entertainer, along with a large orchestra, is engaged to headline the festivities. Guests dine on blini cups filled with caviar and Individual Beef Wellingtons. As midnight approaches, the countdown begins; and at precisely twelve o'clock, one thousand balloons are released from a net on the ceiling of the Grand Ballroom, cascading down onto the merrymakers below.

Recipes from the Del's historic Crown Room and gourmet Prince of Wales room are featured in this holiday chapter.

A Selection of Holiday Entrees. Left: *Herb-Roasted Turkey with Corn Bread, Pecan and Oyster Dressing.* Lower Right: *Spicy Crusted Ham.* Center: *Pepper-Crusted Prime Rib.*

Thanksgiving

George Washington declared the first official national Thanksgiving day in 1789. Some ninety-nine years later, the Del opened its first holiday season to guests from around the world. Many now make it an annual tradition to dine at the Del. Herb-Roasted Turkey takes on a new dimension, along with a robust preparation of Mashed Turnips and Potatoes, Cranberry Relish Braised in Cabernet Sauvignon Wine, and Steamed Persimmon Pudding with Brandy Sauce for dessert.

Menu for Thanksgiving Day, 1928.

MENU

Mulled Cider

Sourdough Cheese Puffs

Broiled Scallops and Pancetta Salad
Sloe Gin Vinaigrette Dressing

Curried Butternut Squash and Apple Soup

Herb-Roasted Turkey
Corn Bread, Pecan, and Oyster Dressing
Old-Fashioned Giblet Gravy

Cranberry Relish Braised in
Cabernet Sauvignon Wine

Mashed Turnips and Potatoes with Roasted
Garlic and Onions

Zucchini with Pesto and Pine Nuts

Sweet Potato Muffins

Steamed Persimmon Pudding with
Brandy Sauce

Mulled Cider

4 sticks cinnamon
24 whole cloves
4 tsp. whole allspice
2 gal. apple cider
2 cups light brown sugar, firmly
packed
2 lemons, thinly sliced

1. Tie cinnamon sticks, cloves, and allspice in a small cheesecloth bag. Pour apple cider into a large, heavy enamel kettle; then add bag of spices and brown sugar. Simmer uncovered for about 25 minutes, or until thoroughly heated.

2. Remove the bag of spices. Pour cider into a heatproof punch bowl, float lemon slices on top, and serve hot.

Yields 24 servings.

Sourdough Cheese Puffs

¼ cup butter or margarine
1 tsp. Dijon-style mustard
1 tsp. minced garlic
1 tsp. caraway seeds
2 tbsp. minced shallots
1 tbsp. dried dill
¼ tsp. white pepper
8 oz. sharp cheddar cheese, grated
1 8-oz. pkg. cream cheese,
softened
2 egg whites, beaten until stiff
1 loaf sourdough bread, sliced,
crusts removed, and cut into
1-inch cubes

1. Preheat oven to 400 degrees.

2. Melt butter or margarine in the top of a double boiler. Add mustard, garlic, caraway seeds, shallots, dill, and pepper.

3. Add the cheeses and stir until they melt.

4. Cool slightly, stir in part of the beaten egg whites, then fold in the remaining egg whites.

5. Using tongs, dip bread cubes in mixture to coat. Place on cookie sheet and flash freeze until firm, about 30 minutes. Bake frozen for 8 to 10 minutes, or until golden and puffed. Transfer to a tray for serving.

Note: Sourdough Cheese Puffs may be prepared in advance and frozen for up to two months.

Yields about 60 1-inch cheese puffs.

Broiled Scallops and Pancetta Salad with Sloe Gin Vinaigrette Dressing

Scallops:
24 large scallops
24 slices pancetta bacon,
thinly sliced
3 tsp. salt
6 tbsp. fresh lemon juice
6 cups baby oak leaf and
baby romaine lettuce
2 grapefruit, peeled and
divided into segments

1. Preheat oven to 450 degrees.

2. Wrap scallops in pancetta and thread them on eight 10-inch bamboo skewers. Season with salt and sprinkle with lemon juice.

3. Broil scallops for approximately 10 minutes, leaving them juicy. Remove from oven, then remove from skewers. Slice each scallop in half lengthwise.

Note: Pancetta, an Italian bacon roll with peppercorns, may be found in most Italian delicatessens.

Sloe Gin Vinaigrette:

6 oz. sloe gin
3 tsp. chopped shallots
1 tbsp. fresh lemon juice
3 egg yolks
6 oz. olive oil
1 tsp. salt
½ tsp. white pepper

1. In a medium saucepan, combine gin, shallots, and lemon juice. Bring to a boil.
2. Cool, then whisk in egg yolk, olive oil, salt, and pepper. Cover and chill until ready to serve.

To Assemble:
1. Chop baby greens and arrange ½ cup on each of twelve salad plates.
2. Place two scallop slices on baby greens.
3. Drizzle Sloe Gin Vinaigrette over salads.

Serves 12.

Curried Butternut Squash and Apple Soup

2 tbsp. butter or margarine
2 medium onions, coarsely
  chopped
1 large or 2 medium butternut
  squash (about 3 lb.), peeled,
  seeded, and cut into chunks
4 tart green apples, peeled,
  cored, and cut into chunks
2 large boiling potatoes, peeled
  and cut into chunks
6 cups Chicken Stock
  (see recipe)
2½ tsp. curry powder
Salt and freshly ground black
  pepper to taste

1. Melt butter or margarine in a heavy stock pot or dutch oven over medium-low heat. Add onions and sauté until golden but not browned, about 15 minutes. Add the squash, apples, potatoes, stock, and curry powder. Increase the heat and bring the mixture to a boil. Reduce heat and simmer until the vegetables are very tender, about 30 minutes.
2. In batches, purée the mixture until smooth in a food processor fitted with a steel chopping blade. Return soup to the stock pot or dutch oven and season to taste with salt and pepper. Serve hot.

Note: To store, ladle the soup into quart jars and refrigerate. Soup may be stored for up to four days.

Yields about 2½ quarts.

Herb-Roasted Turkey

1 12- to 16-lb. fresh turkey
  (hen preferably)
Corn Bread, Pecan, and Oyster
  Dressing (recipe follows)
Salt and freshly ground black
  pepper
2 tsp. dried sage
2 tsp. dried thyme
1 tsp. dried oregano, crumbled
½ cup (1 stick) butter, softened
16-oz. bag fresh cranberries
  (for garnish)
12 sprigs fresh rosemary
  (for garnish)

1. Preheat oven to 350 degrees.
2. Remove giblets from the turkey and reserve for gravy. Rinse turkey well, inside and out, and pat dry with paper towels.
3. Stuff both cavities loosely with Corn Bread, Pecan, and Oyster Dressing, and close both ends with trussing skewers and string. Place the turkey, breast side up, on a rack in a large roasting pan. Insert a meat thermometer into the thickest part of the thigh without touching the bone.
4. Sprinkle the breast with salt, pepper, sage, thyme, and oregano. Melt the butter in a small saucepan and soak a 12-inch square double layer of cheesecloth in it. Gently lay the cheesecloth over the breast.

5. Place the turkey in the oven, and roast for about 20 minutes per pound, or 4 to 4 ½ hours, basting every 30 minutes with the pan juices. Remove the cheesecloth after 3 hours of roasting. The turkey is done when the meat thermometer registers 180 degrees, or when the juices run clear when the thigh is pricked with a meat fork. (If any part of the turkey begins to get too brown during roasting, cover loosely with aluminum foil.)

6. Remove the turkey to a warm platter, cover the turkey loosely with aluminum foil, and let it rest for 20 to 30 minutes before carving, while you make gravy.

Note: Any stuffing that does not fit into the turkey can be placed into greased half-cup molds and heated in the oven for about 30 minutes. Unmold and place on the platter around turkey. Decorate turkey platter with fresh rosemary sprigs and cranberry strands. To make cranberry strands, wash and dry cranberries, thread a heavy needle with string, and thread the cranberries into various lengths. Tie off ends.

Serves 14 to 16.

Corn Bread, Pecan, and Oyster Dressing

1 cup (2 sticks) butter
1 cup finely chopped onions
1 cup finely chopped celery
6 cups crumbled Corn Bread (recipe follows)
1 qt. shucked oysters in oyster liquor
1½ cups coarsely chopped pecans
¼ cup chopped parsley
1 tsp. salt
1 tsp. freshly ground pepper
1 tsp. poultry seasoning
½ tsp. dry mustard
2 eggs, lightly beaten
1 tsp. dried thyme
1 tsp. dried sage
1 cup Chicken Stock (see recipe)

1. Melt the butter in a skillet over medium heat; add the onions and celery. Sauté for about 7 minutes. Transfer the mixture to a large mixing bowl, add the corn bread, and toss to mix. Set aside.

2. Place the oysters and their liquor in a medium-size saucepan over medium heat. Bring to a boil, reduce heat, and simmer for 2 minutes. Remove from heat and use a slotted spoon to transfer the oysters to a cutting board. Reserve the oyster liquor. Cut the oysters in half.

3. Add the oysters to the corn bread mixture, add the remaining ingredients, and mix with your hands until all ingredients are evenly distributed. Add about 2 cups of the reserved oyster liquor to moisten the dressing, or 1 cup of reserved oyster liquor and 1 cup of chicken stock.

Note: Shucked oysters may be found in the fresh fish section of local supermarkets. If using oysters in a jar, you will need four 8-ounce jars.

Corn Bread:

1 cup white cornmeal
1 cup all-purpose flour
1 tbsp. baking powder
½ tsp. salt
¼ cup sugar
1 cup milk
¼ cup vegetable oil
1 egg, beaten

1. Preheat oven to 400 degrees.
2. Grease a 9-inch baking pan.
3. In a large mixing bowl, combine cornmeal, flour, baking powder, salt, and sugar. Stir in milk, oil, and egg. Mix until dry ingredients are moistened.
4. Pour batter into prepared pan. Bake for 20 to 25 minutes, or until light golden brown. Remove from oven; cool.

Old-Fashioned Giblet Gravy

Giblets from turkey
1 large garlic clove, crushed
¼ tsp. salt
¼ cup fat (skimmed from roasting pan)
¼ cup flour
Pan drippings and enough Chicken Stock to make 2 cups (see Chicken Stock recipe)

1. While the turkey is roasting, place giblets, garlic, and salt in a small saucepan with water to cover. Place over medium heat and simmer the giblets for 20 minutes, until cooked through. Remove the giblets and discard the garlic and cooking liquid. Finely chop the giblets, cover, and store in the refrigerator until the turkey is done.
2. When the turkey is done, skim off the fat from the roasting pan. Place ¼ cup fat in a medium-size saucepan over medium heat (discard any remaining fat), and whisk in the flour. Cook, whisking constantly, until the flour is absorbed and a thick paste forms.
3. Scrape the bottom of the roasting pan to remove any browned bits, and stir them into the pan drippings. Pour the pan drippings into a measuring cup and add enough chicken stock to measure 2 cups. Whisk the stock mixture into the flour-fat mixture until smooth. Add the stored giblets and simmer the gravy until it thickens, about 7 minutes.

Cranberry Relish Braised in Cabernet Sauvignon Wine

1 16-oz. bag fresh cranberries
1 cup cabernet sauvignon wine
1½ cups sugar
Peel of 1 orange, finely chopped
1 cinnamon stick

Note: Prepare three days in advance to ensure that the flavors blend and intensify.

1. Sort through cranberries and discard any unripe or soft berries.
2. Bring wine and sugar to a boil in a saucepan. Add the cranberries and the remaining ingredients. Cover partially and reduce heat to medium.
3. Cook until cranberries have burst and sauce is slightly thickened, about 20 minutes. Cool to room temperature.

Serves 10 to 12.

Mashed Turnips and Potatoes with Roasted Garlic and Onions

4 tbsp. olive oil
2 large onions (about 1 lb.), chopped
6 large heads garlic, unpeeled
2½ lb. turnips, peeled
3 lb. russet potatoes, peeled
3 cups Chicken Stock (see recipe)
½ cup milk
2 tsp. salt
½ tsp. white pepper
3 tbsp. chopped fresh basil
1½ tbsp. chopped fresh tarragon
5 tbsp. brandy

1. Preheat oven to 375 degrees.

2. Pour oil into a 13 x 9 x 2-inch baking pan. Add onions and mix until evenly coated. Push onions to one side to make room for garlic. Cut garlic heads in half vertically. Set garlic, cut sides down, in baking dish.

3. Roast onions and garlic until garlic is very tender when pierced all the way through and onions are browned, about 45 minutes. Stir onions occasionally during cooking (without disturbing garlic). Set aside until cool enough to handle.

4. Quarter the turnips and potatoes. Place them in a 6-quart saucepan with the chicken stock. Bring to a boil over high heat, then cover and simmer until vegetables are very tender when pierced with a fork and cooking liquid is almost gone, about 35 minutes.

5. While turnips and potatoes are cooking, squeeze garlic out of husks (discard husks) and place in a small bowl. With the back of a spoon, mash garlic into a smooth paste. Mix in roasted onions. Set mixture aside.

6. Transfer turnips and potatoes to a large bowl and, with an electric mixer or potato masher, beat hot vegetables until they are in small lumps. (If desired, run vegetables through a food processor to break down any tough turnip fibers.)

7. Add the milk, garlic-onion mixture, salt, pepper, basil, tarragon, and brandy. Beat until vegetables are smooth and creamy. Spoon into a shallow 3- to 4-quart casserole. Broil 4 inches from heat until top is dappled with golden brown spots, about 5 minutes.

Serves 12.

Zucchini with Pesto and Pine Nuts

Salt
12 small zucchini, unpeeled and
  cut into julienned strips
4 cups chopped fresh basil
1 cup olive oil
6 tbsp. pine nuts
4 cloves garlic, peeled
2 tsp. salt
2 cups grated Parmesan cheese
4 tbsp. butter or margarine,
  softened
½ cup pine nuts
½ cup unsalted butter

1. Lightly salt zucchini and drain in colander for 30 minutes; pat dry with paper towels. Set aside.
2. Preheat oven to 350 degrees.
3. Purée basil, olive oil, 6 tablespoons of pine nuts, garlic, and salt in a food processor or blender. Transfer to a bowl, stir in Parmesan cheese and 4 tablespoons butter or margarine, and mix well. Set aside.
4. Spread ½ cup of pine nuts on a nonstick cookie sheet; sprinkle lightly with salt. Bake for 3 minutes, or until toasted.
5. In a large, heavy skillet melt ½ cup of unsalted butter over medium-high heat. Stir in zucchini; sauté until heated through. Add basil sauce and toasted pine nuts; then toss, mixing well.

Serves 12.

Sweet Potato Muffins

1¾ cups all-purpose flour
⅓ cup sugar
2 tsp. baking powder
½ tsp. salt
1 tsp. ground cinnamon
⅛ tsp. ground nutmeg
¾ cup mashed baked sweet
  potato, cooled
¾ cup pure maple syrup
2 eggs, lightly beaten
¼ cup butter or margarine,
  melted and cooled
¼ cup vegetable oil
2 tbsp. water
1 tsp. vanilla extract
½ cup chopped walnuts
½ cup raisins

1. Preheat oven to 400 degrees.
2. Grease a twelve-cup muffin tin. In a large mixing bowl, stir together flour, sugar, baking powder, salt, cinnamon, and nutmeg. In another bowl, stir together sweet potato, maple syrup, eggs, butter or margarine, oil, water, and vanilla until blended. Make a well in center of dry ingredients, add sweet potato mixture, and stir just to combine. Stir in walnuts and raisins.
3. Spoon batter into prepared muffin tins; then bake for 20 to 25 minutes, or until a cake tester inserted in center of one muffin comes out clean.
4. Remove muffin tin to a wire rack. Cool for 5 minutes before removing muffins from cups. Serve warm or cool completely and store in an airtight container at room temperature.

Note: These muffins freeze well.

Yields 12 muffins.

Steamed Persimmon Pudding with Brandy Sauce

Pudding:

2 eggs
1¼ cups sugar
1¼ cups sieved persimmon pulp (from about 3 large ripe persimmons)
¼ cup melted butter
1½ cups sifted all-purpose flour
1½ tsp. baking powder
½ tsp. salt
½ tsp. cinnamon
¾ cup milk
1 cup raisins
¼ cup brandy

1. In a small bowl, beat eggs until light, then beat in sugar until smooth and lemon-colored. In another bowl, combine persimmon pulp and melted butter, then stir into egg mixture.

2. In a medium-size mixing bowl, sift dry ingredients; then stir in milk, beating well after each addition. Add raisins, brandy, and stir in persimmon mixture, blending thoroughly. Transfer to a well-buttered mold and cover tightly with foil.

3. To steam, set the mold on a rack in a large, deep kettle; then add enough water to come halfway up the sides of the mold. Bring water to a gentle boil, cover saucepan, lower heat, and steam for 2½ hours. Remove pudding from water and let cool for 15 minutes. Unmold onto foil; serve warm with Brandy Sauce.

Note: Pudding may be made ahead of time and frozen. If wrapping and freezing, first cool completely, then freeze. Bring to room temperature before reheating.

Brandy Sauce:

1 cup unsalted butter
2 cups sifted confectioners' sugar
2 eggs, separated
1 oz. brandy

1. Cream butter and sugar until soft and fluffy. Beat in egg yolks one at a time, then add brandy and mix well.

2. Beat egg whites until stiff but not dry, then fold into sugar mixture. Serve at room temperature.

Serves 12.

Christmas Eve

Christmas Eve sets the mood for a festive Christmas celebration. Long ago, we unpacked the ornaments for our tree and were ready to embark on the well-polished traditions of Christmas. We decorate our tree and attempt to untangle the blur of many Christmases that are tied together with the common thread of happy familiarity.

Sipping on a cranberry-vodka cocktail is a pleasant way to relax during the Christmas season. December is a perfect time to heat up the oven for Pepper-Crusted Prime Rib and individual Yorkshire Puddings, both of which require minimal preparation. A dazzling Chocolate Truffle Tree acts as a centerpiece and a fabulously elegant dessert.

MENU

Cranberry-Vodka Sippers

Caviar Torte

Bibb Lettuce and Sliced Pears
Walnut Vinaigrette Dressing

Pepper-Crusted Prime Rib
Broiled Peaches
Creamed Horseradish Sauce

Yorkshire Pudding

Corn Soufflés with Basil Cream

Zesty Green Beans

Maple-Walnut Biscuits

Chocolate Truffle Tree

Cranberry-Vodka Sippers

4 cups chilled cranberry juice cocktail
3 cups chilled orange juice
1½ cups vodka
1 lime

1. Combine first three ingredients in a pitcher; stir.
2. Pour into chilled champagne flutes and garnish with lime peel.

Serves 8 to 10.

Caviar Torte

8 hard-cooked eggs, peeled
and chopped
3 tbsp. mayonnaise
Salt and freshly ground black
pepper to taste
2 bunches (1¼ cups) minced
scallions (green and white
parts)
8 oz. cream cheese, softened
⅔ cup dairy sour cream
1 3½-oz. jar lumpfish black
caviar
1 3½-oz. jar red caviar
1 lemon, cut into wedges (for
garnish)
6 parsley sprigs (for garnish)

1. Generously grease a 9-inch springform pie pan.

2. Combine eggs with mayonnaise, salt, and pepper; then spread over bottom of prepared pie pan and top with scallions.

3. Combine cream cheese with sour cream in a blender or food processor until smooth. Spread over scallions, cover, and chill overnight.

4. Just before serving, using black and red caviar alternately, make six triangle shapes to form pie wedges making a red and black color scheme.

5. Run knife around springform pan sides, loosen, and lift off. Garnish with lemon wedges and parsley sprigs. Serve with toast points or water crackers.

Note: A wet spatula helps to spread cream cheese and sour cream layers over the scallions. Drain caviars in a small strainer to remove excess oil before spreading them on top.

Serves 10 to 12.

Bibb Lettuce and Sliced Pears with Walnut Vinaigrette Dressing

½ cup walnut oil
4 tbsp. white wine vinegar
½ tsp. salt
⅛ tsp. freshly ground black
pepper
1 tsp. dried basil
2 large ripe Bosc pears
3 heads Bibb or butter lettuce,
leaves separated, washed, and
patted dry
½ cup walnut pieces

1. In a small mixing bowl, combine oil, vinegar, salt, pepper, and basil. Whisk until the ingredients are blended. Set the vinaigrette dressing aside.

2. Wash pears and pat them dry. With a small, sharp knife cut the pears into quarters and remove the cores. Cut each quarter lengthwise into five slices. Place the slices in a bowl, add about 4 tablespoons of the vinaigrette, and stir gently to coat the slices to prevent them from turning brown. Cover the bowl with plastic wrap and refrigerate.

3. Just before serving, arrange the lettuce leaves on individual plates and top them with the pear slices. Whisk vinaigrette to blend it again, then pour over the salad. Sprinkle each portion with walnut pieces.

Serves 8 to 10.

Pepper-Crusted Prime Rib

1 center-cut beef standing rib roast (about 8 lb.)
Vegetable oil
2 tbsp. kosher salt
2 tbsp. black pepper, coarsely ground
2 tbsp. red peppercorns, mashed
2 tbsp. green peppercorns, mashed

1. Preheat oven to 350 degrees.

2. Remove the strings and the layer of surface fat from roast. Place fat side up in an open roasting pan.

3. Rub oil evenly over surface of roast.

4. In a small mixing bowl, mix the remaining ingredients together. Pat salt and peppers evenly over surface of roast.

5. Insert meat thermometer into the thickest part of roast; make sure that it does not rest on bone or fat.

6. Roast meat at 350 degrees to desired doneness (18 to 20 minutes per pound for rare, 22 to 25 minutes per pound for medium, 27 to 30 minutes per pound for well-done).

7. Remove roast from oven, place on a platter, cover with foil, and let it stand for 15 to 20 minutes before carving. To carve, turn roast on a cut end, then cut rack of bones away from the meat. Cut bones apart and set aside for guests who love this portion of the roast. Carve boneless meat across grain into thin slices. Pour off drippings for use in Yorkshire Pudding.

Serves 12.

Broiled Peaches

8 canned peach halves
8 tbsp. dark brown sugar
4 tsp. butter
8 tsp. brandy, heated

1. Arrange peach halves, cut sides up, in a baking pan.

2. Place 1 tablespoon dark brown sugar and ½ teaspoon butter in the cavity of each peach half.

3. Set under the oven broiler until the butter and sugar melt.

4. Remove from the oven and pour 1 teaspoon of heated brandy over each peach half; ignite if you wish. Serve with Pepper-Crusted Prime Rib.

Serves 8.

Creamed Horseradish Sauce

2 cups sour cream
¾ cup prepared white horseradish
2 tsp. Dijon-style mustard
½ tsp. salt
⅛ tsp. white pepper

1. In a medium-size mixing bowl, combine all ingredients, stirring until smooth.

2. Cover and chill overnight. Serve with Pepper-Crusted Prime Rib.

Yorkshire Pudding

Drippings from Pepper-Crusted
  Prime Rib
1 cup milk
6 eggs
1 cup all-purpose flour
½ tsp. dried thyme leaves
2 tsp. salt
¼ tsp. nutmeg
¼ tsp. black pepper

1. Preheat oven to 400 degrees.
2. Divide roast beef drippings among cups in a twelve-cup muffin tin, about 1 tablespoon per muffin cup. Place in oven and heat for 5 minutes.
3. In a blender, combine milk, eggs, flour, thyme, salt, nutmeg, and pepper. Blend well. Fill each muffin cup two-thirds full of batter.
4. Bake for 20 minutes, then turn oven down to 350 degrees and bake for an additional 20 minutes. Do not open oven before baking time is completed. Puddings should be puffed and crisp. Serve immediately alongside Pepper-Crusted Prime Rib.

Yields 12 individual puddings.

Corn Soufflés with Basil Cream

Corn Soufflés:
3 tbsp. butter, softened
½ cup fresh bread crumbs
4 ears fresh corn (or 3 cups
  frozen corn, drained)
¼ cup sugar
6 eggs, separated
2 tbsp. butter, melted
2 tbsp. flour
1 cup half-and-half
½ tsp. mace
1 tsp. salt
½ tsp. freshly ground pepper

1. Preheat oven to 375 degrees.
2. Butter twelve ⅔-cup soufflé dishes; sprinkle with bread crumbs.
3. Cut corn kernels off cobs and mix with sugar. Beat 6 egg yolks, then add corn and remaining ingredients, except egg whites. With a rotary beater or whisk, beat the egg whites until stiff; then fold into corn mixture.
4. Spoon mixture into soufflé dishes; place dishes in a baking pan. Pour enough boiling water into baking pan to rise ½ inch up the sides of soufflé dishes. Bake for 20 minutes, or until puffed and golden brown.
5. Unmold onto a heated serving platter. Spoon Basil Cream (recipe follows) around soufflés.

Serves 12.

Basil Cream:
1½ cups heavy cream
⅛ cup chopped fresh basil

In a heavy saucepan, boil cream until reduced by half; stir in basil and blend.

Zesty Green Beans

8 slices bacon
⅔ cup sliced almonds
1 cup chopped onions
2 cloves garlic, peeled and
  minced
2 tsp. lemon juice
½ tsp. chili powder
2 lb. fresh green beans, ends
  removed
½ cup water
½ cup dry white wine
½ tsp. salt

1. In a 12-inch skillet, cook bacon over medium heat until evenly browned. Remove bacon and drain on paper towels. Crumble when cool.

2. In the same skillet, heat bacon drippings over medium heat, add almonds, and stir until lightly toasted, about 4 minutes. Remove from skillet and set aside.

3. Discard all but 4 teaspoons of bacon drippings from skillet. Add onions, garlic, lemon juice, and chili powder. Cook over medium heat, stirring often, until onions are limp, about 7 to 10 minutes.

4. While onions cook, rinse beans and cut into 2-inch lengths. When onions are limp, add beans, water, and wine to skillet. Cover and cook until beans are just tender, about 10 minutes. Stir in bacon and almonds. Season with salt and transfer to a serving dish.

Serves 10 to 12.

Maple-Walnut Biscuits

4 cups all-purpose flour
1 tbsp. baking powder
1 tbsp. sugar
1½ tsp. salt
½ tsp. baking soda
½ cup shortening
1¼ cups buttermilk
⅓ cup plus 1½ tbsp. maple
  syrup
½ cup chopped walnuts

1. Preheat oven to 450 degrees.

2. In a large mixing bowl, combine flour, baking powder, sugar, salt, and baking soda. With a pastry blender or two knives, cut in shortening until mixture resembles coarse crumbs. Stir in buttermilk, ⅓ cup maple syrup, and walnuts. Quickly mix, just until mixture forms soft dough that leaves sides of bowl.

3. Turn dough onto lightly floured cutting board; knead 6 to 8 strokes to mix thoroughly. With a floured rolling pin, roll dough into a 12 x 8-inch rectangle. Using a floured knife, cut dough into 2-inch squares; then place on a large, ungreased cookie sheet about 1 inch apart. Brush biscuits with 1½ tablespoon maple syrup, then bake for 12 to 15 minutes, or until golden.

Yields 24 biscuits.

Chocolate Truffle Tree

Chocolate Truffles:

**8 oz. semisweet chocolate
  (use good quality)**
4 oz. unsalted butter
3 egg yolks
1 tbsp. Amaretto liqueur
**20 white rose buds with leaves
  (for decoration)**

1. Coarsely chop chocolate. In a double boiler, melt butter. Stir in chocolate and melt over low heat, stirring with a whisk to form a smooth paste. Whisk in egg yolks, then stir in Amaretto. Cover and refrigerate overnight.

2. The next day, form balls with a small 1-inch scoop or melon ball cutter. Place balls on cookie sheets and refrigerate.

Chocolate Truffle Tree.

Dark Dipping Chocolate:
1 lb. dark chocolate
2 tbsp. white chocolate, melted

1. In a double boiler, melt dark chocolate over low heat, stirring until smooth. Remove from heat.
2. When truffles are firm, dip them into the melted dark chocolate. When chocolate has hardened, dip a fork into white chocolate and drizzle a little white chocolate on each truffle. Refrigerate until ready to assemble truffle tree.

White Truffles:
10 oz. white chocolate
2½ oz. salad oil
3 egg yolks
1 ½ tbsp. Grand Marnier liqueur

1. Coarsely chop white chocolate. In a double boiler, combine chocolate and oil. Melt over low heat, stirring with a whisk to form a smooth paste. Whisk in egg yolks, then stir in Grand Marnier liqueur. Cover and refrigerate overnight.
2. The next day, form balls with a small 1-inch scoop or melon ball cutter. Place balls on cookie sheets and refrigerate.

White Dipping Chocolate:
1 lb. white chocolate
1 tbsp. salad oil
2 tbsp. dark chocolate, melted

1. In a double boiler, combine white chocolate and oil. Cook over low heat until chocolate is melted, stirring until smooth. Remove from heat.
2. When truffles are firm, dip them into the melted white chocolate. When chocolate has hardened, dip a fork into dark chocolate and drizzle a little chocolate on each truffle. Refrigerate until ready to assemble truffle tree.

To Assemble Truffle Tree:
1. Purchase one 12-inch styrofoam cone with a 4-inch base (available at local party supply stores).
2. Place 62 toothpicks in cone, distributed evenly. Place truffles on toothpicks, alternating the dark chocolate and white chocolate truffles. Attach the rose buds to the cone with straight pins. Poke leaves in between spaces to form a truffle tree.

Note: Elevate truffle tree on a pedestal cake plate and use as a centerpiece for your Christmas Eve dinner.

Yields approximately 62 truffles.

Christmas Day

Christmas is a slow-paced day. While the children and grandchildren play with their toys and gifts, the adults relax with Sparkling Holiday Punch and nibble on crackers topped with a blend of smoked almonds and cheese. The aroma of Spicy Crusted Ham awakens their senses and chestnut soup simmers on the stove. For dessert, the Del's version of Bûche de Noél takes the form of Chocolate-Chocolate Yule Log. This French Christmas 'log' is always a hit and a perfect complement to a Christmas dinner.

MENU

Sparkling Holiday Punch

Cream of Winter Chestnut Soup

Christmas Cheese Wreath

Spicy Crusted Ham with Two Sauces

Stir-Fried Brussels Sprouts

Festive Potato Cups

Cranberry Muffins

Chocolate-Chocolate Yule Log

Menu for Christmas Day, 1936.

Sparkling Holiday Punch

1 10-oz. pkg. frozen strawberries
 in syrup, thawed
2 tbsp. fresh lime juice
1 bottle (750 ml) sparkling white
 zinfandel wine
1 bottle (750 ml) chilled
 champagne

1. In a blender, purée strawberries and lime juice. Strain to remove seeds and chill.
2. Pour chilled strawberries and lime juice mixture into a punch bowl. Slowly add wine and champagne.

Yields 14 4-oz. servings.

Cream of Winter Chestnut Soup

½ cup butter or margarine
¾ lb. (about 2 medium) potatoes,
 peeled and chopped
1 cup chopped onion
1 cup chopped celery
1 cup chopped carrots
2 cups beef broth
3 cups chicken broth
¼ cup chopped fresh parsley
1 tsp. dried basil
1 tsp. dried thyme
1 tsp. dried sage
1 (15½-oz.) can chestnuts in
 water, drained (reserve
 ½ cup of crumbled chestnuts
 for garnish)
1 cup Madeira wine
1 cup heavy cream
Salt
White pepper

1. In a large saucepan or dutch oven, melt butter or margarine. Add potatoes, onion, celery, and carrots; then cook over medium-low heat for about 20 minutes, stirring occasionally, until vegetables are soft but not brown. Stir in beef broth and chicken broth, parsley, basil, thyme, and sage. Add chestnuts to soup, cover, and simmer for 20 minutes.
2. Stir in wine and cream; simmer for 5 minutes. Season to taste with salt and pepper.
3. Sprinkle reserved crumbled chestnuts over each serving or over the top of soup if you are serving from a soup tureen.

Note: Soup may be prepared ahead of time and frozen or prepared two days in advance, covered tightly, and stored in refrigerator.

Serves 10 to 12.

Christmas Cheese Wreath

2 8-oz. pkg. cream cheese, softened
½ cup mayonnaise
½ cup grated Parmesan cheese
10 slices bacon, cooked and crumbled
½ cup chopped smoked almonds
¼ cup sliced scallions (white part only)
1 bunch flat-leaf parsley, chopped
Pimiento strips (for garnish)

1. In a medium-size mixing bowl, blend together cream cheese, mayonnaise, and Parmesan cheese until smooth.

2. Mix in bacon, almonds, and scallions. Refrigerate for 30 minutes.

3. Remove from refrigerator and form cheese mixture into a long roll; shape roll into a wreath shape, approximately 8 to 10 inches in diameter. Cheese will be soft, although chilled.

4. Liberally cover wreath with chopped parsley. Shape long strips of pimiento into a bow on the wreath. Dot wreath with bits of pimiento to resemble berries. Chill and serve with water crackers.

Serves 10 to 12.

Spicy Crusted Ham with Two Sauces

1 5- to 6-lb. fully cooked, boneless smoked ham
⅓ cup light brown sugar, packed
¼ cup fine dry bread crumbs
¼ tsp. dry mustard
¼ tsp. allspice
¼ tsp. freshly ground black pepper
⅓ cup dark corn syrup
8 to 10 whole cloves

1. Preheat oven to 325 degrees.

2. Place ham, fat side up, on a rack in a shallow roasting pan. Score ham by using a sharp knife to cut long, shallow lines into the fat at 1-inch intervals. Score ham in the opposite direction, creating an all-over diamond pattern. Insert meat thermometer, so bulb is in the center of the thickest part of the ham; then cover ham with aluminum foil to keep it moist.

3. Bake for about 2 hours, or until thermometer registers 140 degrees.

4. While ham is baking, combine brown sugar, bread crumbs, mustard, allspice, and pepper; mix well. Set aside.

5. In a small saucepan, bring corn syrup to a boil, set aside.

6. Thirty minutes before ham is done, stud ham with whole cloves, brush tops and sides of ham with syrup, and sprinkle on about a third of the crumb mixture.

7. Bake 10 minutes more, then drizzle with half of the remaining syrup and sprinkle with half of the remaining crumbs. Bake another 10 minutes, then repeat using remaining ingredients.

8. Serve with two sauces (recipes follow).

Serves 10 to 12.

Raisin Sauce:
1 cup sugar
1 cup water
1 cup raisins
2 tbsp. butter
2 tbsp. cider vinegar
⅛ tsp. cloves, crushed
⅛ tsp. cinnamon
Pinch salt
¾ cup grape jelly
**2 tsp. cornstarch dissolved in
  2 tsp. water**

1. In a 1-quart saucepan, bring sugar and water to a boil.
2. Add raisins, butter, vinegar, cloves, cinnamon, salt, and jelly. Stir over low heat until jelly is dissolved.
3. Add cornstarch to sauce and heat until raisins are plump and sauce thickens slightly.
4. Remove from heat and transfer to a sauce boat.

Yields 3 cups.

Fig Sauce:
**1 8-oz. pkg. dried Calimyrna
  figs, diced**
**1 medium-size apple, peeled and
  diced**
1¼ cup apple juice
½ cup brown sugar, packed
½ cup cider vinegar
¼ tsp. ground allspice
¼ tsp. ground ginger
¼ tsp. ground cinnamon
¼ tsp. salt
½ cup chopped walnuts

1. Place all ingredients except walnuts in a 1-quart saucepan. Bring to a boil over high heat. Reduce heat to low and simmer uncovered, stirring occasionally, until mixture thickens slightly, about 20 minutes.
2. Remove from heat, stir in walnuts, and transfer to a sauce boat.

Yields about 2⅔ cups.

Note: Both sauces may be prepared three days in advance, covered tightly, and stored in refrigerator. Allow sauces to come to room temperature before heating on simmer just until heated through. You may also heat sauces in a microwave oven on medium-high heat for 3 to 4 minutes.

Stir-Fried Brussels Sprouts

**4 12-oz. containers Brussels
  sprouts**
⅓ cup Canola oil
**1 16-oz. can water chestnuts,
  drained**
½ tsp. salt
½ tsp. garlic salt
⅛ tsp. coarsely ground pepper
½ cup water

1. Cut each Brussels sprout in half.
2. In a 5-quart dutch oven, heat half the oil over high heat. Cook half the Brussels sprouts, stirring quickly and frequently, until lightly browned, about 5 minutes. Remove to bowl; reserve. In the same dutch oven, heat remaining oil and cook remaining Brussels sprouts until lightly browned.
3. Add reserved Brussels sprouts to dutch oven; then add water chestnuts, salt, garlic salt, pepper, and water. Reduce heat to medium, cover, and cook for 8 to 10 minutes, stirring occasionally, until Brussels sprouts are tender-crisp. Keep warm until served.

Serves 10 to 12.

Festive Potato Cups

9 red-skinned medium
   potatoes (about 3 lb.), cooked
   and drained
6 medium-size yams (about 3
   lb.), cooked and drained
6 tbsp. butter or margarine
3 egg whites
¾ tsp. onion powder
3 egg yolks
1 ½ tsp. orange peel, finely
   shredded
6 tbsp. butter or margarine,
   melted (for topping)
Salt
White pepper
Vegetable cooking spray

1. Remove skins from the potatoes and yams.

2. In two separate mixing bowls, mash the potatoes and the yams with an electric mixer on low speed until each is smooth and not lumpy. Add 3 tablespoons of butter to each mixture.

3. Beat egg whites and onion powder into white potatoes. Beat the egg yolks and orange peel into the yams. Season each mixture with salt and pepper to taste.

4. Spray two cookie sheets with nonstick vegetable spray. Using a wooden spoon, form about ¼ cup of the yam mixture into a 2 ½- to 3-inch nest on the cookie sheet. Repeat with the rest of the yam mixture, making twenty-four nests.

5. Spoon the potato mixture into a pastry bag fitted with a decorative tip. Pipe potato mixture into the center of the yam nests. Loosely cover nests with plastic wrap and chill overnight.

6. When ready to serve, preheat oven to 450 degrees. Remove nests from refrigerator and bring to room temperature. Drizzle melted butter or margarine over the nests, then bake, uncovered, for 10 to 12 minutes, or until golden. Let stand for 1 to 2 minutes. Use a wide spatula to carefully transfer the nests to dinner plates or to a warmed serving platter.

Serves 12 (2 per person).

Cranberry Muffins

2¼ cups all-purpose flour
¾ cup granulated sugar
1 tsp. baking soda
¼ tsp. salt
1 egg, slightly beaten
1¼ cups buttermilk
4 tbsp. butter, melted
1 cup chopped cranberries
½ cup chopped pecans
Confectioners' sugar

1. Preheat oven to 400 degrees.

2. Lightly grease a twelve-cup muffin tin. In a large mixing bowl, combine flour, ¼ cup granulated sugar, baking soda, and salt. Toss lightly with a fork.

3. In a small bowl, combine egg, buttermilk, and butter; blend well. Add to the dry ingredients and stir just enough to moisten.

4. Toss the cranberries with the remaining granulated sugar, then add to the batter along with the chopped nuts. Spoon batter into the muffin tins, filling them two-thirds full.

5. Bake for 20 minutes, or until a cake tester comes out clean. Sprinkle with confectioners' sugar and serve warm.

Yields 12 muffins.

Chocolate-Chocolate Yule Log

Cake Roll:

3 eggs
¼ cup plus 2 tbsp. sugar
1 tbsp. simple syrup
¼ cup cake flour
4 tbsp. cornstarch
¼ cup dark cocoa
**3½ tbsp. unsalted butter,
  melted and cooled**
Parchment paper

1. Preheat oven to 400 degrees.

2. In a medium-size mixing bowl, combine eggs, sugar, and simple syrup. Beat on high speed with an electric mixer for 4 minutes, or until light and fluffy.

3. Sift together flour, cornstarch, and cocoa. Add to egg mixture, then fold in melted butter.

4. Spray a 15 x 10 x ¾-inch jellyroll pan with nonstick vegetable spray. Line with parchment paper and spray again. Spoon on cake batter, then bake for 7 to 8 minutes, or until cake tester comes out clean. Do not overbake. Remove from oven and cool to room temperature. Place in refrigerator for 1 hour.

5. Remove from refrigerator and turn upside down on parchment paper. Set aside.

Note: Simple syrup is available at your local liquor store.

*Chocolate Buttercream
Filling and Frosting:*

3 cups sifted confectioners' sugar
**¼ cup unsalted butter, cut
  into bits**
½ cup cocoa
2 egg yolks
3 tbsp. coffee

1. In a large mixing bowl, combine confectioners' sugar, butter, and cocoa. With an electric mixer, beat mixture at medium speed for 4 to 5 minutes.

2. Add egg yolks, one at a time, and blend for 2 minutes, scraping down sides of bowl with a spatula. Add coffee and blend for 1 more minute. Set aside.

To Assemble:

1. Spread chocolate buttercream over top of cake. Roll up lengthwise, jellyroll-style. End with seam side down. Cut a 1-inch slice (on the bias) off each end of the cake roll. Set aside.

2. Frost the outside of the cake roll. Frost the end slices, and place them on top of cake, about ¾ inch from each end of cake (to resemble ends of a cut log). Transfer to a cake platter lined with a holiday doily. Garnish with Christmas holly.

Serves 12.

New Year's Eve

New Year's Eve gives us one more chance to celebrate, and there is no nicer way to welcome the new year than with your close friends around you. In Western civilization, the New Year's Eve bash has become a ritual and pleasant obligation that is eagerly anticipated. It is a time to reminisce and relive the good memories from the old year—a way to end the holiday season in high style by enjoying an elegant, but simple-to-prepare dinner.

This is the time of year that calls for champagne and caviar to start off your evening celebration. Blinis, the Russian version of miniature pancakes filled with red and black caviar, are a luxurious start. A rose-shaped salad with a chambord vinaigrette dressing leads up to the entree of Individual Beef Wellingtons, which can be prepared early in the day, leaving you ample time to relax before your guests arrive. Cherries Jubilee is a festive treat and a fitting finale for your New Year's Eve feast.

MENU

French Champagne Cocktails

Miniature Blini Cups with Red Caviar

Rose Salad
Chambord Vinaigrette

Individual Beef Wellingtons
Madeira-Currant Sauce

Duchesse Potatoes

Asparagus and Prosciutto Bundles

Cherries Jubilee

New Year's Eve invitation for 1927.

French Champagne Cocktails

3 oz. cognac, chilled
6 oz. framboise (raspberry
  liqueur), chilled
2 (750-ml) bottles champagne,
  chilled
6 lemon twists

1. Pour ½ ounce of cognac into each of six champagne glasses. Add 1 ounce of framboise.
2. Fill champagne glasses with champagne, stir lightly, and garnish with a lemon twist.

Serves 6.

Miniature Blini Cups with Red Caviar

1 pt. small-curd cottage
  cheese
½ cup plus 1 tbsp. sour cream
1 tbsp. vanilla extract
1 tsp. sugar
3 tbsp. butter or margarine,
  melted
3 eggs
½ cup buttermilk biscuit mix
Vegetable cooking spray
2 oz. red caviar
½ cup minced red onion

1. Preheat oven to 350 degrees.
2. In a food processor fitted with a metal blade (or an electric mixer), mix together cottage cheese, 1 tablespoon sour cream, vanilla, sugar, and butter or margarine until thoroughly blended. Add eggs, one at a time. Add biscuit mix and beat until blended.
3. Spray a miniature muffin tin with nonstick vegetable cooking spray, then fill each ¾-full of batter. Bake for 35 to 40 minutes, or until tops are golden brown. Remove from oven, ease a small knife around edges of cups, and remove contents to a rack to cool. (Cups may be stored at room temperature in an airtight container for two days.)
4. Place cups on a serving platter. Fill cups with remaining sour cream, caviar, and minced red onions.

Note: Cups may be prepared ahead and frozen. Do not defrost before reheating. Preheat oven to 350 degrees, then place frozen cups on cookie sheets and bake for 10 to 15 minutes, or until they are hot and crisp.

Yields about 36 cups.

Rose Salad with Chambord Vinaigrette Dressing

Salad:

6 heads Boston lettuce
16 Belgian endive spears
24 raspberries
6 tsp. pink peppercorns, crushed

1. Wash and dry lettuce; remove hearts (store remainder of lettuce in the refrigerator for use at a later date). Cut off excess core from bottom, so lettuce will sit flat on plate.
2. Cut and trim root end of Belgian endive, cut into quarters.

Chambord Vinaigrette:

2 tsp. Dijon-style mustard
2 tbsp. raspberry vinegar
4 tbsp. olive oil
2 tbsp. walnut oil
2 tbsp. vegetable oil
4 tbsp. Chambord Royal liqueur

1. In a small bowl, whisk mustard and vinegar until well blended. In a separate medium-size bowl, blend all the oils together; then slowly drizzle and whisk into mustard-vinegar mixture until incorporated into a smooth sauce.
2. Slowly whisk in Chambord Royal liqueur.

Note: This dressing may be used on any combination of salad greens and is also good when tossed with strawberries and raspberries topped with orange zest and whipped cream.

Yields 1 cup.

To Assemble:

1. Arrange endive quarters like wheel spokes on six salad plates. Place lettuce heart in center of plate, opening slightly to give a rose appearance. Place a raspberry between each spoke of endive.
2. Drizzle 2 tablespoons of Chambord Vinaigrette over the 'rose.' Sprinkle with 1 teaspoon crushed pink peppercorns.

Serves 6.

Individual Beef Wellingtons with Madeira-Currant Sauce

Beef Wellingtons:

6 4-oz. beef tenderloin filets
Garlic powder
Salt
Pepper
3 tbsp. butter or margarine
10 oz. fresh mushrooms, finely chopped
½ cup finely chopped onion
¼ cup plus 2 tbsp. dry sherry wine
3 tbsp. finely chopped fresh parsley
6 frozen unbaked patty shells, thawed
1 egg, beaten with 1 tbsp. water (egg wash)

1. Preheat oven to 425 degrees.

2. Lightly sprinkle filets with garlic powder, salt, and pepper. Melt butter or margarine in a large skillet, then sauté filets for 2 to 4 minutes on each side. Remove from pan and drain filets on paper towels. Refrigerate.

3. To the pan drippings in the skillet, add chopped mushrooms, onion, wine, and parsley. Cook and stir until onion is tender and all liquid is absorbed.

4. Remove filets from refrigerator and spread equal portions of filling over the top of each chilled steak. Return filets to refrigerator.

5. Grease a 15 x 10 x ¾-inch jellyroll pan.

6. On a lightly floured surface, roll each patty shell into a 6-inch square. Place filets, mushroom side down, on crusts; then fold dough over meat, enclosing it completely. Using a pastry brush, seal edges with egg wash. Place seam side down in prepared pan. Brush all over with egg wash.

7. Bake at 425 degrees for 15 minutes, or until crust is golden.

Madeira-Currant Sauce:

3 tbsp. dried currants (or raisins)
½ cup cabernet sauvignon wine
3 cups Brown Stock (see recipe)
⅓ cup Madeira wine
2 tbsp. butter
8 oz. fresh mushrooms

1. Soak currants or raisins in cabernet sauvignon for 20 minutes. Drain liquid into a small saucepan, discard currants, then add stock. Reduce stock mixture by half over medium-high heat, about 10 minutes.

2. In a medium-size saucepan, combine reduced mixture and Madeira wine, then cook over high heat until mixture is reduced by half. Set aside.

3. Melt the butter in a large skillet, then sauté mushrooms until brown and moisture is evaporated, about 2 minutes. Add mushrooms to Madeira mixture, deglaze skillet with a few tablespoons of Madeira sauce, then add drippings to saucepan and stir. Serve sauce over filets.

Serves 6.

Duchesse Potatoes

3 tbsp. butter or margarine, melted
2 eggs, beaten
⅛ cup Parmesan cheese
½ tsp. salt
⅛ tsp. pepper
1 tsp. nutmeg
4 medium potatoes (about 4 cups), peeled, cooked, and mashed

1. Preheat oven to 500 degrees.
2. In a small mixing bowl, beat 2 tablespoons of butter or margarine with eggs, cheese, salt, pepper, and nutmeg. Add the mashed potatoes and blend mixture thoroughly.
3. Spoon mixture into a pastry bag. Using a large star tip, pipe 2-inch rosettes onto a nonstick cookie sheet. Drizzle remaining butter or margarine over top of rosettes.
4. Bake for 10 to 12 minutes.

Serves 6.

Asparagus and Prosciutto Bundles

30 spears fresh pencil-thin asparagus
6 slices prosciutto ham
½ cup grated Parmesan cheese
¾ tsp. freshly ground pepper
2 cloves garlic, peeled and minced
½ cup butter or margarine, melted

1. Preheat oven to 350 degrees.
2. Grease 13 x 9 x 2-inch baking pan; set aside.
3. Steam asparagus until tender-crisp, 4 to 5 minutes. Immediately chill under cold running water.
4. Wrap 5 asparagus spears in each slice of prosciutto. Place bundles, seam side down, in prepared baking pan.
5. Sprinkle Parmesan cheese across center of each ham bundle. Season generously with pepper.
6. Combine garlic and melted butter or margarine; drizzle over bundles. Bake at 350 degrees for 10 to 15 minutes, or until cheese is melted and light brown and asparagus is heated through. Remove bundles with slotted spoon; place in a heated serving dish. Spoon any melted butter that is left in the baking pan over the cooked bundles.

Serves 6.

Cherries Jubilee

¼ tbsp. granulated sugar
¼ cup orange juice
1 pinch cinnamon
3 cups canned bing cherries, pitted and drained
1 oz. brandy
2 oz. Cherry Heering liqueur
6 large scoops vanilla ice cream
1 cup heavy cream, whipped
6 tsp. chopped almonds

1. In a medium-size saucepan or chafing dish, combine sugar and orange juice over medium heat. Add cinnamon, stirring constantly until sugar is dissolved; then add cherries and cook over high heat for 5 minutes.
2. Heat brandy and Cherry Heering in a small saucepan, then pour over sugar and orange juice mixture. Ignite just before serving.
3. Scoop ice cream into six individual champagne glasses or bowls. Pour cherries over ice cream, and top with whipped cream and chopped almonds.

Serves 6.

CHAPTER SEVEN
Celebrity Selections

Celebrity watching is an enjoyable hobby indulged in by many guests at the Del.
If you are a celebrity, everything about you is noticed—where you go, how you look, what you wear, whom you meet, and what you eat—which brings us to the subject of this chapter. Celebrities, who are out of the ordinary to begin with, often have food preferences that are also out of the ordinary.

The Del has been graced, over the years, with visits from many celebrities—some performing at events such as a New Year's Eve party or the once-in-a-lifetime Centennial celebration, and others are guests just luxuriating in the Old World elegance and Victorian splendor that the Del offers. Let's do a little celebrity watching at the Del.

In 1987, Milton Berle was engaged as the headline star for the New Year's Eve party held in the Grand Ballroom. Mr. Berle arrived early because he had a rehearsal scheduled in the afternoon. Between his arrival and the rehearsal, he requested his version of a screwdriver—a luncheon of Vodka-Steamed Lobster with two glasses of freshly squeezed orange juice. When he arrived at the ballroom for the rehearsal, he immediately expressed his displeasure with the location of the stage and requested that it be moved before the performance that evening. With some difficulty, he was

George Burns' Five-Way Banana Split: pistachio, French vanilla, strawberry, chocolate, and butter pecan ice cream topped with Hot Chocolate Fudge Sauce, Butterscotch Sauce, and Strawberry Sauce and crowned with Whipped Cream, chopped peanuts, and Maraschino cherries.

persuaded that the stage would stay where it was permanently built one hundred years before. An alternative would have to be considered. After additional colorful complaints, he agreed to perform on the dance floor, using the stage only for the band. He performed to a capacity audience of over 850 guests. They loved him.

Dionne Warwick was one of the star attractions at the Centennial celebration held on February 20, 1988. Shortly after she arrived, she placed a triple order for the Del's Oriental Chicken Wings and Cristal Roederer champagne to dampen her vocal cords before what turned out to be a smashing performance.

George Burns was one of the one hundred guest celebrities who attended the Centennial. While enjoying a midnight musical revue, he ordered a double martini and a banana split to be made with five different flavors of ice cream—a small amount of each flavor. The pantry chef dished up five different flavors of ice cream with a melon-ball scoop and topped them with all of the trimmings. Thus, George Burns' Five-Way Banana Split was created.

Also on the Del's celebrity Centennial guest list was Zsa Zsa Gabor. Her only special request was that Pepe, her French poodle, be seated next to her and Cesar Romero. The dining room manager tactfully overlooked the strict health department regulation that did not permit pets in restaurants and seated the trio, after which Ms. Gabor shared her crab cakes with Pepe. Pepe, of course, wore a Hotel Del napkin around his neck to ensure that his immaculate ringlets would remain spotless.

Beverly Sills chose cuisine from Italy at her retirement dinner party. Red Skelton dined on the Del's Thai-Style Halibut en Papillote while he sketched one of his famous clowns on the back of a Crown Room menu.

On April 24, 1984, a tribute to Billy Wilder, producer of the screen classic *Some Like It Hot* that starred Marilyn Monroe, Jack Lemmon, and Tony Curtis, was held at the Del. It had been twenty-five years since the screening of *Some Like It Hot,* which had been filmed at the Hotel del Coronado. To celebrate the anniversary, the San Diego Chamber of Commerce Motion Picture and Television Bureau held a black-tie dinner dance in the Grand Ballroom. The executive chef created a star-studded menu, highlighted with a fish course of Salmon Napoleon Florentine and delicately prepared Noisettes of Lamb with Fines Herbes and Cabernet Sauvignon Sauce. The grand finale was Monroe's favorite, Chocolate Soufflé with Vanilla Sauce. Five hundred guests attended this anniversary celebration, where Jack Lemmon and Tony Curtis reminisced about Marilyn, her sense of dialogue, and her dazzling beauty. Billy Wilder said, "I would get on my knees and beg Marilyn to film another movie under my direction if she were here."

Lawrence Welk was honored at a five-course dinner on July 2, 1982, with every course prepared with champagne. The San Diego County Chapter of the American Red Cross presented Mr. Welk with the Spirit of America Award in recognition of his role in developing and promoting the musical heritage of our country in this century. The chef in the Del's gourmet dining room created palate enticements of Lobster and Blue Point Oysters in Champagne and Mustard Cream, with an intermezzo of Champagne Sorbet served over frozen grapes. Fresh Strawberries in Pink Champagne with Zabaglione Sauce was the dessert.

Celebrity choices of Milton Berle's Vodka-Steamed Lobster, Dionne Warwick's Oriental Chicken Wings, George Burns's Five-Way Banana Split, and Zsa Zsa Gabor's Crab Cakes are included in this chapter, along with Debbie Reynolds' favorite selection of Fresh Fruit Fantasy, a combination of seasonal fruit assembled like a painting by the great masters—in this case, the chefs at the Del.

In 1984, the hotel celebrated the 25th anniversary of the filming of the Marilyn Monroe classic Some Like it Hot. *Stars Tony Curtis* (left) *and Jack Lemmon* (right) *and director Billy Wilder were among those who attended the gala event.*

Some Like It Hot Twenty-Fifth Anniversary Dinner for Six

MENU

Exotic Greens
Balsamic Vinaigrette Dressing

Salmon Napoleon Florentine
Mustard-Dill Sauce

Mango Fruit Sorbet

Noisettes of Lamb with Fines Herbes
Cabernet Sauvignon Sauce
Fennel Stuffed with Rice Medley

Amaretto Pea Pods

Chocolate Soufflé
Vanilla Sauce

The Grand Ballroom of the Hotel del Coronado was the location chosen to celebrate the twenty-fifth anniversary of Oscar-winning director Billy Wilder's film *Some Like It Hot*. Tony Curtis and Jack Lemmon starred in the film as out-of-work musicians so desperate for employment that they join an all-girl band, disguising themselves in wigs, dresses, and makeup as *femmes fatales*.

Exotic Greens with Balsamic Vinaigrette Dressing

1 head radicchio lettuce
1 head limestone lettuce
2 bunches watercress
1 cup sliced mushrooms

1. Wash and dry lettuce leaves and watercress. Cut radicchio into julienned strips. Tear limestone into bite-size pieces. Coarsely chop watercress.
2. Place all greens in a large mixing bowl. Add mushrooms and toss.

Balsamic Vinaigrette:
⅔ **cup olive oil**
⅓ **cup balsamic vinegar**
1 tsp. minced fresh garlic
1 shallot, peeled and minced
½ **tsp. minced fresh marjoram**
½ **tsp. minced fresh sage**
½ **tsp. salt**
¼ **tsp. white pepper**

1. In a medium-size mixing bowl, whisk oil into the vinegar.
2. Add remaining ingredients and whisk again. Cover and refrigerate until ready to serve. Shake well before serving.

Yields 1 cup.

To Serve:
1. Add Balsamic Vinaigrette to greens and toss.
2. Divide greens onto six salad plates and serve.

Serves 6.

Salmon Napoleon Florentine with Mustard-Dill Sauce

Salmon Napoleon:

**2½ lb. (approximately) salmon
  fillets, skinned**
2 8-oz. russet potatoes
2 bunches fresh spinach
**1 cup Mushroom Duxelle (recipe
  follows)**
1 cup chardonnay wine
4 sprigs fresh dill (for garnish)
Parchment paper

1. Preheat oven to 375 degrees.

2. Slice salmon fillets into eighteen 2-ounce portions. With a mallet, lightly pound and flatten fillets to ⅛-inch thickness. Fillets should be approximately 4 x 2 inches in size. Set aside.

3. Clean and peel potatoes. In a medium-size saucepan, bring 2 quarts of water to a boil. Blanch potatoes for about 10 to 12 minutes. Remove potatoes from water, drain, and rinse in cold water. Cut into ⅛-inch slices. Set aside.

4. Clean spinach, remove stems, and place in a colander. Pour boiling water over spinach leaves to wilt. Rinse in cold water. Set aside.

5. On a cutting board, lay out six salmon fillets. Place one layer of potato slices on each. Spread Mushroom Duxelle very thinly over potato layer; then add two spinach leaves and top with second salmon fillet. Repeat process and top with third salmon fillet. Carefully trim edges of Salmon Napoleons.

6. Grease a 14 x 10 x 2-inch baking pan. Transfer Salmon Napoleons to baking pan, pour chardonnay wine over them, cover with parchment paper, and bake for 15 to 20 minutes until salmon is cooked through. Remove from oven.

Mushroom Duxelle:

½ lb. mushrooms
2 tbsp. butter or margarine
2 tbsp. olive oil
1 tsp. salt
¼ tsp. white pepper
1 medium onion, chopped
2 shallots, chopped
1 tbsp. chopped fresh parsley
1 tbsp. chopped fresh dill
2 tbsp. white wine

1. Clean mushrooms, trim off stems, and chop fine.

2. In a small skillet, heat butter or margarine with olive oil, add mushrooms, salt, and pepper. Cover immediately and cook on medium-high heat until moisture has evaporated.

3. Add onion, shallots, parsley, dill, and wine. Continue cooking, uncovered, until mixture is moist. Set aside.

Mustard-Dill Sauce:

½ **cup dry white wine**
2 **tbsp. finely chopped fresh dill**
1 **cup heavy cream**
4 **tsp. Dijon-style mustard**
1 **tsp. salt**
¼ **tsp. white pepper**

1. In a medium-size saucepan, combine wine and dill. Bring to a simmer and cook for 5 minutes, or until liquid reduces to 2 tablespoons, stirring constantly to prevent burning.
2. Blend in cream and simmer for 10 minutes, or until sauce reduces to about ¾ cup. Whisk in mustard, salt, and pepper. Keep sauce warm.

To Serve:
1. Spoon about 2 tablespoons of Mustard-Dill Sauce onto each of six salad plates.
2. Lay a Salmon Napoleon on top of sauce on each plate. Garnish with fresh dill sprig.

Serves 6.

Mango Fruit Sorbet

2 **mangos (about 2 lb.)**
2 **cups sugar**
¾ **cup water**
1 **tbsp. plus 1 tsp. orange juice**
  concentrate

1. Peel and scoop out flesh from mangos. Coarsely chop and set aside.
2. In a small saucepan, combine sugar and water. Bring mixture to a boil, stirring until sugar is dissolved. Set aside.
3. Place the chopped mangos, orange juice concentrate, and sugar-water mixture in a blender. Blend for about 1 minute.
4. Refrigerate mixture until cold, then freeze it in an ice cream maker according to the manufacturer's directions. Transfer sorbet to a covered container and freeze until ready to serve.

To Serve:
Place one small scoop of sorbet in each chilled parfait glass or other suitable stemware.

Note: Sorbet may be prepared up to three weeks in advance.

Yields about 2 pints.

Noisettes of Lamb with Fines Herbes and Cabernet Sauvignon

1 tbsp. minced fresh rosemary
1 tbsp. minced fresh parsley
1 tbsp. minced fresh oregano
1 tbsp. minced fresh thyme
  (or 1 tsp. dried)
1 tsp. coarsely ground black
  pepper
12 3-oz. lamb noisettes
3 tbsp. olive oil
1 tbsp. minced fresh garlic
1 tbsp. finely chopped shallots
½ cup cabernet sauvignon wine
2 cups Lamb Stock (see recipe)
½ cup butter, cut into pieces
½ tbsp. ground coriander seed
2 tsp. salt
½ tsp. pepper

1. Preheat oven to 200 degrees.

2. In a small bowl, combine rosemary, parsley, oregano, thyme, and black pepper.

3. Lay out lamb noisettes and pat mixed herbs on both sides of noisettes. Heat olive oil in a large skillet. Add lamb and cook for 3 minutes on each side for medium-rare. Remove noisettes from skillet and transfer to a 13 x 9 x 2-inch baking pan. Cover and keep warm in the oven.

4. In the same skillet, combine garlic, shallots, wine, and lamb stock. Bring to a boil, then reduce heat to a simmer. Cook and stir until sauce is reduced by half. Whisk in butter; then add coriander seed, salt, and pepper. Remove from heat and strain sauce into the top of a double boiler. Keep warm.

To Serve:

1. Spoon sauce onto one side of each of six dinner plates. Place two lamb noisettes on top of sauce on each.

2. Serve with Fennel Stuffed with Rice Medley and Amaretto Pea Pods (recipes follow) arranged on the other side of plate.

Note: You can purchase twelve loin lamb chops and remove bones, gristle, and fat, then trim into round noisettes; or ask your butcher to cut the noisettes for you.

Serves 6.

Fennel Stuffed with Rice Medley

3 tbsp. butter or margarine
⅓ cup pistachio nuts
12 small fennel bulbs
1½ cups wild rice
2 tsp. salt
1½ cups long-grain rice
1 tbsp. butter or margarine
3 shallots, peeled and minced
1 clove fresh garlic, minced
¼ cup plus 2 tbsp. sherry wine
¼ tsp. white pepper
1 tsp. fines herbes

1. In a small skillet, melt butter or margarine, then add pistachio nuts. Cook and stir for about 3 minutes, or until nuts are browned. Remove from heat and set aside.

2. Clean fennel and place in a medium-size saucepan. Add enough water to cover fennel, and simmer for 30 minutes. Drain and slice fennel in half; scoop out flesh and chop. Set aside fennel halves and flesh.

3. In another medium-size saucepan, cook wild rice in salted water, covered for 20 minutes. Add long-grain rice, cover, and cook for 25 to 30 minutes more. Drain and set aside.

4. In a medium-size skillet, melt butter or margarine. Add chopped fennel, shallots, and garlic. Sauté mixture gently until blended. Add rice, sherry wine, white pepper, and fines herbes. Blend mixture together. Remove from heat.

To Serve:
1. Pile the rice medley into the hollowed-out fennel halves.
2. Sprinkle with toasted pistachio nuts.

Serves 6 (2 per person).

Amaretto Pea Pods

Water
1 tsp. salt
¾ lb. fresh pea pods
3 tbsp. unsalted butter
1½ tbsp. Amaretto liqueur
1½ tsp. fresh lime juice
1 egg yolk, slightly beaten

1. Fill a large skillet ⅔ full of water, bring to a boil, and add salt.
2. Place pea pods in boiling water. Cover, return to a boil, and cook for about 2 minutes. Pea pods will be slightly crunchy. Remove from heat, drain, cover, and set aside. Keep warm.
3. In a small saucepan, melt unsalted butter over low heat, watching carefully to avoid burning, until it is a golden color. Remove from heat and pour into a small mixing bowl. Cool slightly. With a fork, whisk in Amaretto until smooth. Add fresh lime juice.
4. Add a small amount of mixture to beaten egg yolk and whisk again. Add the remainder of the Amaretto butter to egg yolk mixture and whisk until smooth. Pour over pea pods and serve. (If Amaretto butter separates, warm it slightly and whisk again.)

Serves 6.

Chocolate Soufflé with Vanilla Sauce

Chocolate Soufflé:

Sugar
¾ cup milk
2 oz. bitter chocolate
7 tbsp. sugar
3 tbsp. butter
3 tbsp. flour
5 egg yolks
7 egg whites

1. Preheat oven to 375 degrees.

2. Sprinkle inside of buttered 6-cup soufflé dish (or 6 individual soufflé cups) with a little sugar. Set aside.

3. In a small saucepan, combine milk, chocolate, and 2 tablespoons of sugar. Stir constantly over low heat until chocolate is melted. Set aside.

4. Melt butter in a medium-size saucepan. Remove from heat. Stir in flour and 4 tablespoons of sugar. Gradually stir in chocolate mixture, then return to heat. Stir until mixture thickens and resembles a chocolate cream sauce. Remove from heat. Beat egg yolks into chocolate mixture, then transfer to a large mixing bowl and set aside.

5. In a small mixing bowl, beat egg whites until stiff, but not dry. Add the remaining tablespoon of sugar. Beat for 30 seconds, the fold into chocolate mixture. Pour into prepared soufflé dish and bake for 20 minutes.

6. Remove from oven and serve immediately with warm vanilla sauce on the side.

Serves 6.

Vanilla Sauce:

2 cups milk
2 tbsp. sugar
1 tsp. vanilla extract
½ tsp. butter
1 tbsp. cornstarch dissolved in
   1 tbsp. water

1. Bring milk to a boil; then add sugar, vanilla extract, butter, and cornstarch. Whisk over low heat until thickened.

2. Keep warm, then transfer to a serving dish before serving.

Yields 2 cups.

Beverly Sills Retirement Dinner for Eight

The San Diego Opera hosted a retirement dinner for the opera diva Beverly Sills, also known as "Bubbles" for her effervescent personality. The Grand Ballroom, where the birthday bash was held, was decorated with hundreds of helium-filled pink balloons and orchids banking the tables. Joan Sutherland and Ms. Sills' daughter joined in the celebration. An all-Italian menu was chosen by the San Diego Opera committee.

MENU

Venetian Antipasto Salad
Hotel del Coronado House Dressing

Penne Pasta Agliata

Lime and Basil Sorbet

Chicken Saltimbocca
Marsala Sauce

Risotto Milanese

Braised Belgian Endive

Fig and Raspberry Clafouti

An autographed program signed by Beverly Sills and Joan Sutherland at Beverly Sills's retirement dinner.

Hotel Del Coronado House Dressing

1 cup Canola oil
½ cup red wine vinegar
¼ cup fresh lemon juice
1 tbsp. Dijon-style mustard
¼ cup water
1 tsp. sugar
1 tsp. salt
1 tsp. finely ground black pepper
1 tbsp. garlic salt
1 tbsp. dried oregano

1. Place all ingredients in a large mixing bowl. Whisk thoroughly to form an emulsion.
2. Store in a covered jar. Shake well before using.

Yields about 2 cups.

Venetian Antipasto Salad

6 large red bell peppers
6 large yellow bell peppers
8 large mushrooms (about 1 lb.), sliced
2 cups Hotel del Coronado House Dressing (recipe above)
2 heads romaine lettuce
8 slices Cotto salami
8 slices provolone cheese
8 slices mortadella
16 anchovy fillets
2 tsp. capers, washed and dried
8 Roma tomatoes, cut in half (for garnish)
16 Kalamata (Greek) black olives (for garnish)
8 fresh basil leaves (for garnish)

1. Preheat oven to 400 degrees.

2. Place peppers on a nonstick cookie sheet. Bake for 35 minutes, turning them twice. Allow peppers to cool, then remove skin and seeds. Cut into strips and place in a 13 x 9 x 2-inch baking pan. Add sliced mushrooms and ¾ cup Hotel del Coronado Dressing. Cover and refrigerate to marinate for 6 hours or overnight.

3. Trim outer leaves from romaine. Cut 3 inches off the top of each head. Cut each head into quarters. Wash and allow to drain on paper towels. Refrigerate until ready to serve.

To Assemble:

1. Place romaine wedge in the center of each of eight salad plates. Top each wedge with a slice of salami, cheese, and mortadella.

2. Remove peppers and mushrooms from dressing. Arrange red and yellow pepper strips and mushrooms on romaine wedges. Top with anchovy fillets and capers.

3. Place two tomato halves on right side of plate and two olives on left side of plate. Top with remaining dressing over all salads. Garnish with a basil leaf.

Serves 8.

Penne Pasta Agliata

1 tbsp. salt
¼ cup vegetable oil
1 lb. penne pasta
3 tbsp. olive oil
3 cloves garlic, minced
1 cup half-and-half
1 cup freshly grated Parmesan cheese
Salt
White pepper
¼ cup Italian parsley, finely chopped (for garnish)

1. In a large saucepan, bring 1½ quarts of water to a boil. Add salt, vegetable oil, and pasta; then cook for 8 to 10 minutes. Drain and rinse in cold water. Set aside.

2. In a large skillet, heat olive oil, then add garlic and sauté for 1 minute. Do not allow garlic to brown. Add pasta, and cook, stirring, for 2 minutes. Add half-and-half, and simmer for 3 minutes. Add cheese and salt and pepper to taste.

3. Divide pasta onto the centers of eight plates. Sprinkle top with parsley and serve immediately.

Serves 8.

Lime and Basil Sorbet

2 cups water
2 cups sugar
2 cups lime juice
24 fresh basil leaves, finely
  chopped
2 tsp. lime zest (outer skin of
  lime)
6 fresh basil leaves (for garnish)

1. In a small saucepan, combine water and sugar. Bring to a boil, stirring until sugar is dissolved.
2. Remove from heat and cool; then stir in lime juice, chopped basil, and zest.
3. Pour into several undivided ice trays, cover, and place in freezer. Freeze to a slush.
4. In a food processor or blender, process the semi-frozen sorbet until smooth. Return to trays. Freeze until firm.

To serve:
Place one small scoop of sorbet in a chilled sherry glass or other suitable stemware. Garnish with a basil leaf.

Note: Sorbet may be prepared up to three weeks in advance.

Yields about 1 pint.

Chicken Saltimbocca with Marsala Sauce

8 6-oz. whole boneless
  chicken breasts
8 2 x 4-inch thin slices prosciutto
8 2 x 4-inch thin slices Fontina
  or Bel Paese cheese
16 fresh sage leaves (or 2 tsp.
  crumbled sage)
1 cup plus 2 tbsp. Chicken Stock
  (see recipe)
1½ cups Marsala wine
4 oz. (1 stick) butter or
  margarine, cut into small
  pieces
1 tbsp. cornstarch dissolved in
  1 tbsp. water
½ tsp. salt
⅛ tsp. white pepper
1 bunch fresh basil leaves (for
  garnish)

1. Preheat oven to 375 degrees.
2. Lay out chicken breasts skin side down. Flatten breasts by hitting with a mallet. Cover each breast with a slice of prosciutto and a slice of Fontina or Bel Paese cheese. Sprinkle sage over cheese. Roll up chicken breasts and place in a greased 14 x 10 x 2-inch baking pan, seam side down. Add 2 tablespoons of chicken stock.
3. Bake for 30 to 40 minutes, or until thoroughly cooked. Remove breasts from oven, transfer to a warm platter, cover, and keep warm.
4. Pour drippings from baking pan into a medium-size saucepan. Add remaining chicken stock and wine. Cook and stir over medium heat until mixture is reduced by half.
5. Lower heat and whisk in butter or margarine, one piece at a time, until well blended. Add cornstarch, salt, and pepper. Strain sauce into the top of a double boiler. Keep warm.

To Assemble Plate:
1. Slice each chicken breast into five slices. Place on a dinner plate and fan the breast slices down the right hand side of the plate. Spoon about 2 ounces of Marsala Sauce over chicken on each plate.

2. On the lower left-hand side of plate, arrange Braised Belgian Endive (recipe follows).

3. On the upper left hand side of the plate, tap out Risotto Milanese cup (recipe follows).

4. Garnish center of plate with fresh basil leaves.

Serves 8.

Risotto Milanese

½ cup butter or margarine
1 onion, chopped
2 cups Italian (Arborio) rice
  or long-grain rice
3 cups Chicken Stock (see recipe)
½ cup chablis wine
½ tsp. nutmeg
1 tsp. saffron threads
½ cup freshly grated Parmesan
  cheese

1. In a large saucepan, combine 2 tablespoons of the butter or margarine and the onion; then sauté for 3 minutes. Add rice and stir until mixture is blended. Add stock; then reduce heat, cover, and cook rice slowly over low heat for 20 minutes. Do not stir.

2. Add wine, nutmeg, and saffron threads. Cook and stir for 7 to 10 minutes. Add remaining butter and Parmesan cheese; stir thoroughly.

3. Pack into greased custard cups, pressing rice down with the back of a spoon. When ready to serve, loosen sides carefully with a knife, invert cup on dinner plate, and tap lightly to release rice.

Serves 8.

Braised Belgian Endive

8 heads Belgian Endive
2 slices bacon, chopped
1 onion, chopped
2 cloves garlic, peeled and
  minced
6 fresh basil leaves, chopped
1 cup Chicken Stock (see recipe)
1 cup white wine
¼ cup butter or margarine,
  melted
½ cup Brown Stock (see recipe)
Salt
Pepper
Parchment paper

1. Preheat oven to 350 degrees.

2. Trim base of endive heads and discard outer leaves. Using the hearts only, rinse under cold water and pat dry. Set aside.

3. In a large skillet, combine bacon, onion, garlic, and basil leaves. Sauté for about 3 minutes, until onion is transparent.

4. Transfer mixture to a 13 x 9 x 2-inch baking pan. Lay endive over bacon mixture. Pour chicken stock and wine over endives. Brush endives with melted butter or margarine; then lightly brush each endive with brown stock. Season with salt and pepper.

5. Cover baking pan with parchment paper. Brush remaining butter over parchment paper. Bake for 1 hour. Remove from oven and serve immediately.

Serves 8.

THE HOTEL DEL CORONADO COOKBOOK

Fig and Raspberry Clafouti

2 lb. fresh figs, cut in half
  lengthwise
1 cup fresh raspberries
½ cup blanched whole almonds
¼ cup all-purpose flour
1½ cups milk
¾ cup sugar
4 large eggs
2 tbsp. port wine
½ tsp. salt
¼ cup unsalted butter, cut into
  pieces
Whipped cream (for garnish)

1. Preheat oven to 400 degrees.

2. Arrange figs cut side up in two greased 11 x 7 x 1½-inch gratin pans. Sprinkle raspberries around figs.

3. In a blender or food processor, grind almonds fine with the flour; then add milk, ½ cup sugar, eggs, wine, and salt. Blend mixture well, scraping down the sides as necessary.

4. Pour batter slowly over the fruit. Dot fruit with butter and sprinkle it with remaining sugar.

5. Bake in the middle of the oven for 30 to 40 minutes, or until the top is golden and custard is set. Transfer pans to racks and allow to cool for 20 minutes.

6. Serve warm, spooned into dessert dishes and topped with a dollop of whipped cream if desired.

Serves 8.

Lawrence Welk's Champagne Dinner for Ten

Chef James Waller from the Prince of Wales gourmet dining room created this five-course masterpiece that features a melody of exquisitely harmonized flavors for a dinner honoring band leader Lawrence Welk. Chef Waller is a graduate of the California Culinary Academy in San Francisco, where he studied with well-known chefs including Jeremiah Towers and Wolfgang Puck. Chef Waller has been a member of the Del's culinary team since 1982.

These champagne-touched courses created a memorable evening for the 650 guests in attendance. Lawrence Welk, the man with the golden baton and smiling eyes, led the band in some of his popular numbers.

MENU

Nest of Baby Greens with Quail Eggs
Champagne Vinaigrette Dressing

Lobster and Blue Point Oysters
Champagne Mustard Cream

Champagne Sorbet with Frozen Grapes

Grilled Veal Médaillons
Sorrel and Chanterelle Champagne Sauce

White Radishes with Cashews

Rosemary Potatoes

Strawberries in Pink Champagne
Zabaglione Sauce

Nest of Baby Greens with Quail Eggs and Champagne Vinaigrette Dressing

Greens:
20 fresh quail eggs
1½ quarts water
Salt
1 bunch baby spinach
1 bunch baby red swiss chard
1 bunch baby butter lettuce
1 bunch baby limestone lettuce
30 small yellow pear tomatoes

1. In a medium-size saucepan, bring salted water to a boil. Add eggs and cook for 4 minutes. Drain eggs, chill, and peel. Quarter the eggs and reserve for salad.
2. Wash and dry the baby greens; then tear into bite-size pieces. Divide greens onto ten chilled salad plates. Pile high to resemble a nest. Place two quail eggs in the center of the greens on each plate. Cut tomatoes in half. Place three halves around the rim of the plate.
3. Sprinkle with Champagne Vinaigrette Dressing (recipe follows) and serve.

Serves 10.

Champagne Vinaigrette Dressing:
6 egg yolks
½ cup champagne vinegar
1 tsp. salt
¼ tsp. pepper
1 cup olive oil

1. In a medium-size mixing bowl, combine egg yolks, vinegar, salt, and pepper.
2. Slowly whisk in olive oil.

Yields 2 cups.

Lobster and Blue Point Oysters with Champagne Mustard Cream

1 bunch spinach leaves, washed and stems removed
5 6-oz. lobster tails, shucked (save ends for garnish)
2 tbsp. olive oil
¼ cup minced shallots
20 Blue Point oysters, shucked (oyster liquor reserved)
1½ cups champagne
⅓ cup fresh lemon juice
2¼ cups heavy cream
½ tsp. salt
Pinch cayenne pepper
2 tbsp. whole grain mustard
2 firm tomatoes, cut into thin strips (for garnish)

1. Place spinach in colander. Pour boiling water over spinach to wilt. Set aside.
2. Cut each lobster tail into four slices. In a large, heated skillet, place olive oil, shallots, and lobster slices. Sauté over low heat for 2 minutes on each side. Add oysters with their liquor, champagne, and lemon juice. Bring to a boil. Remove oysters and lobster slices and set aside. Continue to cook sauce for 25 minutes.
3. Add cream to champagne mixture and bring to a simmer. Add salt and cayenne pepper. Reduce mixture until it coats the back of a spoon. Return oysters and lobster slices to the skillet to reheat. Stir in mustard. Remove from heat.

To Serve:
1. Arrange three spinach leaves on each of ten fish plates. Slice ten leaves into thin strips and pile into center of each plate.

2. Arrange two lobster slices and two oysters alternately on the plate. Spoon sauce over lobster and oysters. Garnish with ends of lobster tails and four thin strips of tomato.

Serves 10.

Note: Shucked oysters may be found in the fresh fish section of local supermarkets. To shuck oysters youself, scrub oysters thoroughly with a stiff brush under cold running water. Hold each oyster, flat side up, on a work surface with the hinge away from you. Insert an oyster knife between the shells at the hinged end. Twist the knife to pop open the shell, then slide the blade against the flat upper shell to cut the large muscle and free the upper shell. If the shell crumbles and cannot be opened at the hinge, insert the knife between the shells at the curved end of the oyster, pry the shells open, and sever the large muscle. Break off and discard the upper shell and slide the knife under the oyster to release it from the bottom shell.

Lobster and Blue Point Oysters with Champagne Mustard Cream.

Champagne Sorbet with Frozen Grapes

3 cups prepared or canned applesauce

2 cups plus 2 tbsp. chilled champagne

2 tbsp. apple jelly

4 drops red food color

1 bunch red or green grapes, separated, washed, and thoroughly dried

3 egg whites

⅓ cup sugar

1 bunch mint leaves, washed and dried (for garnish)

1. In a medium-size mixing bowl, combine applesauce, 1½ cups champagne, and apple jelly. Add food color to tint light pink. Freeze for at least 2 hours.

2. Thaw frozen mixture slightly; break into chunks. Place chunks in food processor; process until slushy. Transfer to a bowl, then freeze for about 30 minutes.

3. In a medium-size mixing bowl, beat egg whites thoroughly until peaks form.

4. Dip grapes in egg whites, remove and roll in sugar to coat them. Freeze grapes on a cookie sheet for about 30 minutes.

To Serve:

1. Remove grapes from freezer. Place three or four grapes into each of ten 6-ounce champagne flutes. Pour 1 tablespoon of reserved champagne over grapes in each glass.

2. Place a small scoop of sorbet on top of grapes. Garnish with a mint leaf and serve immediately.

Note: Sorbet may be prepared up to three weeks in advance.

Yields about 1 quart.

Grilled Veal Médaillons with Sorrel and Chanterelle Champagne Sauce

10 5-oz. veal médaillons

2 tsp. salt

2 tsp. freshly ground black pepper

1 tbsp. olive oil

2 cups champagne

2 tbsp. chopped shallots

2 cups heavy cream

2 cups Demi-Glacé (see recipe)

¼ lb. chanterelle mushrooms, julienned

20 large sorrel leaves, julienned

1. Place veal médaillons on a cutting board. Trim off all fat. Tap médaillons with flat side of knife to flatten a little. Season with salt and pepper.

2. In a large skillet, heat oil; then add veal and sear for 1 minute on each side. Drain off drippings. Add champagne and shallots and stir to deglaze skillet. Turn off heat. Remove veal, place in a greased 13 x 9 x 2-inch baking pan. Bake in oven at 350 degrees for approximately 25 minutes, or until veal is medium doneness.

3. Bring champagne mixture to a simmer, then cook and stir until reduced by half. Add cream and stir, cooking until mixture is reduced by half. Add demi-glacé; continue to cook and stir until mixture is slightly thickened.

4. Add mushrooms and bring to a simmer; then add sorrel strips. Cook and stir for about 1 minute (do not overcook sorrel or it will turn brown). Remove from heat. Cover and keep warm.

To Assemble Plate:

1. Place Veal Médaillons and Sorrel and Chanterelle Champagne Sauce onto the lower area of each of ten dinner plates.

2. On the upper left, spoon on White Radishes with Cashews (recipe follows). Sprinkle parsley leaves over radishes.

3. On the upper right, place Rosemary Potatoes (recipe follows).

Serves 10.

White Radishes with Cashews

2½ tbsp. butter or margarine
2 tbsp. curry powder
2½ tsp. caraway seeds
½ tsp. white pepper
2 cloves garlic, peeled and minced
6 pearl onions, peeled and finely chopped
2½ tbsp. freshly ground ginger
12 large radishes (about ½ lb.), peeled and cut into strips
½ tsp. salt
2 tbsp. soy sauce
5 medium tomatoes (about 1¼ lb.), peeled and chopped
1 cup coarsely chopped cashew nuts
1½ cups plain yogurt
2½ tsp. fresh lemon juice
1½ cups chopped parsley

1. In a large skillet, melt butter or margarine. Add curry powder, caraway seeds, and pepper. Gently sauté for 3 minutes. Add garlic, onions, and ginger. Simmer for 5 more minutes. Add radishes, salt, and soy sauce. Cook for 15 minutes.

2. Add tomatoes, nuts, yogurt, and lemon juice. Cook for 2 more minutes. Remove from heat, sprinkle with parsley, and serve.

Serves 10.

Rosemary Potatoes

3 lb. large red-skinned
unpeeled potatoes, washed
and quartered
¾ cup olive oil
3 cloves garlic, peeled and
minced
3 tbsp. chopped fresh rosemary
(or 1 tbsp. dried crushed
rosemary)
3 tbsp. chopped fresh thyme
(or 1 tsp. dried crushed thyme)
1 tsp. salt
¼ tsp. pepper

1. Preheat oven to 450 degrees.

2. Arrange raw potatoes in a 13 x 9 x 2-inch baking pan. Set aside.

3. In a medium-size bowl, combine olive oil, garlic, rosemary, thyme, salt, and pepper. Stir and blend thoroughly. Pour over potatoes; toss to coat evenly.

4. Bake uncovered for about 40 minutes, or until tender and brown, stirring occasionally. Remove from oven and serve.

Serves 10.

Strawberries in Pink Champagne Zabaglione Sauce

Strawberries:
50 strawberries
5 oz. sugar
1 cup pink champagne
**4 oz. semisweet dark chocolate,
grated (for garnish)**

Pink Champagne Zabaglione:
12 egg yolks
¾ cup sugar
2 tsp. fresh lemon juice
¾ cup pink champagne

1. Wash strawberries and remove stems. Pat dry, place in a large bowl, and set aside.

2. In a medium-size bowl, combine sugar and champagne. Mix well and pour over strawberries. Cover and refrigerate. Allow strawberries to marinate overnight.

Place all the ingredients in the top of a double boiler. Whisk briskly over hot water. Continue to whisk until the egg mixture takes on the consistency of whipped cream. Remove from heat.

To Serve:
1. Remove strawberries from refrigerator. Place five strawberries in each of ten champagne glasses.

2. Spoon warm Zabaglione over the strawberries and top with grated chocolate.

Serves 10.

Celebrity Choices

Celebrities are often known to have special preferences in food and drink. Those who are guests at the Hotel del Coronado are no exception. Here are the selections of several celebrities for the fascination of all of you who are fans. Prepare one of these recipes, and you will be a celebrity in the eyes of your family and friends.

CHOICES

Milton Berle's
Vodka-Steamed Lobster with Dijon Sauce

Dionne Warwick's
Oriental Chicken Wings

George Burns'
Five-Way Banana Split

Zsa Zsa Gabor's
Crab Cakes with Cilantro Mayonaise

Red Skelton's
Thai-Style Halibut en Papillote

Debbie Reynolds'
Fresh Fruit Fantasy with Pecan-Yogurt Dressing

Cesar Romero and Anne Jeffreys at the hotel's Centennial Gala.

Milton Berle's Vodka-Steamed Lobster with Dijon Sauce

On New Year's Eve of 1987, Milton Berle was the star attraction at the Hotel del Coronado, arriving with an entourage of assistants and his own favorite pillow and sheets. He chose to dine on Vodka-Steamed Lobster for lunch with two glasses of freshly squeezed orange juice. Eight hundred and fifty guests, including some who had made reservations a year in advance, enjoyed Milton Berle's performance and gave him a standing ovation.

2 cups lemon-pepper vodka
1 (1- to 1¼-lb.) whole lobster

1. Pour vodka into a dutch oven; bring to a boil. Add lobster and cover tightly. Cook for 10 minutes.
2. Remove lobster from the vodka. Plunge cooked lobster into cold water for 1 minute to stop the cooking process.
3. Remove lobster from cold water, then set it on its back on a wooden cutting board. Twist off large claws. Cut lobster from head to tail with a large, sharp knife. Do not cut through the shell. Remove tail and serve on a platter with Dijon Sauce (recipe follows) on the side.

Note: Mr. Berle requested the lobster tail only. However, the meat in the claws is juicy and sweet and can be served alongside the lobster tails. Provide metal lobster crackers and tiny forks for the enthusiast who desires to tackle the whole lobster.

Serves 1.

Dijon Sauce:
1 egg
1 tbsp. fresh lemon juice
1 tbsp. Dijon-style mustard
¼ tsp. white pepper
¾ cup extra-virgin olive oil

1. In a blender or food processor, combine egg, lemon juice, mustard, and pepper. Process thoroughly for about 1 minute. While machine is running, add olive oil slowly in a thin stream until it is incorporated.
2. Remove from blender or food processor and place in a small serving dish or gravy boat.

Yields about 1 cup.

Dionne Warwick's Oriental Chicken Wings

Dionne Warwick was one of the celebrities who performed in a star-studded musical review held after the Centennial dinner. During her rehearsal, the hotel employees who were setting up the ballroom for the performance stopped simultaneously to listen to the songbird, spellbound by her talent. After her rehearsal, she retired to her suite and ordered the Del's Oriental Chicken Wings for a snack before her evening performance.

3 lb. chicken wings (disjointed)
2 tsp. salt
¼ tsp. pepper
3 tbsp. Canola oil
1 clove garlic, peeled and minced
1 tsp. onion powder
1 tsp. Chinese 5-spice powder
1 tsp. honey
½ cup soy sauce
1 tsp. ground ginger
¼ cup ketchup
½ cup dry sherry wine

1. Preheat oven to 375 degrees.
2. Place chicken wings in a 13 x 9 x 2-inch baking pan. Sprinkle with salt and pepper. Brush on oil.
3. In a medium-size bowl, combine garlic, onion powder, Chinese 5-spice powder, honey, soy sauce, ginger, ketchup, and wine. Blend thoroughly, then pour over wings.
4. Bake uncovered for 50 minutes, basting frequently. Remove from oven and serve on a heated serving platter or chafing dish.

Note: These chicken wings may be served as an hors d'oeuvre. They may be prepared in advance, wrapped in foil, and frozen. To serve, remove from freezer and open foil wrapping. Allow chicken wings to reach room temperature, then place in a preheated 300-degree oven for 15 minutes, or until heated through.

To disjoint chicken wings:
1. Cut wings off at the joint (do not use the tips).
2. Loosen the meat away from the bone.
3. Pull back all of the skin and meat.

Serves 8.

George Burns' Five-Way Banana Split

George Burns attended a floor show during the Del's Centennial celebration in February of 1988. He requested a double martini and a banana split made with every flavor of ice cream that the hotel had to offer. The *garde-manger* (pantry chef) picked up a melon-ball scoop and went to work creating a banana split with five flavors. So was the creation of George Burns' Five-Way Banana Split.

1 ripe banana
1 scoop pistachio ice cream
1 scoop french vanilla ice cream
1 scoop strawberry ice cream
1 scoop chocolate ice cream
1 scoop butter-pecan ice cream
2 tbsp. Hot Chocolate Fudge Sauce (recipe follows)
2 tbsp. Butterscotch Sauce (recipe follows)
2 tbsp. Strawberry Sauce (recipe follows)
Whipped cream (for garnish)
1 tbsp. peanuts, coarsely chopped (for garnish)
2 maraschino cherries (for garnish)

1. Peel and split banana lengthwise, place halves, cut side up, on a dessert dish. Top with 1 scoop each of pistachio, french vanilla, strawberry, chocolate, and butter pecan ice creams.

2. Pour 2 tablespoons each of Hot Chocolate Fudge Sauce, Butterscotch Sauce, and Strawberry Sauce on ice cream. Top with a large dollop of whipped cream. Sprinkle on chopped peanuts and add maraschino cherries.

Serves 1.

Hot Chocolate Fudge Sauce:
1 cup sugar
1 cup whipping cream
2 tbsp. butter
1 tbsp. light corn syrup
4 squares (1 oz. each) unsweetened chocolate
1 tsp. vanilla extract

1. In a medium-size saucepan, combine all ingredients except vanilla extract. Heat over medium-high heat, stirring constantly. Bring to a boil, then reduce heat to simmer and cook and stir for 5 minutes.

2. Remove from heat, add vanilla extract, and transfer to a small serving bowl.

Yields 1⅓ cups.

Butterscotch Sauce:
1 cup packed light brown sugar
¼ cup half-and-half
2 tbsp. butter
2 tbsp. light corn syrup

1. In a small saucepan, combine all of the ingredients. Heat over medium-high heat. Stir and bring to a boil.

2. Remove from heat and transfer to a small serving bowl.

Yields 1 cup.

Strawberry Sauce:

½ cup red currant jelly

1 10-oz. pkg. frozen sliced strawberries, thawed and drained (reserve ½ cup juice)

1 tbsp. cornstarch

1. In a small saucepan, melt jelly over low heat. Set aside.

2. In another small saucepan, combine strawberry juice and cornstarch; blend until smooth. Gradually stir in jelly over medium heat. Cook and stir until mixture has thickened. Stir in strawberries.

3. Remove from heat. Cool and transfer to a small serving bowl.

Yields about 1½ cups.

Whipped Cream:

½ pt. whipping cream

1 tbsp. sugar

1 tsp. vanilla extract

1. Chill a medium-size mixing bowl and beaters in the refrigerator for at least 4 hours (or overnight).

2. Remove mixing bowl and beaters from the refrigerator. Pour cream into bowl and beat for about 1 minute; then add sugar and vanilla extract. Continue to beat until mixture forms a peak. Transfer to a small serving bowl.

Yields about 1 cup.

Serves 1.

Zsa Zsa Gabor's Crab Cakes with Cilantro Mayonnaise

Zsa Zsa Gabor was one of the celebrities invited to the Del's Centennial birthday bash. She, Pepe (her French poodle), and Cesar Romero dined on Crab Cakes in the outdoor bistro-style Ocean Terrace restaurant. Pepe was well behaved and did not beg for even a taste of Ms. Gabor's Crab Cakes, although she did pass him a morsel under the table.

Cilantro Mayonnaise:

1 cup mayonnaise

1 tbsp. fresh lemon juice

1 tbsp. sherry wine vinegar

⅛ tsp. cayenne pepper

2 tbsp. finely minced cilantro

1. Place all the ingredients in a small mixing bowl. Whip until well blended.

2. Transfer mixture to a small serving bowl. Cover and refrigerate.

Yields about 1¾ cups.

Crab Cakes:

2 eggs
2 tbsp. mayonnaise
½ tsp. dry mustard
⅛ tsp. cayenne pepper
½ tsp. salt
¼ tsp. white pepper
1 drop Tabasco sauce
1 tbsp. minced scallions, white part only
1 tsp. minced fresh thyme (or ½ tsp. dried)
1 tsp. minced fresh oregano (or ½ tsp. dried)
1 lb. fresh crabmeat, flaked
1 tbsp. minced parsley
8 soda crackers, crushed
¼ cup butter or margarine
1 lemon, cut into wedges (for garnish)
Cilantro-Mayonnaise (recipe above)

1. In a large mixing bowl, beat eggs with a whisk. Add mayonnaise, mustard, cayenne pepper, salt, white pepper, Tabasco sauce, scallions, thyme, and oregano. Whisk until mixture is smooth.

2. Add crabmeat and parsley. Blend with a fork, then shape into eight round crab cakes. Roll cakes in crushed soda crackers, then wrap cakes in waxed paper and chill for 30 minutes.

3. Remove cakes from refrigerator, and melt 2 tablespoons of butter or margarine in a large, heavy skillet. Add four crab cakes and sauté for about 5 minutes on each side, until lightly browned. Set aside and keep warm. Repeat process with remaining crab cakes and butter or margarine. Remove from heat.

To serve:

1. Place two crab cakes onto each of four salad plates.

2. Garnish with lemon wedges and serve with Cilantro Mayonnaise.

Serves 4.

Zsa Zsa Gabor and husband Prince Frederic von Anhalt at the hotel's Centennial weekend.

THE HOTEL DEL CORONADO COOKBOOK

Red Skelton's Thai-Style Halibut en Papillote

Red Skelton arrived quite unexpectedly one evening and politely requested a quiet table for dinner, out of the main flow of traffic. He was so impressed with Executive Sous-Chef Brian Florida's creation of Thai-Style Halibut en Papillote that he asked his waiter the name of the food and beverage director at the Del. After being advised, he wrote the following message on the back of his menu: "Dear Beverly Bass, Thank you for your kindness, dear heart," signing it "Red Skelton," with one of his famous clowns drawn below his message.

½ **cup sesame oil**

4 **(6 ½-oz.) halibut fillets**

½ **yellow bell pepper, cored, seeded, and julienned**

½ **red bell pepper, cored, seeded, and julienned**

3 **scallions (green and white parts), cut on a bias**

1 **rib celery, washed and cut on a bias**

½ **leek, washed and julienned**

1 **carrot, washed, scraped clean, and julienned**

2 **ribs bok choy, washed and thinly sliced**

10 **chili peppers, washed and cut in half**

1 **tbsp. minced fresh ginger**

1 **clove minced garlic**

¼ **cup coarsely chopped cilantro**

¾ **cup sake**

1 **cup oyster sauce**

2 **tbsp. soy sauce**

1 **orange, peeled and separated into segments (for garnish)**

4 **12-inch sheets rice paper**

1. Preheat oven to 350 degrees.

2. In a large skillet, heat 2 tablespoons of sesame oil. Add halibut and sear briefly on each side. Remove from skillet. Set aside.

3. Place yellow pepper, red pepper, scallions, celery, leek, carrot, bok choy, chili peppers, ginger, and garlic in skillet. Sauté for 5 minutes, stirring constantly. Add cilantro and sauté for 15 seconds. Add sake to deglaze skillet; then add oyster sauce and soy sauce. Toss vegetables in sauce. Set aside.

4. Fill another large skillet with water to ¾-full level. Heat water to just below a simmer, then remove from heat. Place a sheet of rice paper in water to soften. Remove and brush with sesame oil. Set aside on countertop. Repeat procedure with remaining rice paper.

5. Divide sautéed vegetables into four portions. Spoon ¼ of vegetable mixture into center of each softened rice paper sheet. Place halibut fillet atop vegetables.

6. Fold rice paper up toward halibut to partially cover fish. Fold left and right sides of rice paper up to enclose fish, making the fish packets oblong in shape. Cut off any excess rice paper.

7. Transfer fish packets to an oiled baking pan. Brush packets with sesame oil. Bake for 15 minutes. Remove from oven, transfer fish packets onto four dinner plates. Open edible packets and garnish halibut with orange segments.

Note: Rice paper is available at Asian markets.

Serves 4.

Debbie Reynolds' Fresh Fruit Fantasy.

THE HOTEL DEL CORONADO COOKBOOK

Debbie Reynolds' Fresh Fruit Fantasy with Pecan-Yogurt Dressing

Debbie Reynolds and Donald O'Connor performed at the Centennial weekend celebration. They sang and danced their way to a standing ovation from the seven hundred guests who enjoyed their combined performance. Ms. Reynolds, clad in a skin-tight royal blue sequin gown and known to be a health-conscious star, chose the Del's Fresh Fruit Fantasy for dinner before her spectacular performance.

1 1-inch slice seedless watermelon, peeled

¼ fresh papaya, peeled, seeded, and cut into parallel slices lengthwise (leaving intact at the base, fan-style)

¼ cantaloupe, peeled, seeded, and cut into parallel slices lengthwise (leaving intact at the base, fan-style)

3 slices pineapple, peeled

4 pink grapefruit sections

3 orange sections

1 kiwi, peeled and cut into 3 slices

¼ plum, unpeeled, pitted, and sliced, fan-style

1 fresh blueberry (for garnish)

4 mint sprigs (for garnish)

11 fresh raspberries (for garnish)

1. Cut watermelon slice into quarters, place in center of plate.

2. Arrange papaya fan on the center of watermelon, on the right side.

3. Arrange cantaloupe fan on the center of watermelon, on the left side.

4. Arrange pineapple slices on top of the watermelon slice, below the papaya and cantaloupe.

5. Arrange two pink grapefruit sections on each side atop the watermelon slice. Place the orange sections at the twelve o'clock position.

6. Place the kiwi slices down the center of plate.

7. Place plum fan atop pineapple slices; arrange blueberry at the base of plum.

8. Garnish with sprigs of mint placed at the 3, 6, 9 and 12 o'clock positions; place 2 raspberries in the center of each mint sprig and 1 raspberry in the center of each kiwi slice. (You have now recreated the Del's Fresh Fruit Fantasy!) Serve with Pecan-Yogurt Dressing (recipe follows).

Serves 1.

Pecan-Yogurt Dressing:
1 cup plain yogurt
1 tbsp. honey
2 tsp. lemon juice
¼ cup finely chopped pecans

1. In a small mixing bowl, combine all the ingredients and blend thoroughly.

2. Transfer to a small serving bowl, cover, and refrigerate for at least 2 hours (or overnight). Serve in a small bowl to accompany Fresh Fruit Fantasy.

Yields about 1¼ cups.

CHAPTER EIGHT

Beach Bash

The all-American backyard barbecue becomes a Beach Bash at the Del. The Del's esplanade overlooking Coronado's white sandy beach is transformed into an informal outdoor buffet. Appetites piqued by the fresh sea air and the aroma of Kentucky Bourbon-Glazed Ham and dill butter-basted corn on the cob roasting on the barbecue. Highlight recipes of Barbecued Baked Beans, Rip-Roaring Ribs, Firecracker Chicken Drumsticks, and Feta Grilled Lamb Chops in foil have been included. At the Del, to match the casual ambiance of the occasion, all servers and bus boys are dressed in Levis and plaid shirts.

This sets the scene for the story of the "Ice Cream Bandit." Naturally, the Beach Bash is held close to the beach, far (it seems like two miles) from the main kitchen and the storage area where all tables, chairs, and reserve food supplies are located. One ill-fated evening, the Beach Bash was overwhelmed by a crowd of more than one hundred guests who arrived without reservations. As a result, the Fresh Peach Ice Cream that was being served on the Down-Home Peach Cobbler had nearly run out. One of the Levis-clad bus boys was told by the manager to run to the main kitchen for more ice cream. The bus boy, on his own, decided that it would be more expedient to get the ice cream from the

kitchen of the Prince of Wales gourmet dining room, which was much closer to the beach. So he ran, without a word of explanation, to the nearby Prince of Wales kitchen, grabbed two gallons of ice cream, and bolted back to the Beach Bash. When the manager asked him if he had flown, he felt quite proud of his speedy accomplishment. However, within minutes the hotel's security department had been alerted by the Prince of Wales staff, and every security officer was searching for an ice cream bandit dressed in Levis and a plaid shirt. When the search reached the Beach Bash, there they were—eight suspects (bus boys) fitting the description of the ice cream bandit. At this point, the enterprising bus boy felt that maybe he should have run the distance back to the main kitchen as instructed.

No other atmosphere lends itself better to a relaxed, informal party than the outdoor barbecue. There is no need to worry about red wine spills on your best white linen tablecloth, and clean-up is much easier as well. Remind your guests when you invite them that the attire is casual. They will arrive relaxed and ready to enjoy a glass of wine or a cold beer (pre-iced in a large bucket).

Buffet menus for eight follow to celebrate Memorial Day, July Fourth, and a laborless Labor Day. The chapter finale is the "Just the Four of Us" dinner that is prepared almost completely on the barbecue—including a dessert of Barbecued Banana Splits! This intimate grilled menu allows you to relax and enjoy your easiest party of the year.

Fourth of July Beach Bash. Clockwise from bottom: *Rip Roaring Ribs; Intoxicating Minted Watermelon; Red, White, and Blueberry Dessert; Green and Yellow Bean-Pepper Salad; Artichoke, Crab, and Red Onion Salad.*

Memorial Day Bash

Memorial Day signals the unofficial beginning of summer and the return of casual, fun entertaining. Part of a three-day weekend, it is the perfect occasion to kick off the summer season with a bash of flavors hot off the barbecue. The aroma of barbecued ham glazed with Kentucky bourbon will awaken the taste buds of all your lucky guests.

Prepare the chili two days before your bash to allow the flavors to intensify and blend over time. This leaves the preparation of Confetti Coleslaw, Seafood-Laced Potato Salad, and Down-Home Peach Cobbler for the day before the bash. Beefsteak Tomatoes and Mozzarella with Basil Vinaigrette Dressing may be prepared on the morning of your party. The last few minutes before the dinner are dedicated to grilling the corn.

A little advance preparation will leave you free to enjoy the compliments of your guests.

MENU

Beefsteak Tomatoes and Mozzarella
Basil Vinaigrette Dressing

Confetti Coleslaw

Seafood-Laced Potato Salad

Beach Bash Chili

Grilled Corn with Dill Butter

Kentucky Bourbon-Glazed Ham

Jalapeño Corn Muffins

Fresh Peach Ice Cream

Down-Home Peach Cobbler

Early post card showing the surf breaking close to Ocean Boulevard. In the years since then, the beach has widened and now boasts an expanse of fine sand.

Tent City was created in 1902, when the hotel was closed for remodeling, and hotel guests were housed in tents along the beach. The tents gained popularity as a seaside resort, and it lasted until 1939.

Beefsteak Tomatoes and Mozzarella with Basil Vinaigrette Dressing

¼ cup olive oil
1½ tbsp. balsamic vinegar
1 tbsp. chopped fresh basil
¾ tsp. Dijon-style mustard
½ tsp. salt
⅛ tsp. freshly ground pepper
4 beefsteak tomatoes, thinly
    sliced
1 lb. mozzarella cheese, sliced
    ¼ inch thick
1 tbsp. finely chopped fresh dill
Salt

1. Whisk oil, vinegar, basil, mustard, salt, and pepper together in a large nonmetal bowl. Set aside.
2. Alternate slices of tomatoes and mozzarella cheese on a platter. Pour oil mixture over tomatoes and cheese, coating them thoroughly. Sprinkle dill and salt over tomatoes.
3. Refrigerate, covered, until serving.

Serves 8.

Confetti Coleslaw

6 slices bacon
4 cups shredded green cabbage
2 large carrots, shredded
½ red bell pepper, cored,
    seeded, and minced
½ green bell pepper, cored,
    seeded, and minced
1 small red onion, finely
    chopped
1 cup mayonnaise
½ cup sour cream
¼ cup milk
2 tsp. Dijon-style mustard
½ tsp. salt
¼ tsp. freshly ground pepper
½ tsp. chili powder

1. Cook bacon until crisp; drain and crumble. Reserve 2 tablespoons of bacon drippings.
2. Combine bacon, cabbage, carrots, red pepper, green pepper, and onion in a large bowl.
3. In a small mixing bowl, whisk mayonnaise and bacon drippings thoroughly. Add remaining ingredients. Mix well. Pour over cabbage mixture; toss. Refrigerate until serving.

Serves 8.

Seafood-Laced Potato Salad

6 cups cooked potatoes, pared
    and cubed
½ cup finely chopped onion
1 small red bell pepper, finely
    chopped
½ cup thinly sliced celery
¾ lb. fresh crabmeat (or 2 6-oz.
    cans crabmeat)
½ lb. cooked bay shrimp,
    shelled
1 ¼ cups mayonnaise
2 tsp. prepared mustard
1 ½ tsp. lemon juice
2 tsp. chili sauce
1 tsp. sea salt
⅛ tsp. pepper

1. In a large mixing bowl, combine potatoes, onion, pepper, celery, crabmeat, and shrimp. Set aside.
2. In a small mixing bowl, whisk together mayonnaise, mustard, lemon juice, chili sauce, salt, and pepper. Pour over potato mixture; gently mix until well blended. Transfer to a serving bowl and refrigerate until serving.

Serves 8.

Beach Bash Chili

4 tbsp. unsalted butter
4 medium onions, finely chopped
2 green bell peppers, cored,
    seeded, and finely chopped
4 lb. lean ground beef
2 cups beer
1 28-oz. can crushed tomatoes
    in purée
2 cups beef broth
4 cloves garlic, peeled and
    minced
3½ tbsp. chili powder
2 tsp. ground cumin
¾ tsp. paprika
1½ tsp. dried oregano, crumbled
1½ tsp. dried basil, crumbled
1½ tsp. cayenne pepper
2 tsp. salt
1 tsp. freshly ground black
    pepper

Toppings:
2 cups sour cream
2 cups grated cheddar cheese
1 cup chopped scallions (white
    part only)
2 cups chopped fresh tomatoes

1. Melt butter in a dutch oven. Sauté onions and peppers over medium heat until golden. Add ground beef and brown over high heat, stirring until crumbly. Drain off fat.
2. Add beer and allow to boil; add remaining ingredients and stir to combine.
3. Bring to a boil, reduce heat, cover, and simmer for 2 hours.
4. Serve hot with bowls of toppings.

Note: Chili freezes well for up to three months.

Place the condiments in separate bowls.

Serves 12.

Grilled Corn with Dill Butter

8 ears fresh corn in husks
½ cup butter, at room
  temperature
1 roasted red bell pepper,
  chopped
2 tbsp. finely chopped fresh dill
½ tsp. salt
⅛ tsp. pepper

1. Peel back husks from corn without detaching them from stems; remove silk. Rewrap husks around each ear; tie them at top with kitchen string. Soak corn in cold water for 20 minutes.

2. Place butter in food processor; process until smooth. Add red pepper; process until smooth. Add dill, salt, and pepper; process until well blended. Place butter mixture in a serving dish.

3. Remove corn from water; shake to remove excess water.

4. Grill corn over hot coals for about 20 minutes, turning every 5 minutes, until a kernel pulls away from ear easily. Serve with dill butter.

Serves 8.

Kentucky Bourbon-Glazed Ham

1 fresh ham (about 5 lb.)
1 cup Kentucky bourbon
  whiskey
1 cup firmly packed brown sugar
½ tsp. ground cloves
Grated rind of 1 orange
⅓ cup steak sauce

1. Trim rind from ham and score fat into diamonds. Mix remaining ingredients in a bowl to make a glaze.

2. Tie ham every 2 inches with string. Spear ham on a rotisserie rod and fasten the ends. If desired, insert a meat thermometer into the center of the thickest part of the ham, not touching the bone.

3. Make a drip pan by placing a pan in the grill and arranging the coals around it. Prepare hot coals for grilling. Place rotisserie rod 8 inches above gray coals. Grill for 3 to 4 hours, adding more coals when needed.

4. During the last hour of grilling, brush glaze over all sides of ham; repeat glazing every 10 minutes.

5. Remove rod and carve ham into thin slices. Serve at room temperature.

Note: If using a meat thermometer, allow the ham to cook until it registers 170 degrees. Ham may also be roasted successfully in a dome-type covered grill, or baked in an oven at 350 degrees until the thermometer registers 170 degrees.

Serves 8 to 10.

Jalapeño Corn Muffins

1½ cups cornmeal
½ cup all-purpose flour
2 tbsp. sugar
2 tsp. baking powder
½ tsp. baking soda
½ tsp. salt
1¾ cups sour cream
3 eggs
1 4-oz. can diced green chiles

1. Preheat oven to 350 degrees.

2. Grease a twelve-cup muffin tin. In a large bowl, combine cornmeal, flour, sugar, baking powder, baking soda, and salt.

3. In a small bowl, mix sour cream, eggs, and green chiles until blended. Stir into cornmeal mixture until just moistened.

4. Spoon into muffin cups, then bake for 20 to 25 minutes, or until wooden toothpick inserted in center comes out clean.

5. Remove from pan. Serve with unsalted butter.

Yields 12 muffins.

Fresh Peach Ice Cream

5 fresh peaches (about 1½ lb.)
1½ cups sugar
1½ cups milk
1½ cups heavy cream
1 tsp. vanilla extract

1. Blanch peaches in boiling water for 1 minute. Drain, then immerse them in a bowl of ice water to stop the cooking process.

2. Peel and pit the peaches; place in a blender or food processor and purée.

3. In a large mixing bowl, combine sugar, milk, and cream, stirring until the sugar is dissolved. Stir in purée and vanilla extract. Refrigerate mixture until it is cold, then freeze it in an ice cream maker according to the manufacturer's directions.

Yields 1½ quarts.

Early post card showing the open-air school on the beach for the children of the winter season visitors.

Early post card of the hotel by moonlight.

Down-Home Peach Cobbler

8 cups sliced fresh peaches
  (4 to 5 lb.)
2 cups sugar
3 tbsp. all-purpose flour
½ tsp. ground nutmeg
1¼ tsp. almond extract
⅓ cup melted butter
2 frozen 8-inch pastry crusts

1. Combine peaches, sugar, flour, and nutmeg in a large saucepan. Let sit for 20 minutes, or until a syrup forms.

2. Bring peach mixture to a boil, reduce heat, and cook for 10 minutes. Remove from heat; blend in almond extract and butter.

3. Preheat oven to 475 degrees.

4. Grease an 8 x 12 x 2-inch baking pan. Place one pastry crust in the baking pan. Spoon half of the peach mixture onto the crust.

5. Roll out the remaining pastry crust, then cut into ½-inch-wide strips. Place half the pastry strips over the peach mixture in the pan. Bake for 12 minutes.

6. Remove from oven and spoon remaining peach mixture over the baked pastry. Arrange the remaining pastry strips in a lattice design over the peaches. Bake again at 475 degrees for 10 to 15 minutes, or until lightly browned.

Serves 8.

Fourth of July Bash

God bless America, land that we love—it's the Fourth of July, our country's birthday, and a time to celebrate the land of the free and the home of the brave!

A patriotic color scheme of red, white, and blue reflects the day's theme. Start with a red tablecloth and alternate red, white, and blue napkins. Place a miniature American flag that has been inserted into a red gumdrop base at each place setting. For the centerpiece, tie together a bouquet of red, white, and blue helium-filled balloons. Fasten them to the handle of a basket that you've filled with red and white carnations and American flags.

This Independence Day menu allows you to avoid the hot kitchen by preparing the salads and the dessert the day before, leaving only the chicken drumsticks and baked beans to bake in the oven, while you are outside in the fresh air sipping a cool drink and toasting your heritage with special friends.

MENU

Artichoke, Crab, and Red Onion Salad

Green and Yellow Bean-Pepper Salad

Intoxicating Minted Watermelon

Barbecued Baked Beans

Rip-Roaring Ribs

Firecracker Chicken Drumsticks

Crispy Herbed French Rolls

Red, White, and Blueberry Dessert

MISS INDEPENDENCE

Hotel Del Coronado
Coronado Beach
California
Mel S. Wright, Manager

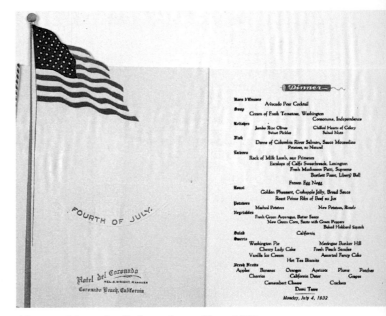

Above: *Menu for Independence Day, 1932.*

Left: *Cover of the Independence Day menu, 1926.*

Artichoke, Crab, and Red Onion Salad

½ cup olive oil

½ cup white wine vinegar

1 tsp. dry mustard

½ cup mayonnaise

½ cup sour cream

1 tsp. grated lemon peel

½ tsp. salt

¼ tsp. freshly ground black pepper

2 medium-size red onions, thinly sliced

2 lb. fresh crabmeat (or 5 6-oz. cans)

2 ripe avocados, peeled, pitted, and sliced

2 6-oz. jars marinated artichoke hearts, drained

1 bunch romaine lettuce, washed, dried, and tops cut into sharp points with scissors

1. In a small glass bowl, combine oil, vinegar, mustard, mayonnaise, sour cream, lemon peel, salt, and pepper. Fold in onions, cover, and marinate for 4 hours.

2. With a slotted spoon, lift onion slices from marinade, reserving marinade. Combine onion and crabmeat.

3. Arrange romaine leaves on a platter, points facing outward. Place onion-crabmeat mixture on romaine. Top with avocado slices and artichoke hearts. Pour reserved marinade over all. Refrigerate until serving.

Serves 8.

Green and Yellow Bean-Pepper Salad

Salad:
¾ lb. fresh green beans
¾ lb. fresh wax beans
1 large green bell pepper,
 cored, seeded, and cut into
 ¼-inch strips
1 large yellow bell pepper,
 cored, seeded, and cut
 into ¼-inch strips

Dressing:
½ cup olive oil
3 tbsp. white wine vinegar
Juice of ½ lemon
1 tbsp. Dijon-style mustard
1 small garlic clove, peeled
 and crushed
2 shallots, peeled and minced
½ tsp. dried sweet basil
½ tsp. dried oregano
1 tbsp. chopped parsley
½ tsp. salt
½ tsp. freshly ground black
 pepper

1. Layer beans and peppers in a steamer rack. Place over a saucepan of simmering water, cover, and steam the vegetables for about 12 minutes until crisp-tender.
2. Combine remaining ingredients in a screw-top jar, cover, and shake well to mix.
3. When the vegetables are done, transfer them to a bowl and pour the dressing over them. Cover tightly and refrigerate for a few hours or overnight before serving.

Serves 8.

Intoxicating Minted Watermelon

1 cup sugar
2 cups water
2 bunches mint
1 large ripe watermelon
Vodka
Mint sprigs (for garnish)

1. Place sugar and water in a medium-size saucepan. Stir to dissolve sugar. Bring to a boil and gently boil for 5 minutes.
2. Remove from heat, add mint, then let syrup cool completely. Remove mint.
3. Measure syrup into a mixing bowl. For every cup of syrup, add 2 ounces of vodka.
4. Using a kitchen hypodermic syringe, inject watermelon every 2 to 3 inches with the syrup.
5. Chill for 4 hours. Cut into wedges and garnish with mint sprigs.

Note: The kitchen hypodermic syringe can be found in most stores specializing in kitchen equipment.

Serves 8.

Barbecued Baked Beans

2 lb. navy beans
8 slices bacon, cut crosswise
   into thin strips
2 cups chopped onion
2 large cloves garlic,
   peeled and minced
1½ cups ketchup
2 cups dark brown sugar, packed
2 tsp. mustard powder
2 tbsp. ground red chili powder

1. Place navy beans in a dutch oven, cover with water, and soak overnight.

2. Cook beans in soaking water for about 1 hour or until tender. Drain thoroughly.

3. Preheat oven to 325 degrees.

4. Sauté bacon strips in a heavy skillet over medium heat for about 3 minutes. Add onion and garlic and continue cooking until onion is transparent, but not browned.

5. Transfer bacon, onion, garlic, and any fat from skillet to a large mixing bowl. Add remaining ingredients and combine thoroughly.

6. Pour mixture into a 4-quart baking pan. Bake, uncovered, for 3 hours.

Serves 8.

Rip-Roaring Ribs

1 navel orange
¾ cup soy sauce
1½ cups firmly packed dark
   brown sugar
2 tbsp. Worcestershire sauce
½ cup minced shallots
¼ cup minced scallions
1½ cups Dijon-style mustard
¾ cup bourbon whiskey
8 slabs (1½ to 2 lb. each)
   pork or beef spare ribs
½ cup coarsely chopped scallions
   (for garnish)

1. Peel orange, remove all white pith, section, and chop flesh fine. Combine orange with soy sauce, brown sugar, Worcestershire sauce, shallots, scallions, mustard, and bourbon; whisk to blend. Cover and refrigerate marinade for 24 hours.

2. Place ribs in a large glass casserole. Pour marinade over meat, cover, and refrigerate overnight.

3. Preheat oven to 350 degrees. Place ribs on racks in baking pans (ribs should not touch each other). Roast for 1½ hours or until tender, basting occasionally with pan drippings and marinade.

4. Prepare a hot charcoal fire.

5. Grill ribs, turning once, until well browned (5 to 10 minutes on each side). Baste once or twice with any remaining marinade while grilling. Pile ribs high on large platter; garnish with chopped scallions.

Serves 8 to 10.

THE HOTEL DEL CORONADO COOKBOOK

Firecracker Chicken Drumsticks

1 cup ketchup
½ cup white vinegar
½ cup honey
3 tbsp. Tabasco sauce
16 chicken drumsticks

1. Preheat oven to 400 degrees.

2. In a small bowl, combine ketchup, vinegar, honey, and Tabasco sauce. Set aside.

3. Rinse drumsticks and pat dry. Line two baking pans with heavy aluminum foil.

4. Bake drumsticks, uncovered, for 40 minutes. Gently shift drumsticks every 10 minutes to loosen them from foil. When drumsticks are golden, pour sauce over them, turning to coat evenly.

5. Continue to bake until sauce is bubbling and drumsticks are lightly browned, about 20 minutes more, turning drumsticks once or twice. Drumsticks may be served at room temperature.

Serves 8.

Crispy Herbed French Rolls

½ cup olive oil
4 cloves garlic, peeled and
  minced
1 tsp. dried oregano
½ tsp. dried rosemary
4 French rolls (5 to 7 inches
  long)

1. Preheat oven to 375 degrees.

2. In a small mixing bowl, whisk together olive oil, garlic, and herbs.

3. Slice rolls in half lengthwise; place face up on a baking sheet. Brush with herbed oil.

4. Bake for 8 to 12 minutes, until lightly browned with crusty edges. Serve immediately.

Note: Rolls may be prepared ahead of time, covered with foil, held at room temperature overnight, then warmed before serving. They may also be frozen and brought to room temperature before baking.

Serves 8.

Red, White, and Blueberry Dessert

1 cup coarsely crushed pretzels
1 cup pecans
1 cup butter, melted
3 tbsp. sugar
1 8-oz. package cream cheese,
    softened
2 8-oz. cartons nondairy whipped
    topping
1 cup confectioners' sugar
1 6-oz. package strawberry gelatin
1½ cups boiling water
1 16-oz. package frozen
    strawberries, thawed in
    their juice
1 carton fresh blueberries,
    washed and air dried

1. Preheat oven to 375 degrees.

2. Combine pretzels, pecans, butter, and sugar in a food processor and process until thoroughly blended. Pat crust into 13 x 9 x 2-inch baking pan, then bake for 10 minutes. Cool.

3. Combine cream cheese, 1 carton of nondairy whipped topping, and confectioners' sugar in a mixing bowl; beat until mixture is light and fluffy. Spread filling evenly over cooled crust.

4. To prepare topping, stir together gelatin and boiling water in a mixing bowl until dissolved. Add strawberries with their juice, then chill until partially set. Pour over cream cheese mixture, then refrigerate for 24 hours.

5. Cut into squares or cut into star-shaped portions with a cookie cutter. Top with a dollop of nondairy topping and blueberries.

Yields 15 squares or 9 stars.

Laborless Labor Day Bash

Labor Day originated in Europe in the 1800s when workers sought by direct action to enforce a holiday on the first of May. The United States decided to be different, selecting the first Monday in September as the date for almost everyone to kick back and take the day off. The Hotel del Coronado was six years old in 1894, when Congress passed the bill that made Labor Day a legal holiday throughout the Union.

Now that we have given due credit to our forefathers who made this holiday possible, let's have a party! But let's not make too much work of it—it seems only fair that it should be the cook's day off as well. Here is a menu that allows the cook a laborless Labor Day for the last outdoor party of the season. You can definitely be a guest at your own bash because all the dishes are prepared the day before—with only the last thirty minutes dedicated to grilling the Feta Grilled Lamb Chops.

MENU

Layered Bacon and Egg Salad

Molded Citrus-Avocado Salad

Ham and Cheese Salad

Potato Scallops in Garlic Cream

Deviled Green Beans and Tuna

Feta Grilled Lamb Chops

Sourdough Onion-Garlic Bread

Milky Way Layer Cake

Layered Bacon and Egg Salad

1 head iceberg lettuce, cut
  into bite-size pieces
½ cup chopped scallions (green
  and white parts)
½ cup chopped celery
½ cup sliced water chestnuts
1 cup mayonnaise
1½ tbsp. sugar
3 hard-cooked eggs, peeled and
  chopped
4 slices bacon, cooked and
  crumbled
½ cup grated cheddar cheese

1. In a clear glass salad bowl, layer the vegetables in the order given.

2. Combine the mayonnaise and sugar; then spread the mixture over the vegetables, covering them completely with a very thin layer.

3. Sprinkle with egg, bacon, and cheese. Cover tightly with plastic wrap and refrigerate for 24 hours.

4. Do not toss before serving.

Serves 8.

Molded Citrus-Avocado Salad

1 3-oz. package orange gelatin
1 3-oz. package lemon gelatin
1½ cups boiling water
1 tbsp. grated orange rind
1 tsp. grated lemon rind
1 cup cold water
3 tbsp. plus ¼ cup fresh
  lemon juice
1 large avocado
1 cup canned sliced cling
  peaches, well drained
1 cup pink grapefruit sections
½ cup drained halved red
  maraschino cherries
2 oranges, peeled and cut into
  wedges (for garnish)

1. In a large mixing bowl, blend orange and lemon gelatins with the boiling water. Mix in grated orange and lemon rinds.

2. When the gelatin is completely dissolved, pour in the cold water and 2 tablespoons of fresh lemon juice.

3. Chill mixture until it begins to thicken. Peel and slice the avocado into twelve lengthwise segments. As you slice, drop each segment into the ¼ cup of fresh lemon juice to prevent discoloration, then drain. Carefully stir avocado, peaches, grapefruit, and cherries into the chilled gelatin.

4. Brush the inside of a 4-cup mold with remaining lemon juice. Ladle the fruit gelatin mixture into the mold. Chill overnight.

5. At serving time, unmold on a large platter or tray and garnish with orange wedges.

Serves 8.

Ham and Cheese Salad

1½ lb. baked ham, sliced ¼
  inch thick and cut in
  julienned strips
1½ lb. Gruyère cheese, sliced
  ¼-inch thick and cut into
  julienned strips
1 10-oz. box frozen green peas,
  defrosted and drained
¼ cup thinly sliced scallions
  (white part only)
¼ cup chopped red bell pepper
¼ cup chopped green bell
  pepper
2 tbsp. chopped parsley
2 tbsp. white wine vinegar
2 tbsp. Dijon-style mustard
½ tsp. salt
¼ tsp. freshly ground black
  pepper
⅛ tsp. cayenne pepper
½ cup extra-virgin olive oil

1. In a large mixing bowl, combine ham, cheese, green peas, scallions, red pepper, green pepper, and parsley.
2. In a small mixing bowl, whisk together vinegar, mustard, salt, black pepper and cayenne pepper. Gradually whisk in the olive oil in a thin stream.
3. Pour dressing over ham and cheese mixture and toss thoroughly. Cover and refrigerate overnight. Transfer mixture to a glass bowl and serve at room temperature.

Serves 8.

Potato Scallops in Garlic Cream

8 russet potatoes (about 4 lb.),
  peeled
6 cloves garlic, peeled and
  minced
2 tsp. nutmeg
2 cups heavy cream
2 tsp. salt
1 tsp. pepper

1. Preheat oven to 350 degrees.
2. Cut potatoes into ⅛-inch slices.
3. Grease a 9 x 13 x 2-inch baking pan. Using half the potatoes, cover the bottom of the pan. Sprinkle with half the garlic and nutmeg. Add the remaining potatoes and top with the remaining garlic and nutmeg.
4. Bring cream to a boil in a small saucepan, then pour it over the potatoes. Top with salt, pepper, and additional nutmeg, if desired.
5. Bake for 1 hour and 15 minutes. Potatoes should be tender and lightly brown on top.

Note: This dish may be prepared the day before serving. Bake potatoes for 30 minutes, cool, and refrigerate. When ready to serve, allow potatoes to reach room temperature, then complete baking at 350 degrees for 30 minutes.

Serves 8.

Deviled Green Beans and Tuna

4 tbsp. butter
4 tbsp. flour
1 tsp. salt
½ tsp. pepper
2½ cups milk
2 tbsp. prepared mustard
2 tsp. horseradish
2 10-oz. boxes French-style
  frozen green beans, defrosted
  and drained
2 6½-oz. cans solid white tuna,
  drained and lightly flaked
2 hard-cooked eggs, peeled and
  chopped
2 tbsp. chopped parsley
2 3½-oz. cans French-fried
  onion rings

1. Preheat oven to 375 degrees.
2. Butter a 2-quart casserole and set aside.
3. Melt butter in a medium-size saucepan; then blend in flour, salt, and pepper. Gradually add milk; cook and stir until mixture comes to a boil.
4. Stir in mustard, horseradish, green beans, tuna, eggs, and parsley.
5. Transfer mixture to casserole. Spread onion rings over the top.
6. Bake for 35 minutes.

Note: This dish may be prepared a day early. Bake casserole at 375 degrees for 15 minutes, then refrigerate. When ready to serve, allow string beans to reach room temperature. Complete baking at 375 degrees for 20 minutes, or until thoroughly baked.

Serves 8.

Feta Grilled Lamb Chops

8 loin lamb chops (2 inches
  thick)
Vegetable oil
1½ tsp. salt
½ tsp. freshly ground black
  pepper
2 cloves garlic, peeled and
  minced
½ tsp. dried thyme
½ tsp. dried oregano
½ lb. feta cheese, crumbled

1. Prepare hot coals for grilling.
2. Rinse and dry lamb chops. Cut eight pieces of heavy-duty aluminum foil 12 inches long. Lightly oil the foil, then place one chop in center of each.
3. Mix together all remaining ingredients and divide the mixture evenly among the chops, coating the tops. Fold up foil, sealing the edges completely.
4. Arrange the packages on grill, 5 inches above the heat.
5. Grill for 30 minutes. To serve, remove from foil.

Serves 8.

Sourdough Onion-Garlic Bread

2 1-lb. oval loaves sourdough
  bread, unsliced
3 sticks unsalted butter, at
  room temperature
½ cup finely chopped parsley
½ cup finely minced scallions
1 tsp. salt
1 tsp. dried basil
1 tsp. dried thyme
1 tsp. dried oregano
½ tsp. dried rosemary
4 medium cloves garlic, peeled
  and crushed
6 tbsp. grated Parmesan cheese

1. Preheat oven to 400 degrees.

2. Trim crusts from top and sides of bread. Cut 2-inch diagonal slices across bread, leaving bottoms of bread intact. Cut 2-inch diagonal slices in opposite direction, forming diamond shapes.

3. Combine and blend butter, parsley, scallions, salt, basil, thyme, oregano, rosemary, and garlic in a mixing bowl or a food processor with a metal blade.

4. Spread butter mixture between cuts and over top and sides of loaves.

5. Sprinkle tops with Parmesan cheese, then bake for 35 to 45 minutes until golden brown.

Note: Bread may be wrapped in foil and refrigerated overnight or prepared ahead of time and frozen. Before serving, place on baking sheet and bring to room temperature. Heat at 300 degrees for 10 minutes. Leftovers can be wrapped in foil and reheated in low oven.

Serves 8.

Milky Way Layer Cake

Cake:
8 1¾-oz. Milky Way candy bars
1 ½ cups butter or margarine
2 cups sugar
4 eggs, well beaten
2½ cups flour
½ tsp. baking soda
1¼ cups buttermilk
1 tsp. vanilla extract
1 cup chopped pecans
Confectioners' sugar (for
  dusting)

1. Preheat oven to 325 degrees.

2. Melt candy bars with ½ cup of butter or margarine. Remove from heat and allow mixture to cool.

3. Cream remaining cup of butter with sugar. Add beaten eggs and cooled candy bar mixture.

4. Sift flour and baking soda together. Alternately add flour mixture and buttermilk to the batter, blending thoroughly. Add vanilla extract and nuts and mix.

5. Grease three 9-inch cake pans, then dust with confectioners' sugar. Pour equal amounts of batter in each; then bake for 35 to 45 minutes.

6. Cool cake in pans on wire racks for 10 minutes. Invert cake layers onto racks and cool completely.

Icing:
2½ cups sugar
1 cup evaporated milk
½ cup butter or margarine
1 cup marshmallow cream
1 6-oz. package semisweet chocolate chips
1 cup chopped pecans (for topping)

1. Combine sugar and evaporated milk in a small saucepan. Cook over low heat to a soft ball stage.
2. Remove from heat, add butter or margarine, marshmallow cream, and chocolate chips. Stir well until all ingredients have melted.

To Assemble:
1. Spread icing evenly between layers and over tops and sides of cake.
2. Top with pecans.

"Just the Four of Us" Bash

This menu is designed to follow a foursome at golf, doubles at tennis, mark a reunion of close friends, or note any other occasion that calls for entertaining a special couple informally. Please your friends and delight yourself with this easygoing dinner for four. Except for the salad, it's all prepared on the grill so you won't be tied up in the kitchen, missing the intimacy and conversation of the occasion.

MENU

Bibb Lettuce Salad
Honey-Mustard Dressing

Filet Mignon
Red Pepper Hollandaise Sauce

Best Barbecued Potatoes

Grilled Herbed Asparagus

Bacon-Cheese Crescents

Barbecued Banana Splits

Bibb Lettuce Salad with Honey-Mustard Dressing

Salad:
2 heads Bibb lettuce
3 scallions (both green and white parts), chopped
Honey-Mustard Dressing (recipe follows)
2 hard-cooked eggs, peeled and grated

1. Rinse lettuce well, pat dry, and break into bite-size pieces. Add scallions and mix thoroughly.
2. Toss greens and scallions with Honey-Mustard Dressing. Divide onto four salad plates; sprinkle tops of salads with grated egg.

Serves 4.

Honey-Mustard Dressing:

1 qt. mayonnaise
1 cup prepared mustard
½ cup honey
1 tsp. white vinegar

1. Combine mayonnaise and mustard in a large mixing bowl. Mix briskly with a whisk, then add honey and vinegar.
2. Continue mixing until all ingredients are thoroughly blended.

Note: Leftover dressing may be stored in tightly covered jar in the refrigerator for up to four months.

Yields about 5 ½ cups.

Filet Mignon and Red Pepper Hollandaise Sauce

Filet Mignon Steaks:

4 filet mignon steaks (about 1½ inches thick)
Vegetable oil
8 cloves unpeeled garlic, soaked in water for 30 minutes
Salt
Freshly ground black pepper

1. Prepare hot coals for grilling.
2. Brush each filet mignon lightly with oil.
3. Place the garlic cloves on top of the hot coals in the area where you will be grilling the steaks. Brush the grill lightly with oil.
4. Sear the steaks over high heat for 1 minute per side, then sear edges. Raise the grill to reduce heat, place steaks on grill, and barbecue for 4 minutes on the first side, then 5 to 6 minutes on the second side for rare, or 7 to 8 minutes for medium-rare. Sprinkle with salt and pepper. Serve with Red Pepper Hollandaise Sauce. Discard garlic cloves.

Serves 4.

Red Pepper Hollandaise Sauce:

1 red bell pepper
2 egg yolks
2 tbsp. lemon juice
¼ tsp. Dijon-style mustard
6 tbsp. unsalted butter, frozen
¼ tsp. Tabasco sauce
1 tsp. salt

1. Pierce the stem end of the red pepper using a long fork with a heat-proof handle, and hold it as close as possible to a high flame. Turn frequently until the pepper is charred and the skin has puffed away from the flesh. Immediately place the hot pepper into a paper bag and seal it tightly. Allow the pepper to set for 10 minutes, then remove from the bag and gently pull off the charred skin. Core, seed, and roughly chop the pepper.
2. Place pepper in food processor and process until smooth. Pour the puréed pepper into the top of a double boiler. Place over simmering water; add egg yolks, lemon juice, and mustard. Stir mixture until it begins to thicken. Add butter, 1 tablespoon at a time. Continue stirring until mixture is smooth and thick. Stir in Tabasco sauce and salt. Keep over warm water until serving time.

Yields about 1 cup.

Best Barbecued Potatoes

4 medium-size russet potatoes
(about 2 ¼ lb.)
4 tbsp. Best Barbecue Sauce
(recipe follows)

1. Prepare hot coals for grilling.
2. Scrub potatoes and prick all over with a fork. Brush each potato with barbecue sauce.
3. Place potatoes on outer edges of grill, then cook for 55 minutes, or until tender.

Serves 4.

Best Barbecue Sauce:
1 tbsp. unsalted butter
1 onion, finely chopped
¾ cup ketchup
3 tbsp. Worcestershire sauce
2 tbsp. A-1 steak sauce
1 tbsp. cider vinegar
3 tbsp. brown sugar
¼ cup water
Dash Tabasco sauce

1. Melt butter in a small saucepan over medium-low heat. Add onion and cook for 5 minutes, but do not brown.
2. Stir in the remaining ingredients. Heat to boiling; then reduce heat. Simmer uncovered for 20 minutes.

Note: Leftover barbecue sauce may be used for baked chicken. Pour sauce over raw chicken parts and bake at 350 degrees for 1 hour or until tender.

Yields about 1 cup.

Grilled Herbed Asparagus

1 lb. fresh asparagus
¼ cup olive oil
4 large fresh basil leaves, chopped
⅛ tsp. chopped fresh thyme
1 tsp. chopped fresh parsley
1 small scallion (green and white parts), minced

1. Prepare hot coals for grilling.
2. Break the tough bottoms off the asparagus spears by bending each spear until it snaps. Peel the stems and place the asparagus in a shallow glass or ceramic dish.
3. Combine the remaining ingredients, then pour over the asparagus. Toss to coat. Let stand, covered, for 30 minutes.
4. Transfer asparagus to a hot grill; cook over high heat for 10 minutes, turning once. Continue to cook over medium heat (use the outer edges of the grill), turning several times until crisp-tender, about 10 minutes.

Serves 4.

Bacon-Cheese Crescents

5 slices bacon
1 8-oz. package crescent
   refrigerator rolls
½ cup sharp cheddar cheese,
   grated
1½ tbsp. fresh chives, chopped

1. Preheat oven to 375 degrees.

2. In a small skillet, fry bacon over medium heat until lightly browned. Drain well on paper towels; then crumble when cool and set aside.

3. Unroll and separate the crescents. Lay each crescent on a lightly greased baking sheet. Sprinkle each crescent with cheese, bacon, and chives, dividing ingredients equally among the eight crescents.

4. Roll up each piece of dough to form a crescent roll, starting with the wide end of the triangle. Tuck point of dough under roll.

5. Bake for 10 to 13 minutes, or until rolls are lightly browned. Serve hot.

Yields 8 rolls.

Barbecued Banana Splits

4 ripe bananas
4 heaping tbsp. peanut butter
6 tbsp. milk chocolate bits
6 tbsp. miniature marshmallows

1. Prepare four 8-inch strips of foil.

2. Peel back one section of the skin on each banana. Spread peanut butter over banana; add chocolate bits and marshmallows. Replace the skin, then wrap each banana in foil.

3. Place the foil packets on the grill over glowing embers. Cook for 10 minutes, turning frequently.

Serves 4.

CHAPTER NINE

Banquets Galore

"You're invited to a banquet." When you hear the word *banquet,* what thoughts or expectations run through your mind? First, you think of a festive and enjoyable occasion. You also expect to be one of many guests there. Last, but not least, you expect a culinary experience that is out of the ordinary—a meal that could be described as sumptuous or elaborate.

At the Del, the banquet customer determines the occasion and invites the guests. The Del does the rest. Banquets range in size from an intimate dinner gathering for as few as four to an elegant banquet for as many fifteen hundred. The Del bases its banquet theory on the idea that eating is one of the most enjoyable pastimes for people of any age. The art of cooking embraces all five senses, giving visual delight to the eye, enticing aromas to the nose, texture to the touch, the tinkle of fine crystal to the ear, and delicious flavors to the taste buds. A successful banquet is indeed a sensory experience. The chef describes the preparation of a banquet dinner as "painting a picture on the plate."

Now, let's talk about your involvement with food. There is a double delight where food is concerned. The first delight is when your tastes become sufficiently adventurous to enable you to acquire a discriminating palate. The second delight is when you are ready to cook and create recipes that you have never tried before. You do not have to be a genius to cook. Take it slowly—as you would any new project—and you can reach amazing heights. All you need is a strong love for good food.

From the International Dinner menu, explore new combinations and experiment with colorful ingredients, starting with *fruits de mer* caught in a net of black linguini and culminating with Wine-Poached Pears in Papaya Sauce. Stimulate your culinary skills by preparing appealing dishes designed especially for the Chefs de Cuisine banquet, featuring Sherry and Cognac-Spiked Consommé and Shrimp and Scallop Tartlet with Two Sauces. An elegant dinner for eight opens with Exotic Baby Greens with Goat Cheese and Sun-Dried Tomatoes and closes with Strawberry Cheese Cake with Strawberry Sauce. Celebrate the Chinese New Year with three exquisite courses of Oriental Stuffed Avocado, Hunan Beef with Pungent Plum Sauce on a bed of buckwheat noodles, and Chocolate-Dipped Bananas and Lychee Nuts on Kiwi Coulis.

Good food and good conversation are the two inseparable ingredients for a successful party. Turn the pages of this chapter and prepare for a culinary treat. Your party will be a time for you to shine.

Following Page: *International Dinner.* Center: *Veal Chops on Red Pepper Sauce, Fresh Spinach Leaves and Pine Nuts, Polenta with Gorgonzola Cheese, and Orange-Glazed Carrots Julienned.* Upper Left: *Netted Fruits de Mer.* Upper Right: *Wine-Poached Pears with Papaya Sauce.*

International Dinner

Worldly dishes with a cornucopia of flavors and appealing colors are highlighted on the international menu. Netted Fruits de Mer won a blue ribbon when the executive chef, Jay Pastoral, entered it in the International Seafood Fair in Baja California, Mexico.

MENU

U.S.A.
California Sunburst Salad
Walnut Vinaigrette Dressing

FRANCE
Netted Fruits de Mer
Saffron Sauce

ITALY
Veal Chops with Red Pepper Sauce
Polenta with Gorgonzola Cheese
Fresh Spinach Leaves and Pine Nuts
Orange-Glazed Carrots Julienned

MEXICO
Wine-Poached Pears
Papaya Sauce

GRAND BANQUET
—GIVEN BY—
AL MALAIKAH
TEMPLE,
(TEMPLE OF THE ANGELS)
A. A. O. N. M. S.
OASIS OF LOS ANGELES,
—AT—
HOTEL DEL CORONADO,
CORONADO, CALIF.
SATURDAY, AUGUST 10, 1889.

MENU
Celery.   Olives.

Green Turtle a l'Anglaise

Columbia River Salmon a la Montpensier,
Cucumber Mayonaise;   Potatoes Duchesse.

Filet of Beef, larded, a la Portugaise,
New Green Peas,   Browned New Potatoes.

Sweetbreads Croquettes a la Perigourdine,
Suprême of Chicken a la Maréchale.

Maraschino Punch.

California Grass Bird on Toast, with Jelly,
Lettuce Salad.

Strawberry Shortcake,   Assorted Cakes
Neapolitan Ice Cream.
Fruit,   Nuts,   Café Noir.

Menu printed on silk for the Al Malaikah Grand Banquet.

California Sunburst Salad with Walnut Vinaigrette Dressing

Salad:
1 head red leaf lettuce
2 oranges
1 avocado
1 medium red onion, thinly sliced
⅓ cup walnuts, coarsely chopped

1. Wash and dry lettuce, then separate into leaves.
2. Peel oranges, remove pith, and thinly slice. Peel avocado, remove pit, and cut into quarters.

Walnut Vinaigrette Dressing:
½ cup walnut oil
3 tbsp. red wine vinegar
1½ tsp. freshly squeezed lemon juice
Pinch sugar
Salt and pepper to taste

1. In a medium-size mixing bowl, whisk oil into the vinegar.
2. Add remaining ingredients and whisk again until well blended. Cover and refrigerate until ready to serve. Whisk again before serving.

To Assemble:
1. Divide lettuce leaves among four salad plates.
2. Divide orange slices into four portions and place on lettuce leaves.
3. Cut each avocado quarter into two slices, leaving the base intact. Place avocado slices on top of orange slices. Press avocado slices gently, so they fan out.
4. Place three onion rings on top of orange and avocado. Sprinkle with chopped walnuts and top with Walnut Vinaigrette.

Serves 4.

Netted Fruits de Mer with Saffron Sauce

Black Linguini:
1 tsp. salt
3 tbsp. vegetable oil
½ lb. black linguini

1. In a large saucepan, bring 2 quarts of water to a boil. Add salt, vegetable oil, and linguini. Cook for 7 minutes.
2. Drain, set aside, and keep warm.

Saffron Sauce:
½ cup Fish Stock (see recipe)
¼ cup white wine
⅛ tsp. saffron strands
½ cup heavy cream

1. In a small saucepan, combine stock, wine, and saffron strands. Stir and simmer until mixture is reduced by half.
2. Add cream. Cook until slightly thickened. Keep warm and set aside.

Seafood:
3 tbsp. butter or margarine, softened
1 clove garlic, peeled and finely minced
Salt and white pepper
1 8-oz. lobster tail, cut into 4 pieces (including shells)
4 large scallops
8 large (16-20/lb.) shrimp, shelled
4 crab claws, cooked and drained
½ tsp. saffron strands

1. Preheat oven to 400 degrees.
2. Place softened butter, garlic, salt, and pepper in a small mixing bowl. Combine thoroughly.
3. Place all seafood except the crab claws in a greased baking pan. Brush seafood with garlic butter, then bake for approximately 8 minutes. Remove from oven and add crab claws. Top only the scallops with saffron strands. Return seafood to oven and continue to bake for 5 minutes. Remove from oven, cover, and keep warm.

To Assemble:
1. Spoon saffron sauce onto each of four salad or fish plates.
2. Lay strands of black linguini horizontally and vertically over the saffron sauce to create a net effect.
3. Arrange seafood on top of the linguini net.

Serves 4.

Veal Chops with Red Pepper Sauce

Veal:
3 tbsp. olive oil
4 7-oz. veal chops
½ tsp. salt
½ tsp. white pepper

1. Preheat oven to 400 degrees.
2. Season veal chops with salt and pepper.
3. Heat the oil in a large skillet, then add chops and sear for 3 minutes on each side.
4. Remove chops from skillet and transfer to a greased baking pan. Bake for 8 to 10 minutes. Remove from oven and keep warm.

Note: Have your local butcher cut four veal chops from a rack of veal ¾-inch thick, leaving the bone attached.

Red Pepper Sauce:
4 red bell peppers
2 tbsp. butter or margarine
1 large red onion, chopped
2 cloves garlic, peeled and coarsely chopped
2 cups red wine
⅛ tsp. cayenne pepper
Salt
Pepper

1. Preheat oven to 350 degrees.
2. Place peppers on a nonstick cookie sheet, then bake for 1 hour. Remove peppers from oven and cool. Carefully remove the skins, cut into halves, remove seeds, and coarsely chop. Set aside.
3. In a medium-size saucepan, melt butter or margarine over medium heat. Add onion, garlic, and pepper. Sauté for 3 minutes. Add wine, bring to a simmer, and cook for 8 minutes. Remove from heat. Add cayenne pepper, salt, and pepper to taste.
4. Transfer mixture to a blender and blend to a purée consistency. Remove and place in a double boiler to keep warm.

To Serve:
1. Spoon Red Pepper Sauce onto one side of each of four dinner plates.
2. Lay a veal chop on top of the sauce on each plate.

Serves 4.

Polenta with Gorgonzola Cheese

2 cups water
½ tsp. salt
¾ cups coarse-ground cornmeal
¼ tsp. white pepper
4 oz. Gorgonzola cheese

1. Preheat oven to 350 degrees.
2. In a heavy saucepan, bring water and salt to a boil. As water begins to boil, sprinkle in the cornmeal, a little at a time, whisking constantly.
3. After all the cornmeal has been added, reduce the heat and cook for 15 minutes, stirring continuously. Mixture will become quite thick. Remove from heat and add pepper.
4. Use a rubber spatula to fill four greased ½-cup timbales with cornmeal mixture. Pack down firmly with the back of the spatula.
5. Invert timbales onto a cookie sheet. Tap lightly to release cornmeal mixture. Place 1 ounce of cheese on top of each timbale. Place in oven and bake for approximately 2 minutes, or until cheese is just melted. Remove from oven and use a spatula to transfer to dinner plates.

Note: Timbales are small custard dishes or pastry molds.

Serves 4.

Fresh Spinach Leaves and Pine Nuts

⅛ cup pine nuts
Salt
4 tsp. butter or margarine
2 bunches fresh spinach leaves, washed, dried, and stems removed
Salt
White pepper

1. Preheat oven to 350 degrees.
2. Spread out pine nuts on a nonstick cookie sheet; sprinkle lightly with salt. Bake for 3 minutes, or until toasted. Remove from oven and set aside.
3. In a large skillet or wok, melt butter or margarine. Add spinach leaves, stirring constantly. Season with salt and pepper. Gently fold in pine nuts. Remove from heat and serve.

Serves 4.

Orange-Glazed Carrots Julienned

¾ lb. carrots, peeled and
    julienned
2 tbsp. butter or margarine
2 cups orange juice
⅓ cup brown sugar
Salt
Pepper

1. In a medium-size saucepan, bring 1 quart of water to a boil. Add carrots and blanch for 2 minutes. Remove from heat, drain, and set aside.

2. In a large skillet, melt butter or margarine. Add carrots and sauté for 3 minutes. Stir in orange juice and brown sugar. Bring to a simmer, cover, and cook for 10 minutes. Season with salt and pepper to taste. Remove from heat and serve with a slotted spoon.

Serves 4.

Wine-Poached Pears with Papaya Sauce

Pears:
4 medium-size firm ripe Bosc
    pears
3 cups red wine
2 cups water
½ cup fresh lemon juice
12 cinnamon sticks
1 cup sugar
½ cup cornstarch
½ cup water
4 cloves
4 mint leaves

1. Peel each pear and core from bottom end, leaving stem intact. Slice about ¼ inch from base of each pear, so it will sit flat.

2. In a dutch oven, combine wine, water, lemon juice, cinnamon sticks, and sugar. Bring to a boil over medium heat; then add pears, standing them upright. Cover, reduce heat, and simmer for about 30 to 40 minutes, or until tender. Remove pears from liquid and allow to cool. Place in a covered dish and chill. Save liquid.

3. While pears are cooling, transfer cooking liquid to a medium-size saucepan and bring to a simmer. In a small bowl, whisk together the cornstarch and water. Pour the cornstarch mixture into the cooking liquid in a slow stream. Reduce the heat and stir sauce until it is thick enough to coat the whisk, about 2 to 3 minutes.

4. Remove chilled pears from refrigerator and spoon thickened sauce over pears to glaze them.

Note: For a more intense flavor, prepare the pears a day in advance and let them steep in the wine mixture overnight.

Papaya Sauce:
1 papaya, peeled and cut into
    chunks
½ cup pineapple juice
½ cup heavy cream
1 tbsp. honey

Place all the ingredients in a blender and purée.

To Serve:
1. Transfer pears to four glass dessert bowls or plates. Top each pear with a clove and a mint leaf.
2. Spoon papaya sauce around each pear and serve.

Serves 4.

Chefs de Cuisine Dinner

The San Diego chapter of the Chefs de Cuisine held its annual awards dinner banquet at the Hotel del Coronado in 1990. One hundred and fifty local chefs gathered together to vote for one of their peers as the chef who was most dedicated and involved in the culinary field.

Executive Chef Jay Pastoral of the Hotel del Coronado hosted this dinner and chose a classic menu for the banquet because he felt that it matched the atmosphere and Old World elegance for which the Del is known.

MENU

Sherry and Cognac-Spiked Consommé
Mushroom and Duck Pouches

Shrimp and Scallop Tartlet with Two Sauces

Lemon Sorbet Intermezzo

Petite Filets Mignon Rossini
Madeira Sauce

Turned Potatoes with Baby Carrots, Baby
Yellow Zucchini, and Haricots Verts

Chocolate-Raspberry Tiramisu

Program for a "Special Musicale" in the Rotunda (main lobby) on Sunday evening, August 26, 1928.

Sherry and Cognac-Spiked Consommé with Mushroom and Duck Pouches

Consommé:

1 10-oz. can chicken consommé
1 10-oz. can beef consommé
½ cup sherry wine
¼ cup cognac

1. In a medium-size saucepan, bring chicken and beef consommés to a simmer; then add sherry and cognac.

2. Cover and simmer for 10 minutes. Turn off heat and keep covered on stove.

Pouches:

1 6- to 7-oz. duck breast
Salt
Pepper
5 sprigs fresh thyme, chopped
2 tbsp. vegetable oil
1 tbsp. minced shallot
⅛ cup sliced oyster mushrooms
¼ cup sliced shiitake mushrooms
2 oz. white wine
¼ tsp. salt
⅛ tsp. pepper
4 scallions (green part only),
   blanched and drained
4 sprigs fresh thyme
   (for garnish)

1. Preheat oven to 350 degrees.
2. Place duck breast in a small baking pan, fat side down. Sprinkle with salt, pepper, and 2 tablespoons chopped thyme. Bake for about 25 minutes, or until duck breast is fork-tender. Set aside to cool, remove skin, then cut into julienned strips.
3. In a medium-size skillet, heat vegetable oil, shallots, and remainder of chopped thyme. Sauté for 1 minute. Add mushrooms and duck. Stir and cook for 2 more minutes; then add wine, salt, and pepper. Turn off heat, cover, and set aside.

Crêpes:

1 cup unsifted all-purpose flour
¼ tsp. salt
4 eggs
1 ¼ cups milk
2 tbsp. butter or margarine,
   melted

1. In a food processor or blender, combine flour, salt, eggs, and milk. Process until smooth.
2. Heat a 7-inch nonstick skillet over medium-high heat. Brush skillet with melted butter or margarine; then pour about 3 tablespoons of batter all at once into center of skillet. Immediately swirl pan to coat bottom with a thin layer of batter. Cook until golden brown. With small metal spatula, loosen edges of crêpe and turn over. Cook until underside is golden brown in spots. Turn crêpes out onto a sheet of waxed paper.
3. Repeat procedure with remaining melted butter or margarine and batter, adjusting heat as necessary.

Note: Crêpes may be prepared ahead of time and refrigerated or frozen and thawed before using. Remaining crêpes may be frozen as well for later use.

Yields 16 to 18 crêpes.

To Assemble:

1. Lay four crêpes out on a flat surface. Spoon 1 tablespoon mushroom-duck filling onto center of each crêpe. Gather ends of crêpe together and tie tightly with a blanched scallion top.
2. Place one pouch in each of four soup bowls. Ladle consommé into bowls. Avoid pouring consommé over pouches. Float a sprig of thyme in consommé as a garnish.

Serves 4.

Shrimp and Scallop Tartlet with Two Sauces

Tartlet:

1 (17¼-oz.) pkg. frozen puff pastry

1 egg beaten with 1 tsp. water (egg wash)

1½ cups Court Bouillon (see recipe)

8 large shrimp (about ½ lb.), shelled and deveined

8 large sea scallops (about ½ lb.)

8 chive strands

1. Preheat oven to 350 degrees.

2. Defrost puff pastry according to the package directions. Lay pastry sheet out on a flat surface.

3. Cut pastry sheet into four rectangles, each 2 ½ x 4 inches. Brush each rectangle with egg wash.

4. Place on a small nonstick cookie sheet and bake for 15 minutes, or until golden brown. Remove from oven and allow to cool at room temperature. Pastry shells will puff up and be very light. Remove a thin slice from the top of each pastry shell. Set aside.

5. In a medium-size saucepan, combine 1½ cups Court Bouillon, shrimp, and scallops. Bring to a simmer and poach for about 2 to 3 minutes. Remove from heat, cover, and set aside.

Note: Puff pastry may be found in the frozen section of local supermarkets.

Nantua Sauce:

5 tbsp. butter or margarine

1½ tbsp. shallots, peeled and finely chopped

1 cup Fish Stock (see recipe)

Dash paprika

1 tbsp. lobster base

½ cup white wine

½ cup heavy cream

½ tsp. salt

¼ tsp. white pepper

1. In a medium-size saucepan, melt 1 tablespoon butter or margarine. Add shallots, cover, and cook over medium heat, shaking the pan occasionally, until shallots are soft.

2. Stir in fish stock, paprika, lobster base, and wine. Cook and stir, reducing mixture by one-half.

3. Stir in cream and simmer for 2 minutes. Strain mixture through a fine sieve into a small saucepan. Place over very low heat and whisk in the remaining butter or margarine. Do not allow the sauce to boil. Season with salt and pepper. Remove from heat and keep warm.

Note: Lobster base may be found in the soup section of most specialty markets.

Champagne Sauce:

3 tbsp. butter or margarine

2 tbsp. shallots, peeled and finely chopped

2 tbsp. all-purpose flour

¾ cup Fish Stock (see recipe)

½ cup champagne

¼ cup heavy cream

¼ tsp. nutmeg

½ tsp. salt

¼ tsp. white pepper

1. In a small saucepan, melt butter or margarine. Add shallots, cover, and cook over medium heat, shaking the pan occasionally until the shallots are soft.

2. Stir in flour and continue to cook for about 2 more minutes. Add fish stock and champagne. Bring to a simmer and cook for 5 minutes.

3. Stir in cream, nutmeg, salt, and pepper; then simmer for 2 minutes. Strain mixture through a fine sieve into a small saucepan. Keep warm.

To Assemble:

1. Spoon Nantua Sauce onto the center of each of four salad plates. Place a puff pastry shell on top of sauce on each plate.

2. Arrange two shrimp and two scallops on each pastry shell.

3. Spoon Champagne Sauce over seafood. Place thin slice of pastry shell on top of seafood. Garnish with two chive strands placed crisscrossed over each tartlet.

Serves 4.

Lemon Sorbet Intermezzo

2 lemons
1 cup sugar
1½ cups water
⅓ cup fresh lemon juice
2 tsp. freshly grated lemon zest
⅛ tsp. salt
12 lemon leaves, washed and dried (for garnish)

1. Cut lemons into halves. Remove fruit with a serrated knife, leaving shell intact. Cut a thin sliver off bottom of lemon shells, so they will stand upright. Set aside.

2. In a small saucepan, combine the sugar and water. Bring mixture to a boil, stirring until the sugar is dissolved. Stir in lemon juice, zest, and salt.

3. Refrigerate mixture until it is cold; then freeze it in an ice cream maker according to the manufacturer's directions. Transfer sorbet to covered container and freeze until ready to serve.

To Serve:

1. Place three lemon leaves on each of four dessert plates.

2. Set a lemon shell on each plate. Scoop sorbet into shells and serve immediately.

Note: Sorbet may be prepared three weeks in advance.

Serves 4.

Petite Filets Mignon Rossini with Madeira Sauce

Madeira Sauce:

3 tbsp. butter or margarine, cut into small pieces
2 tbsp. peeled and chopped shallots
½ cup Brown Stock (see recipe)
½ cup Madeira wine
1 cup Demi-Glacé (see recipe)
Salt
White pepper

1. Melt 1 tablespoon butter or margarine in a small saucepan. Add shallots and sauté for 1 minute. Add brown stock and wine; then cook and stir until mixture is reduced by one-half.

2. Add demi-glacé and continue to cook, stirring, for 10 minutes. Strain mixture through a fine sieve into a small saucepan, then blend in remaining 2 tablespoons of butter or margarine, stirring constantly. Add salt and pepper to taste. Keep warm and set aside.

Yields about 1 cup.

Toasted Croutons:

1 thin French baguette
2 tbsp. butter or margarine, melted

1. Preheat oven to 350 degrees.

2. Cut four ¼-inch slices from baguette. Spread with butter or margarine and place on a nonstick cookie sheet. Bake for about 6 minutes, or until well browned. Remove from oven and set aside.

Petite Filets:

Salt and white pepper
4 6-oz. beef filets mignon
2 tbsp. vegetable oil
4 2-oz. slices raw duck liver

1. Preheat oven to 400 degrees.

2. Season filets with salt and pepper.

3. Heat oil in a large skillet, then sear filets for 2 minutes on each side.

4. Transfer filets to a greased baking pan. Bake for about 10 minutes for medium-rare.

5. While filets are baking, reheat the same skillet, and sauté duck liver for 15 seconds on each side. Remove from heat and place a slice of liver on each toasted crouton.

To Assemble Plate:

1. Place a filet (off-center) on each of four dinner plates. Place crouton with duck liver on the left side of the filet.

2. Spoon Madeira Sauce on half of the filet.

3. Divide and arrange vegetables (recipe follows) around the filet.

Serves 4.

Turned Potatoes with Baby Carrots, Baby Yellow Zucchini, and Haricots Verts

2 large russet potatoes
  (about 1 ¼ lb.)
8 baby carrots
4 baby yellow zucchini
¼ lb. haricots verts (French green
  beans)
Salt and pepper
3 tbsp. butter or margarine,
  melted

1. Peel potatoes, cut off both ends, and cut into quarters. With a small, sharp paring knife, trim the sides of each quarter to make a rectangular shape. Trim the corners to make eight smooth oval-shaped potatoes. Place in a bowl of cold water; set aside.

2. Trim and peel carrots, leaving ¾ inch of the green stems attached. Place in the bowl of water with turned potatoes.

3. Wash zucchini; set aside.

4. In a medium-size saucepan, bring 1 quart of water to a boil. Drain potatoes, add to boiling water, and cook for about 8 or 9 minutes. With a slotted spoon, remove potatoes from boiling water and place in a greased casserole.

5. Add more water to saucepan (if necessary) and bring to a boil. Add carrots and cook for 15 minutes. Add zucchini and cook for 1 minute. Remove vegetables from boiling water and drop them into a bowl of ice water for 1 minute. Drain and line them up in the casserole with the turned potatoes.

6. In a small saucepan, bring 3 cups of salted water to a boil. Add haricots verts and cook for 8 minutes. Remove and place in ice water for 30 seconds; then drain and add to casserole.

7. Season vegetables with salt and pepper. Brush with butter or margarine and place in the microwave for 2 minutes on high heat. Remove from microwave and arrange on plates.

Serves 4.

Chocolate-Raspberry Tiramisu

1½ lb. mascarpone cheese, at room temperature

1 cup confectioners' sugar

4 egg yolks

¾ cup semisweet chocolate chips

3 oz. Kahlua liqueur

3 oz. Marsala wine

3 oz. brewed strong coffee, at room temperature

16 Italian ladyfingers

24 fresh raspberries, washed and air dried (for garnish)

8 oz. semisweet chocolate, finely chopped (for garnish)

1. Place cheese and sugar in the bowl of an electric mixer. Blend on medium-speed for about 3 minutes, or until light and fluffy. Add egg yolks, one at a time, beating for 1 minute on medium-speed after each addition. Fold in chocolate chips; set aside.

2. In a medium-size mixing bowl, combine the Kahlua, wine, and coffee. Cut ladyfingers in half lengthwise, then quickly dip the ends of the ladyfingers into the Kahlua mixture.

3. Place four ladyfingers standing upright into each of eight dessert dishes.

4. Transfer cheese mixture into a pastry bag with a large star tip. Pipe mixture into the center of each dessert dish. Top with three raspberries and sprinkle with chopped chocolate.

Note: Italian ladyfingers are available at Italian markets and gourmet shops. You may also use plain ladyfingers found in your local market.

Serves 8.

Chocolate-Raspberry Tiramisu.

Dinner at Eight

The perfect number for an elegant dinner party is eight—for both the appointed hour and the number of invited guests. Conversation flows easily, and the menu is designed to enhance convivial intimacy. Even when the host or hostess doubles as cook and waiter, the dinner can be as impressive and relaxed as if there were a staff of servants to assist.

Exotic Baby Greens, Goat Cheese, and Sun-Dried Tomatoes with Thai Vinaigrette Dressing

8 arugula leaves
8 baby romaine leaves
8 baby red leaf lettuce leaves
8 curly endive leaves
2 heads radicchio
1 lb. goat cheese, cut into 16 slices
Olive oil
6 tbsp. black sesame seeds
Thai Vinaigrette Dressing (recipe follows)
16 sun-dried tomatoes, cut into julienned strips

1. Preheat oven to 350 degrees.
2. Wash and dry arugula, romaine, and red leaf lettuce leaves. Tear leaves into bite-size pieces and place in a large salad bowl. Set aside.
3. Brush goat cheese slices with olive oil and coat with sesame seeds. Place cheese on a nonstick cookie sheet. Bake for approximately 10 minutes, until cheese is soft.
4. Toss mixed lettuce with enough Thai Vinaigrette to just coat leaves. Arrange a bed of lettuce and arugula on each of eight salad plates. Place two slices of warm goat cheese on top of lettuce and sprinkle with tomato strips.

Note: Black sesame seeds are available at Asian markets. White sesame seeds may be substituted for black.

Serves 8.

Thai Vinaigrette:
1 jalapeño pepper
½ cup olive oil
4 tbsp. sesame oil
½ cup rice wine vinegar
4 tbsp. finely chopped fresh mint
2 cloves garlic, peeled and minced
4 tbsp. ginger, minced
4 tbsp. water
Pinch salt

1. Wash and cut jalapeño pepper in half. Remove seeds and clean out rib. Finely mince ½ teaspoon of pepper; discard remainder.

2. In a medium-size mixing bowl, combine olive oil and sesame oil. Whisk in rice wine vinegar; then add mint, garlic, ginger, water, minced jalapeño pepper, and salt.

Note: Rice wine vinegar is available at Asian markets.

Yields about 1 cup.

Braided Halibut and Salmon with Pesto-Beurre Blanc Sauce

Pesto-Beurre Blanc Sauce:
2 cups heavy cream
¼ cup plus 1 tsp. butter
1 shallot, peeled and chopped
½ cup cider vinegar
½ cup dry white wine
¼ cup pesto

1. In a medium-size saucepan, cook and stir cream until it has been reduced by half. Set aside.

2. In a medium-size skillet sauté shallot in 1 teaspoon of butter for 1 minute. Add vinegar and wine. Simmer until liquid has almost evaporated; then add cream. Simmer for 5 more minutes. Strain sauce into a clean saucepan. Add pesto and gradually whisk in remaining butter. Keep warm in the top of a double boiler.

Note: Pesto sauce can be found in the refrigerated section of most local supermarkets.

Braided Halibut and Salmon:
4 halibut fillets (about 1½ lb.)
3 lb. salmon fillets, cut thin
Salt and freshly ground black pepper
1 cup white wine
½ cup Fish Stock (see recipe)
Parchment paper

1. Preheat oven to 325 degrees.

2. Wash the fillets and pat dry. Remove any remaining bones with tweezers. Cut both the halibut and salmon into strips ½ inch wide and 6 inches long. Lay two salmon strips and one halibut strip side-by-side, alternating colors; then gently braid them. You should have eight braids.

3. Grease a 13 x 9 x 2-inch baking pan. Lay braids side-by-side in pan. Sprinkle with salt and pepper. Pour wine and fish stock into the baking pan. Cover with parchment paper and bake for 15 minutes.

4. Remove the baking pan from oven, and carefully lift braids onto eight dinner plates. Spoon Pesto-Beurre Blanc Sauce around the braids and serve immediately.

Serves 8.

Soufflé Potatoes

4 medium russet potatoes
  (about 1¼ lb.)
2 tbsp. butter or margarine
2 tbsp. half-and-half
1 tsp. fines herbes
1 tsp. salt
½ tsp. freshly ground black
  pepper
¼ tsp. grated nutmeg
1 tbsp. grated Parmesan cheese
2 eggs, separated

1. Preheat oven to 425 degrees.

2. Scrub potatoes and remove any eyes. With a small, sharp knife, pierce each potato several times. Place potatoes on a nonstick cookie sheet. Bake for 1 hour, or until potatoes are tender.

3. Remove potatoes from oven and cut each potato in half lengthwise. Carefully scoop out potato flesh and place in a bowl. Replace potato skins on the cookie sheet and bake for 5 minutes, until crisp and golden.

4. With an electric beater, whip potatoes until smooth; then add butter or margarine, half-and-half, fines herbes, salt, pepper, nutmeg, Parmesan cheese, and egg yolks. Beat until ingredients are thoroughly blended.

5. In a small bowl, whisk egg whites until they are stiff and form peaks. With a spatula, fold whites into potato mixture very gently until well blended.

6. Fill each potato skin with mixture, and return to oven for 10 to 15 minutes, or until potatoes are lightly browned. Serve immediately.

Serves 8.

Asparagus Gâteau

1½ lb. green asparagus,
  trimmed
3 eggs
2 egg yolks
2 cups heavy cream
Pinch nutmeg
Salt
White pepper

1. Preheat oven to 350 degrees.

2. In a medium-size saucepan or asparagus steamer, bring about 1 quart of water to a boil. Add asparagus and cook until tender, about 8 minutes. Remove and drain.

3. Transfer asparagus to a blender, purée, then strain through a fine sieve.

4. In a small saucepan, heat the purée, gently stirring to remove any excess moisture.

5. Remove from heat. Thoroughly blend eggs, egg yolks, and cream into purée. Add a pinch of nutmeg, salt, and pepper.

6. Divide mixture among eight individual buttered ramekins or custard cups. Place dishes in a roasting pan and surround with boiling water. Cover with waxed paper.

7. Place in oven for about 20 minutes, or until lightly set.

8. When ready to serve, carefully loosen edges with a knife and invert cups onto eight dinner plates.

Serves 8.

Strawberry Cheesecake with Strawberry Sauce

Graham Cracker Crust:
1½ cups graham cracker crumbs
½ cup sweet butter, melted

1. Spray bottom and sides of a 10-inch springform pan.
2. In a medium-size mixing bowl, combine graham cracker crumbs and melted butter. Mix thoroughly.
3. Press into pan, covering bottom only. Set aside.

Filling:
30 oz. cream cheese
1½ cups granulated sugar
5 large eggs
¼ cup heavy cream
¾ cup strawberry jam

1. Preheat oven to 200 degrees.
2. In a large mixing bowl, combine cream cheese and sugar. With an electric mixer, blend until smooth at medium speed.
3. Add 1 egg at a time, scraping sides of mixing bowl with a spatula. Mix until well blended. Add cream and continue to mix on slow speed for 1 to 2 minutes. Stir in jam, swirling it gently through the cream cheese mixture.
4. Bake for 3 hours. Remove from oven, cool to room temperature, and refrigerate overnight.

Strawberry Sauce:
1 basket fresh strawberries, washed and air dried
½ cup water
1¼ cups granulated sugar

Combine all ingredients in a blender. Blend on high speed until berries are puréed. Cover and refrigerate.

Yields approximately 1½ cups

To Serve:
1. Remove strawberry cheesecake from the refrigerator. Release sides of spring form pan. Cut cake into twelve slices.
2. Spoon Strawberry Sauce onto each of twelve dessert plates. Set cheesecake on top of sauce and serve.

Serves 12.

Chinese New Year

Chinese cuisine is generally recognized by modern nutritionists as having a distinct, well-balanced composition, healthy ingredients, and a delicious flavor. Asian dishes have made rapid inroads into American eating habits, and the growing appreciation of these dishes gives rise to the urge to prepare them at home. Enjoy this trend and celebrate the Chinese New Year by planning an intimate dinner of three courses for four close friends.

MENU

Oriental Stuffed Avocado

Hunan Beef with Pungent Plum Sauce

Buckwheat Noodles with Shiitake Mushrooms

Julienne of Snow Peas and Yellow and Red Peppers

Chocolate-Dipped Bananas and Lychee Nuts on Kiwi Coulis

Oriental Stuffed Avocado

2 large, ripe avocados
1 tbsp. lemon juice
5 dried Chinese mushrooms, soaked in water
¼ lb. bay shrimp, shelled, cooked, and chopped
3 tbsp. mayonnaise
1 egg yolk
Juice of ½ lemon
½ tsp. curry powder
½ tsp. Tabasco sauce
2 tsp. vegetable oil
¼ tsp. salt
¼ tsp. white pepper
¼ tsp. garlic salt
Paprika (for garnish)
1 head Bibb lettuce, washed and dried

1. Cut avocados into halves lengthwise; remove pits. Carefully remove avocado from shells. Sprinkle with lemon juice, chop, and set aside. Leave enough avocado adhering to shells to form a cup. Cut a thin slice from the bottom of shells, if necessary, to stabilize them.

2. Drain mushrooms and chop. In a medium-size mixing bowl, combine mushrooms, shrimp, avocado, mayonnaise, egg yolk, lemon juice, curry powder, Tabasco sauce, oil, salt, pepper, and garlic salt. Blend thoroughly. Spoon mixture into avocados and sprinkle with paprika.

To serve:
Place three Bibb lettuce leaves on each of four salad plates. Set filled avocado shells on top of lettuce leaves.

Note: Dried Chinese mushrooms are available in Asian markets.

Serves 4.

Hunan Beef with Pungent Plum Sauce

8 3-oz. beef tournedos
Hunan Marinade
(recipe follows)
½ cup butter or margarine
2 tbsp. sesame oil
½ cup red wine

1. Place tournedos in a 13 x 9 x 2-inch baking pan. Pour Hunan Marinade over tournedos and refrigerate for 24 hours.

2. Preheat oven to 350 degrees.

3. In a large skillet, heat butter or margarine and oil. Remove tournedos from marinade, transfer to a skillet, and cook on medium heat for about 2 minutes on each side until browned. Transfer to a greased baking pan and bake for about 8 minutes for medium-rare.

4. While tournedos are baking, deglaze skillet with wine; then add Hunan Marinade, bring to a slow boil, reduce heat, and simmer for 10 minutes. Strain and keep warm.

5. When ready to serve, spoon Hunan Glacé over tournedos.

Serves 4.

Hunan Marinade:
2 tbsp. hoisin sauce
2 tbsp. oyster sauce
4 tbsp. plum sauce
1 tbsp. sherry wine
1 tsp. minced ginger
1 tsp. minced fresh garlic

In a small mixing bowl, combine all of the ingredients. Set aside.

Note: Hoisin sauce, oyster sauce, and plum sauce are available in Asian markets and some supermarkets.

To Assemble Plate:

1. Divide Buckwheat Noodles (recipe follows) into four portions. Place a bed of noodles in the center of each of four dinner plates. Arrange the Julienne of Snow Peas and Yellow and Red Peppers (recipe follows) in a circle around the noodles.

2. Arrange two tournedos on top of noodles, so they overlap slightly. Spoon Hunan Glacé over the top of the tournedos.

3. Arrange julienned shiitake mushrooms on one side of the plate and garnish opposite side with a scallion brush (recipes follow).

Buckwheat Noodles with Shiitake Mushrooms

12 oz. buckwheat noodles
3 tbsp. butter or margarine
1 tsp. sesame oil
4 large shiitake mushrooms, cut into julienned strips
½ tsp. salt
⅛ tsp. white pepper

1. Cook noodles according to package directions. Drain and set aside.
2. While noodles are boiling, melt butter or margarine in a small skillet and add sesame oil. Add shiitake mushrooms, salt, and pepper. Sauté for about 2 minutes. Mushrooms may be spooned on top of noodles or arranged on side of serving plate with Hunan Beef.

Note: Buckwheat noodles are available in Asian markets.

Serves 4.

Julienne of Snow Peas and Yellow and Red Peppers

1 cup julienned snow peas
1 cup julienned yellow bell pepper
1 cup julienned red bell pepper
¼ cup butter or margarine
⅛ tsp. salt
Dash white pepper

1. Wash snow peas and remove strings. Wash yellow and red peppers, cut peppers in half, and remove seeds and rib portion from inside of peppers.
2. Cut vegetables into julienned strips.
3. In a medium-size saucepan, bring 1 quart of water to a boil; then blanch vegetables for 1 minute. Remove and place vegetables in ice water for a few seconds. Drain.
4. In a small skillet, heat butter or margarine over medium heat; sauté vegetables for 3 minutes. Season with salt and pepper. Serve immediately.

Serves 4.

Scallion Brushes (for garnish):
4 large scallions
ice water

1. Trim the roots and the green parts from scallions, leaving about 2½ inches of stalk. Make crisscross cuts about ½ inch deep at both ends of each stalk and spread the fringed ends gently.
2. Place scallions in a bowl of cold water with a few ice cubes. Chill them for 2 hours, or until the fringed ends have curled. Drain scallions well.

Chocolate-Dipped Bananas and Lychee Nuts on Kiwi Coulis

1 20-oz. can lychee nuts
¼ cup rum
12 oz. semisweet chocolate
2 tsp. honey
2 bananas (about 1 lb.)
¾ cup pineapple juice
2 kiwis, peeled and cut into 8 slices

1. Drain lychee nuts and place in a small mixing bowl. Sprinkle rum lightly over lychee nuts. Dry nuts with a paper towel. Set aside.

2. In a double boiler, melt the semisweet chocolate, add honey, and stir over low heat. Remove from heat and set aside.

3. Peel bananas, cut into 1½-inch chunks, and place in a small mixing bowl. Pour pineapple juice over bananas, coating all sides of bananas; wipe dry with a paper towel.

4. Dip lychee nuts onto the melted chocolate. Set them on waxed paper on a cookie sheet. Remove bananas from pineapple juice and dip banana sections halfway in the melted chocolate. Set them on the cookie sheet with the lychee nuts to cool.

Note: Lychee nuts are available in Asian markets.

Kiwi Coulis:
½ cup water
¼ cup sugar
2 cups kiwis, peeled and chopped
2 tbsp. cornstarch dissolved in 2 tbsp. water

1. In a small saucepan, boil the water, sugar, and kiwis for about 5 minutes. Add the cornstarch and boil for 1 minute.

2. Transfer to a blender, blend for about 30 seconds, then strain through a sieve.

Note: Leftover Kiwi Coulis may be refrigerated in a covered jar and kept for up to one week. Serve leftover Kiwi Coulis over ice cream.

Yields about 2½ cups.

To Assemble:
1. Spoon about 2 tablespoons of Kiwi Coulis onto each of four dessert plates.

2. Place two chocolate-dipped banana chunks, four chocolate-dipped lychee nuts, and two slices of kiwi on top of Kiwi Coulis. Refrigerate until ready to serve.

Serves 4.

minute. What do you need?'' Besides additional crushed ice for the four-foot-high ice carving of the numerals *100* looming over seashells of lobster, crab, and shrimp, I needed another pair of feet. After three days of directing the food and beverage operation for this bash, I found that even sneakers were uncomfortable.

Our success kept us going. We knew that we were all part of history and that the centennial at the Hotel del Coronado was the most impressive birthday party we would ever produce or attend. Recipes for the complete centennial dinner follow, so you can prepare them for your own special celebrations—and I promise that you'll be as successful as we were.

Friday, February 19, 1988

The Extraordinary Journey

Decade by Decade

Through 100 Years of Entertainment, Theatrics and History

Throughout the Hotel's Ballrooms, Gardens and Grounds

Dress: Attire From Your Favorite Decade

8 P.M.   The Journey Begins

Hotel del Coronado

Centennial Gala Weekend

An Extraordinary Journey Through 100 Years

The Centennial Ball and Gala Entertainment Spectacular

The invitation for the Centennial Gala weekend.

The White Tie or Very Black Tie Reception

Preceding the magnificent Centennial Dinner, a White Tie or Very Black Tie Reception was held under a canopy of stars in the courtyard of the Hotel del Coronado. Clad in white tails, 'Army Archerd' announced the celebrities as they were ushered into the opening event of the evening.

Tiny morsels of exquisitely prepared Bouchées Filled with Brie were passed on silver trays by tuxedoed waiters. Strolling violinists played to the elegantly attired attendees. You can experience the gala weekend through the recipes on the following pages.

MENU

Champagne

Bouchées Filled with Brie

Cheese Straws

Curried Cocktail Nuts

Celebrities at the hotel's Centennial weekend included Anne Jeffreys and Phyllis Diller.

Bouchées Filled with Brie

1 (17¼-oz.) package frozen puff pastry (or 16 minibouchées)
1 egg beaten with 1 tsp. water (egg wash)
½ lb. Brie cheese, cut into tiny cubes
¼ cup finely chopped pecans
8 Tokay grapes, halved and seeded

1. Preheat oven to 375 degrees.
2. Thaw puff pastry sheets for 20 minutes.
3. Unfold pastry sheets onto a floured cutting board. Brush top of one sheet lightly with water, then lay the other sheet directly on top. Dip a 2¼-inch and a 1½-inch cutter in flour to coat edges.
4. Cut pastry into circles with 2¼-inch cutter. Place circles on a nonstick cookie sheet. Mark center of each circle with the 1½-inch cutter, cutting only through top layer of pastry. Brush with egg wash.
5. Bake for 15 to 20 minutes, or until puffed, crisp, and golden.
6. Remove and cool slightly. Lift out tops with the point of a paring knife and discard. Scoop out slightly undercooked interior.
7. Fill cooled bouchées with Brie cubes; top with pecans. Return to oven for 5 minutes, or until cheese is melted. Remove from oven and top each with a grape half.

Note: Frozen puff pastry sheets may be found in the frozen section of local supermarkets. Minibouchées are available at many specialty markets. Bouchées made from puff pastry freeze well and may be baked two weeks in advance and frozen. Bouchée shells keep for up to ten days in an airtight container or may be frozen and kept for up to eight weeks.

Yields 16 bouchées.

Cheese Straws

2 cups grated sharp cheddar cheese
1 cup all-purpose flour
½ tsp. salt
⅛ tsp. cayenne pepper
½ cup butter, melted

1. Preheat oven to 400 degrees.
2. In a large mixing bowl, combine cheese, flour, salt, and cayenne pepper. Blend well. Add butter, stirring with a wooden spoon until blended. (The dough will be stiff.)
3. Place the dough in a pastry bag. Using a large star tube, pipe onto a nonstick or lightly greased cookie sheet in 1½-inch strips. Bake for about 10 minutes, or until lightly browned.
4. Cool on a wire rack, then store in an airtight container until ready to serve.

Yields 30 to 35 cheese straws.

Curried Cocktail Nuts

½ cup olive oil
2 tbsp. curry powder
2 tbsp. Worcestershire sauce
¼ tsp. cayenne pepper
4 cups assorted nuts (roasted and salted)

1. Preheat oven to 300 degrees.
2. Combine oil and seasonings in medium-size skillet. When mixture is hot, add nuts, stirring constantly until nuts are completely coated.
3. Line baking pan with brown paper. Spread out nuts and bake for 30 minutes. Nuts should be crisp and tasty.

Yields 4 cups.

The Centennial Dinner

The spectacular five-course Centennial Dinner—the birthday party of the century—was served in the famous Crown Room of the Hotel del Coronado on February 20, 1988, on the occasion of the Del's one hundredth anniversary. Guests were seated at tables in an arrangement similar to that of the banquet held at the Hotel del Coronado for Charles Lindbergh when he celebrated the completion of his first transatlantic flight in 1927. Ten-foot-tall arbors covered with twenty thousand roses together with two thousand candles glowing on the tables transformed the room into an aromatic, candlelit paradise. Six trumpeters played a fanfare saluting the guests as they were escorted into the rose-filled fairyland.

Brandied Cream of Mushroom Soup en Croûte, followed by Lobster Ravioli with Cognac Sauce, a salad of Composed Garden Greens, and an entrée of Noisette Trio of Beef, Veal, and Lamb, was served. The grand finale, a dessert called Decadent Chocolate Centennial Surprise, satisfied the palates of the *bons vivants* among the guests.

The Centennial Birthday Dinner menu, February 20, 1988.

Advance Planning for Your Centennial Dinner

Some advance planning may be helpful in the preparation of your Centennial Dinner:

1. Shopping for some ingredients may be done up to three days in advance.
2. Green Peppercorn Mustard Vinaigrette Dressing may be prepared four days in advance.
3. Brandied Cream of Mushroom Soup may be prepared two days in advance.
4. Ravioli, cognac sauce, and fish stock may be prepared three days in advance. Store separately and cover tightly.
5. Petite Vegetable Bundle and Château Potatoes may be prepared the day before.
6. Decadent Chocolate Centennial Surprise may be prepared two days in advance and assembled up to four hours before serving.

This leaves only the médaillons, the sauces, and the Composed Garden Greens to prepare on the day of your party. *Bon appétit!*

MENU

Brandied Cream of Mushroom Soup en Croûte

Lobster Ravioli with Cognac Sauce

Composed Garden Greens
Green Peppercorn Mustard
Vinaigrette Dressing

Noisette Trio of Beaf, Veal, and Lamb
Château Potatoes
Petite Vegetable Bundle

Decadent Chocolate Centennial Surprise

The Crown Room decorated with arbors of roses and other fresh flowers for the hotel's 100th anniversary gala dinner. The crown-shaped chandeliers give the room its name.

Brandied Cream of Mushroom Soup en Croûte

Soup:

1 tbsp. unsalted butter
1 tbsp. minced shallots
1 lb. firm fresh mushrooms,
    cleaned and chopped
¼ tsp. dried thyme
½ bay leaf
1 tsp. salt
½ tsp. white pepper
1 ¾ cups heavy cream
1 (14½-oz.) can chicken broth
¼ cup brandy

1. Melt butter in a heavy saucepan, then lightly sauté shallots. Add mushrooms, thyme, and bay leaf. Sauté over moderate heat for 10 minutes, or until liquid disappears.

2. Add salt, pepper, cream, and chicken broth; bring to a boil. Reduce heat and simmer for 20 minutes. Remove bay leaf and place mixture in a blender. Blend for 30 seconds.

3. Return to saucepan, add brandy, and continue to simmer for 10 minutes more, stirring constantly. Allow soup to cool at room temperature before you place puff pastry circles over soup.

Croûte:

1 (17¼-oz.) package frozen puff
    pastry sheets
1 egg beaten with 1 tsp. water
    (egg wash)

1. Preheat oven to 400 degrees. You will need four 6-ounce ovenproof soup bowls.

2. Unfold one sheet of puff pastry and defrost for 20 minutes. Lay out defrosted puff pastry sheet on a floured cutting board. Roll out lightly.

3. Using a kitchen bowl for a cutter, cut out four 5-inch circles large enough to cover soup bowls.

4. Fill soup bowls with 5 ounces of soup. Place puff pastry circles over bowls, allowing puff pastry to extend ½ inch over top of bowls. Seal pastry to the bowls by pressing down with your fingers. Brush entire surface of puff pastry with egg wash.

5. Bake for 15 minutes.

Note: Frozen puff pastry sheets may be found in the frozen section of local supermarkets. You may omit the croûte if you wish—the Brandied Cream of Mushroom Soup is excellent sprinkled with minced chives and served alone.

Serves 4.

Lobster Ravioli with Cognac Sauce

Ravioli:

1 lobster tail (approximately 4 oz.)

2 tbsp. butter or margarine

2 scallions, finely chopped

½ clove garlic, peeled and minced

2 medium-size mushrooms, minced

2 tbsp. white wine

1 tsp. salt

⅛ tsp. white pepper

16 wonton wrappers

1 egg beaten with 1 tsp. water (egg wash)

3 cups Fish Stock (see recipe)

2 oz. red caviar (for garnish)

2 oz. black lumpfish caviar (for garnish)

1. Preheat oven to 350 degrees.

2. Remove ½ cup lobster meat from shell and chop fine. (Save shell for Cognac Sauce.)

3. In a heavy skillet, melt butter or margarine. Add scallions, garlic, and mushrooms; then sauté over medium heat for 1 minute.

4. Add lobster meat and continue cooking for 1 minute. Add wine, salt, and pepper; stir and cook for 1 minute. Remove from heat; set aside.

5. Place 8 wonton wrappers on a work surface. Place 1 tablespoon of lobster filling in the center of each wonton. Paint the surrounding area with egg wash. Place another wonton wrapper on top of each. Use a fork that has been dipped in flour to press and seal the edges.

6. In a heavy skillet, simmer 3 cups fish stock. Add raviolis and poach until just *al dente*, approximately 5 minutes. Transfer raviolis to a greased casserole.

7. Place casserole in warm oven, maintaining low heat until raviolis are served.

Cognac Sauce:

⅓ cup butter or margarine

2 cloves garlic, peeled and minced

1 large shallot, minced

Lobster shell, chopped

¼ cup cognac

2 tbsp. flour

3 cups Fish Stock (see recipe)

⅓ cup white wine

Pinch salt and pepper

1. In a heavy skillet, melt butter or margarine. Add garlic and shallot and sauté for 1 minute.

2. Add chopped lobster shell; cook and stir for 2 minutes. Add cognac and continue to cook until cognac is reduced by half.

3. Stir in flour; then add fish stock, wine, salt and pepper. Continue cooking until ingredients have been thoroughly heated.

4. Strain sauce and discard shells.

To Serve:

1. Place 4 tablespoons of sauce onto each of four fish plates.

2. Lay two raviolis on sauce on each plate. Garnish with a dot each of red and black caviar.

Serves 4.

Composed Garden Greens with Green Peppercorn Mustard Vinaigrette Dressing

Composed Greens:

16 radicchio leaves
16 baby oak lettuce leaves
4 romaine leaves, ends cut into points (6 inches long)
8 Belgian endive leaves, ends cut into points
16 curly endive leaves
16 spinach leaves
1 cucumber, peeled and cut into four 2-inch slices with center hollowed out to form a ring
1 small red bell pepper, cored, seeded, and julienned
1 small yellow pepper, cored, seeded, and julienned
12 chives
24 enoki mushrooms
4 edible nasturtiums (optional)

1. Wash and dry all leaves. Place cucumber ring in center of each of four plates. Set romaine point behind the ring; then arrange two Belgian endive spears inside cucumber ring, point side up.

2. Arrange four oak lettuce leaves at 3, 6, 9, and 12 o'clock positions.

3. Arrange four curly endive leaves between oak leaves.

4. Place four radicchio leaves around cucumber ring on top of oak leaf. Arrange four spinach leaves on top of curly endive leaves. Fill in spaces as necessary with any of the above greens.

5. In center of cucumber ring, finish bouquet with two red pepper strips, one yellow pepper strip, three chives, and six enoki mushrooms.

6. Place a nasturtium on right side of plate, facing guest. You have formed a floral pattern of greens around the cucumber center.

7. Drizzle Green Peppercorn Mustard Vinaigrette Dressing (recipe follows) lightly over salad.

Note: Save leftover greens to make a colorful tossed salad later. Greens will stay fresh for up to five days if wrapped loosely in dampened paper towels and refrigerated.

Serves 4.

Green Peppercorn Vinaigrette:

⅓ cup olive oil
2 tbsp. hazelnut oil
1 tbsp. champagne vinegar
1 tbsp. lemon juice
2 tsp. Dijon-style mustard
1 tbsp. finely ground green peppercorns
Dash nutmeg

In a small mixing bowl, whisk all ingredients together until well blended.

Yields ¾ cup.

Noisette Trio of Beef, Veal, and Lamb

Beef Médaillons with Sauce
Marchand de Vin:

2 tbsp. butter, melted
4 (2½-oz.) beef médaillons
1 tbsp. chopped shallots
1 clove garlic, peeled and minced
2 tbsp. flour
1 cup beef consommé
1 cup Burgundy wine
Salt and pepper to taste

1. Place 1 tablespoon melted butter in a large skillet; then add beef médaillons and sear quickly on each side. Remove from skillet, and set médaillons in a 13 x 9 x 2-inch baking pan.
2. To the same skillet, add remaining tablespoon of butter. Cook shallots and garlic until soft, but not browned.
3. Add flour and cook for 2 minutes. Add consommé, wine, salt, and pepper. Stir until ingredients are well blended; then simmer for 7 minutes, stirring constantly.
4. Strain sauce and pour into a small ovenproof dish.
5. Fill an 8 x 8-inch ovenproof casserole ¾ full of boiling water. Set dish with sauce in the water to keep it warm.

Veal Médaillons
with Sauce Soubise:

3 tbsp. butter, melted
4 (2½-oz.) veal médaillons
3 tbsp. chopped leek (white portion only)
1 clove garlic, peeled and minced
2 tbsp. flour
2 cups half-and-half, heated
½ cup white wine
Salt and pepper to taste
Dash nutmeg

1. Place 2 tablespoons melted butter in a large skillet; then add veal and sear quickly on each side. Remove from skillet and add veal médaillons to same baking pan as the beef.
2. To the same skillet, add remaining tablespoon of butter, leek, and garlic. Cook for about 1 minute.
3. Add flour and cook for 1 minute. Add half-and-half, wine, salt, pepper, and nutmeg. Stir until well blended and simmer for 7 minutes, stirring constantly.
4. Strain sauce and pour into a small ovenproof dish. Place sauce in same water-filled casserole as the Marchand de Vin sauce.

Lamb Médaillons
with Sauce Pernod:

2 tbsp. butter, melted
4 (2½-oz.) lamb médaillons
1 tbsp. shallots, chopped
1 clove garlic, peeled and minced
2 tbsp. flour
2 cups beef consommé
¼ cup Pernod liqueur
1 tbsp. half-and-half
Salt and pepper to taste

1. Place 1 tablespoon of butter in a large skillet. Add lamb médaillons and sear quickly on each side. Remove from skillet and add lamb to the same baking pan as the beef and veal médaillons.
2. In the same skillet, cook shallots and garlic in remaining tablespoon of butter until soft, but not browned.
3. Add flour and consommé. Stir and cook until mixture is well blended.
4. Add Pernod and continue to stir. Simmer for 7 minutes, then blend in half-and-half, salt, and pepper.
5. Strain sauce and pour into a small ovenproof pan. Place sauce in same water-filled casserole as the Marchand de Vin and Soubise sauces.

To Bake Noisette Trio:
1. Preheat oven to 350 degrees.
2. Bake beef, veal, and lamb médaillons for 15 minutes.

Serves 4.

To Assemble Centennial Dinner Plate:
1. Place a small amount of each sauce on each of four plates. Place each beef, lamb, and veal médaillon on its appropriate sauce.
2. Place a Petite Vegetable Bundle (recipe follows) in center of each plate.
3. Place one Château Potato (recipe follows) between each of the médaillons, star fashion.

Château Potatoes

16 small new potatoes (about 4½ lb.)
¼ cup Clarified Butter (see recipe)
Salt and pepper to taste

1. Peel and shape potatoes into egg-shaped portions.
2. Fill a large saucepan with water and bring to a boil.
3. Blanch potatoes in boiling water for about 5 minutes. Drain.
4. Heat butter in a large skillet. Add potatoes and sauté until browned; sprinkle with salt and pepper.

Serves 4.

Petite Vegetable Bundles

1 leek (green part only), cleaned and trimmed
1 carrot, cleaned and cut into 12 julienned strips
1 zucchini, unpeeled, cut in half lengthwise, seeds removed, and cut into 12 julienned strips
1 yellow crookneck squash, unpeeled and cut into 12 julienned strips
½ lb. pencil-thin asparagus (3-inch asparagus tips only)
1 red bell pepper, cored, seeded, and cut into 12 julienned strips
4 tbsp. butter, melted
Dash salt and pepper

1. Preheat oven to 250 degrees.
2. Bring 2 quarts of water to a boil. Blanch leek until wilted; then rinse in cold water immediately and set aside.
3. Add remainder of vegetables, except red pepper, to boiling water. Cook for about 10 to 12 minutes until vegetables are *al dente*. Do not overcook.
4. Open leek and flatten green part on a cutting board. Cut leek into four 4-inch-long portions. Place three strips each of red pepper, carrot, zucchini, crookneck squash, and asparagus on the leek and roll tightly. Trim bottom of each bundle, leaving bundles 2 inches tall.
5. Place bundles in a greased baking pan. Sprinkle lightly with salt and pepper; then drizzle 1 tablespoon of melted butter over the top of each bundle.
6. Bake for about 10 minutes, or until vegetables are thoroughly heated.

Serves 4.

THE HOTEL DEL CORONADO COOKBOOK

Decadent Chocolate Centennial Surprise

Chocolate Cups:

6 oz. semisweet chocolate
2 tbsp. butter
1 pint basket raspberries, washed
**   and air dried**

1. In a heavy saucepan, heat the chocolate and butter. Stir until chocolate is melted and mixture is smooth.

2. Using a flexible spatula, swirl mixture around bottom and sides of four 2½- to 3-ounce Danish paper cups, covering the entire inner surface with a thin layer of chocolate.

3. Place cups in muffin tins and chill. Peel off paper and keep in refrigerator until ready to fill.

Note: Packaged chocolate cups are available at specialty markets if you prefer to buy them premade.

Chocolate Leaves:

20 lemon leaves
2 oz. semisweet chocolate

1. Wash the lemon leaves and dry thoroughly.

2. In a heavy saucepan, heat the semisweet chocolate over low heat, stirring constantly until the chocolate begins to melt. Immediately remove the chocolate from heat and stir until smooth.

3. With a small paintbrush, brush melted chocolate on the undersides of lemon leaves, building up layers of chocolate, so that leaves will be sturdy. (Save remainder of chocolate for assembling dessert.)

4. Place leaves on a cookie sheet lined with waxed paper; chill until hardened. Just before using, carefully peel the fresh leaves away from the chocolate leaves. Set chocolate leaves aside.

Kahlua Cream:

1 cup heavy cream
3 tbsp. confectioners' sugar,
**   sifted**
2 tbsp. Kahlua

1. In a medium-size mixing bowl, whip heavy cream until cream forms peaks.

2. Add confectioners' sugar and Kahlua. Stir until well blended.

To Assemble:

1. Stand five chocolate leaves upright around the inside edges of each chocolate cup.

2. Pour a small amount of reserved melted chocolate in the bottom of each chocolate cup, then fill with raspberries.

3. Place 4 tablespoons of Kahlua Cream mixture in center of each of four dessert plates. Set chocolate cup atop cream mixture.

4. Place dessert in refrigerator until serving time.

Serves 4.

Victorian Tea

In the Garden Patio, guests sipped on tea and dined on petite tea sandwiches and the tiniest of miniature tartlets. The centennial guests themselves were dressed to the nines as they viewed a fashion show featuring a spectacular collection of authentic Victorian costumes and the latest trendy fashions.

MENU

Cucumber Sandwiches

Chicken Sandwiches

Curried Egg Sandwiches

Watercress Sandwiches

Dilled Shrimp Sandwiches

Assorted Fruit Tartlets

Fruitcake Cookies

Black Bottom Cupcakes

Selected Teas

Afternoon Tea menu from 1931.

Cucumber Sandwiches

2 medium cucumbers (about ½ lb. each)
Salt
2 tbsp. unsalted butter
¼ cup mayonnaise
12 thin slices white bread

1. Peel cucumbers and cut them in half lengthwise. Seed them with a small teaspoon. Cut into paper thin slices and salt lightly.

2. Place cucumbers in a strainer over a bowl and refrigerate for 1½ hours.

3. In a small bowl, cream the butter with a wooden spoon, then mix in mayonnaise. Lightly coat one side of each slice of bread with the butter mixture.

4. Remove cucumbers from refrigerator and squeeze in a tea towel to remove all excess liquid.

5. Spread cucumbers on half the bread slices. Cover with remaining bread slices. Trim crusts and cut each sandwich into four triangles.

Note: For additional color, spread softened unsalted butter on cut edges of the sandwiches and dip them in herbs or paprika. Always place prepared sandwiches on damp (not wet) tea towels and cover them with additional damp towels until ready to serve.

Yields 24 tea sandwiches.

Chicken Sandwiches

1 cup minced chicken (skinned, boned, and poached)
½ tbsp. minced shallots
½ tsp. lemon juice
¼ tsp. salt
⅛ tsp. white pepper
¼ cup mayonnaise
12 thin slices whole wheat bread
5 tbsp. unsalted butter, creamed

1. In a small bowl, combine chicken, shallots, lemon juice, salt, pepper, and mayonnaise. Blend well.
2. Lightly coat one side of each slice of bread with butter.
3. Spread chicken mixture on half of the bread slices. Cover with remaining bread slices. Trim crusts and cut each sandwich into four triangles.

Yields 24 tea sandwiches.

Curried Egg Sandwiches

4 large eggs, hard cooked and peeled
1 tsp. Dijon-style mustard
¼ tsp. curry powder
½ tsp. salt
⅛ tsp. white pepper
¼ cup mayonnaise
12 thin slices pumpernickel bread
5 tbsp. unsalted butter, creamed

1. In a small bowl, chop eggs and mash. Add mustard, curry powder, salt, pepper, and mayonnaise. Blend well.
2. Lightly coat one side of each slice of bread with butter.
3. Spread egg mixture on half of the bread slices; cover with remaining buttered bread slices. Trim crusts and cut each sandwich into four triangles.

Yields 24 tea sandwiches.

Watercress Sandwiches

1 bunch watercress leaves, finely chopped
¼ tsp. salt
⅛ tsp. white pepper
16 thin slices white bread
¼ cup mayonnaise

1. Season watercress with salt and pepper.
2. Lightly coat one side of each bread slice with mayonnaise.
3. Sprinkle watercress on half of the bread slices; cover with remaining bread slices. Trim crusts and cut each sandwich into four triangles.

Yields 32 tea sandwiches.

Dilled Shrimp Sandwiches

8 oz. cooked bay shrimp, shelled
   and coarsely chopped
⅓ cup minced celery
¼ tsp. onion salt
⅛ tsp. white pepper
2 tsp. snipped dill
¼ cup mayonnaise
12 thin slices white bread
5 tbsp. unsalted butter, creamed

1. In a small bowl, combine shrimp, celery, onion salt, pepper, dill, and mayonnaise. Blend well.

2. Lightly coat one side of each slice of bread with butter.

3. Spread shrimp mixture on half of the bread slices; cover with remaining buttered bread slices. Trim crusts and cut each sandwich into four triangles.

Yields 24 tea sandwiches.

Assorted Fruit Tartlets

Rich Tart Pastry:
½ cup butter, chilled
1¾ cups all-purpose flour
¼ tsp. salt
1 egg, slightly beaten (use only
   ½ beaten egg)
⅛ cup vegetable oil
¼ cup cold water

1. Cut chilled butter into ½-inch slices. In a medium-size bowl, combine flour and salt. Using a pastry blender or a fork, cut butter into flour mixture until all particles are the size of small peas; set aside.

2. In a small bowl, combine egg, oil, and water. Using a fork, stir egg mixture into flour mixture until evenly distributed. Divide dough in half; then shape into two balls for easy handling. Wrap in plastic wrap and refrigerate for at least 1 hour.

3. Preheat oven to 400 degrees.

4. Roll out dough on a lightly floured board, then cut into 3-inch circles. Carefully fit dough into 2-inch tart pans or miniature muffin tins. Trim edges even with tops of pan; prick side and bottom of each with fork.

5. Bake tart shells for 10 to 12 minutes, or until golden brown.

Yields 20 tart shells.

Crème Pâtissière:
¼ cup all-purpose flour
⅓ cup sugar
1 cup milk
3 egg yolks, beaten
1 tbsp. butter
⅛ tsp. almond extract

1. In a medium-size saucepan, combine flour and sugar. Gradually add milk, stirring until smooth. Add egg yolks; then cook, stirring over low heat, until thickened (about 3 minutes).

2. Remove from heat and stir in butter and almond extract. Cover with plastic wrap; set aside to cool.

3. Spoon 2 to 3 teaspoons of crème into each cooled tart shell.

Assorted Fresh Fruit:
4 boysenberries
4 halves of green grapes
2 sliced strawberries
2 mandarin orange segments
½ banana, thickly sliced

Place small pieces of any of the fruit on top of the crème in tart shells.

Glaze:

½ cup apricot preserves
1 tbsp. orange juice

1. In a small saucepan, heat apricot preserves and orange juice until mixture is blended and warm. Strain to remove pieces of fruit from glaze.
2. Lightly brush glaze over fresh fruit in tarts.

Yields 20 tartlets.

Fruitcake Cookies

½ lb. butter or margarine
2 cups brown sugar, packed
4 eggs
1 cup bourbon
3 cups flour
3 tsp. baking soda
¼ tsp. nutmeg
¼ tsp. cinnamon
¾ lb. white raisins
¾ lb. dark raisins
½ cup candied pineapple
½ cup (each) green and red candied cherries
¾ lb. pecans, chopped
¾ lb. walnuts, chopped

1. In a large mixing bowl, cream together butter and sugar. Add eggs and bourbon; then slowly add flour, baking soda, and spices. Mix in fruit and nuts.
2. Chill overnight.
3. When ready to bake, preheat oven to 275 degrees.
4. Drop from a teaspoon onto greased cookie sheets. Bake for 20 minutes.

Note: Dough may be kept in refrigerator for three days before baking.

Yields 2 dozen cookies.

Black Bottom Cupcakes

Cake:

1½ cups all-purpose flour
1 cup sugar
¼ cup unsweetened cocoa powder
1 tsp. baking soda
½ tsp. salt
1 cup water
½ cup corn or vegetable oil
1 tbsp. distilled white vinegar
1 tsp. vanilla extract

Filling:

1 8-oz. pkg. cream cheese
1 large egg
⅓ cup sugar
¼ tsp. salt
1 cup semisweet chocolate chips
Sugar

1. Preheat oven to 350 degrees. Line miniature muffin tins with fluted paper cups.
2. In a large mixing bowl, sift together the flour, 1 cup sugar, cocoa, baking soda, and ½ teaspoon salt. Add the water, oil, vinegar, and vanilla extract; then beat together until well blended.
3. To make the filling, combine the cream cheese, egg, ⅓ cup sugar, and ¼ teaspoon salt in a separate mixing bowl. Beat well to blend, then stir in the chocolate chips.
4. Fill each muffin cup half full with batter; then top with ½ teaspoon of the cream cheese filling and sprinkle with sugar.
5. Bake for 20 to 25 minutes, or until a cake tester inserted in the center comes out clean. Remove the cupcakes to a wire rack to cool.

Yields 3½ dozen miniature cupcakes.

Popular Tea Selections

The tea ceremony has long been a tradition in the British Empire. This charming ritual has crossed the ocean to America and has become an elegant way to entertain in the afternoon. Choose one or two of the popular teas listed below, and salute the British for passing along a pleasant custom.

Vintage Darjeeling: The rarest of teas; the ultimate brew for afternoon tea time. Sip it with watercress or chicken sandwiches.

Orange Pekoe: A brisk, smooth, high-grown Ceylon tea; good for lunch or early afternoon.

Lemon-scented: A light, refreshing tea scented and flavored with natural lemon essence.

Irish Breakfast: A robust, pungent, extremely satisfying tea.

Prince of Wales: A richly colored, mellow tea from the Anhwei province of China.

China Oolong: A gentle brown tea with an exquisite flavor often likened to that of ripe peaches. Try it with fruit, crêpes, or tarts.

Earl Grey: A unique blend of China and Darjeeling teas; famous for its fragrance and delicate bergamot flavor.

Note: Tea bags do not need to brew as long as loose tea. They contain broken leaves, designed to release their flavor just a minute or two after immersion in water.

The three-day Centennial Gala weekend concluded on Sunday with a carnival celebration on the beach. Hundreds of balloons were released, and bystanders enjoyed the spectacle from the beach.

Splendor by the Sea Brunch

Opulent displays of Gravlax with Herb-Mustard Sauce, Glazed Baked Ham with Orange Marmalade Sauce, and Bloody Mary Crêpes Filled with Crab and Tomatoes graced the tables of the Splendor by the Sea Brunch—the culmination of the Centennial weekend. The brunch was served in a large, square circus tent that was erected especially for the affair, overlooking the sandy beach and the Pacific Ocean.

A two-foot-tall cheddar cheese carving of the numerals *100* accented the anniversary. The numerals were surrounded by five-pound wheels of domestic and imported cheeses. Chocolate fondue stations with bite-size fruit served to satisfy the palates of dessert devotees.

The guests re-created the year of 1888 by attending the event in all-white Victorian attire. The ladies shaded their Victorian coiffured hairstyles with authentic parasols. The gentlemen were clad in crisp white suits—some even enhancing the theme with white hats and spats.

Recipes from the Splendor by the Sea Brunch follow—including such menu items as Cointreau-Minted Melon Balls, Crustless Jack and Red Pepper Quiche, and Honey-Lemon Muffins with Peach Butter—all of which have been adapted for at-home kitchen preparation.

MENU

Champagne Royale Cocktails

Gravlax with Herb-Mustard Sauce

Marinated Herring in Sour Cream and Scallion Sauce

Cointreau-Minted Melon Balls

Imported and Domestic Cheese Tray

Glazed Baked Ham with Orange Marmalade Sauce

Crustless Jack and Red Pepper Quiche

Bloody Mary Crêpes Filled with Crab and Tomatoes

Honey-Lemon Muffins with Peach Butter

Choconut Fondue

Champagne Royale Cocktails

24 tbsp. crème de cassis
4 750-ml bottles chilled champagne
2 baskets of fresh raspberries (or 12 strawberries)

1. Pour 1 tablespoon crème de cassis into each champagne glass.
2. Fill glasses with champagne.
3. Place three fresh raspberries or one strawberry in each glass.

Note: White wine may be substituted for champagne.

Serves 12 (two glasses each).

Gravlax with Herb-Mustard Sauce

**4 1-lb. pieces center-cut salmon
fillet**
½ cup lemon-flavored vodka
½ cup sugar
½ cup coarse salt
3 tbsp. coarsely ground pepper
1 bunch dill sprigs
1 bunch fresh chives
Minibagels
**Herb-Mustard Sauce (recipe
follows)**

1. Place two salmon fillets in a glass baking pan. Pour vodka over salmon, turning the salmon as necessary to coat.

2. Mix sugar, salt, and pepper. Gently rub the mixture into the flesh side of the salmon.

3. Arrange two fillets in the baking pan, skin side down. Top with remaining two fillets, skin side up.

4. Place half of the dill and chives on top of each pair of fillets. Wrap both pairs of fillets in plastic wrap and replace them in the baking pan.

5. Place another glass baking pan directly on top of the wrapped fillets and weigh the pan down with heavy juice cans or bricks.

6. Refrigerate for 3 days. During the refrigeration, open the plastic wrap and baste salmon every 12 hours. Rewrap salmon and place weights on it carefully after each basting.

7. When ready to serve, remove weights, unwrap fillets, and gently wipe off all the marinade and herbs. Slice thinly on the diagonal of the skin. Serve with Herb-Mustard Sauce and minibagels that have been split.

Note: Minibagels are available at most supermarkets and delicatessens.

Serves 12.

Herb-Mustard Sauce:
6 eggs, hard cooked and peeled
1 tsp. prepared mustard
1 tsp. Dijon-style mustard
½ tsp. salt
2 cups olive oil
8 tbsp. white vinegar
**2 cloves garlic, peeled and
minced**
4 sweet pickles, finely chopped
4 tsp. finely chopped parsley
**2 tsp. finely chopped fresh
tarragon**
**2 tsp. finely chopped fresh
chervil**
2 tsp. finely chopped chives
16 capers, drained and chopped

1. Separate egg yolks from whites. Cut whites into small thin strips; set aside. In a large mixing bowl, mash egg yolks to a paste consistency. Add mustards and salt. Mix thoroughly.

2. Whisk in oil, a little at a time. When mixture begins to thicken, increase oil to a slow stream, and start adding vinegar, beating constantly. Use only the amount of the 2 cups of oil required to reach a velvety consistency. Sauce should not be as thick as mayonnaise.

3. Stir in garlic, pickles, herbs, capers, and egg whites. Mix thoroughly. Cover and refrigerate for several hours to allow flavors to blend.

Yields about 3 cups.

Marinated Herring in Sour Cream and Scallion Sauce

2 lb. salt herring fillets
6 scallions
1 cup sour cream
2 tsp. lemon juice
1 tsp. grated lemon rind
1 tsp. freshly ground pepper

1. Place herring fillets in large bowl of cold water and cover. Refrigerate overnight, changing water once.
2. Pour off water. Drain herring fillets on paper towels.
3. Trim scallions. Cut into thin slices, using both white and green parts.
4. Cut herring into bite-size pieces. Add scallions, sour cream, lemon juice, lemon rind, and pepper. Blend thoroughly with herring.

Serves 12.

Cointreau-Minted Melon Balls

1 firm ripe casaba melon
1 firm ripe honeydew melon
1 firm ripe cantaloupe
1 cup watermelon
⅔ cup plus 2 tbsp. Cointreau liqueur
⅔ cup chopped fresh mint

1. Cut melons in half and scoop out seeds with a wooden spoon. Using a melon ball scoop, cut as many balls as possible. Keep the balls whole and the same size. Place balls in a medium-size mixing bowl, add Cointreau, and stir well.
2. Place melon balls in a serving bowl or a scooped-out watermelon shell.
3. Refrigerate until ready to serve. Sprinkle with fresh mint before serving.

Serves 12.

Imported and Domestic Cheese Tray

7 oz. Edam cheese
7 oz. Gouda cheese
2 Jonathan apples
1 lb. Brie cheese wheel
½ lb. Swiss cheese
1 lb. Provolone cheese
1 lb. Port Salut cheese
1 bunch green seedless grapes
2 bunches red seedless grapes
French baguettes
Water crackers

1. Peel Edam and cut several wedges from it. Arrange in the center of a large serving tray. Cut Gouda into wedges, leaving wax coating on. Fan out cheese wedges, alternating with thick slices of unpeeled apples.
2. Slice sections from Brie cheese; arrange on tray.
3. Overlap slices of Swiss cheese and pile Provolone cut into sticks next to it. Cube Port Salut cheese and pile it in any open spaces. Garnish with green and red grapes. Serve with sliced baguettes and water crackers.

Serves 12.

Glazed Baked Ham with Orange Marmalade Sauce

3 tbsp. orange marmalade
1 tbsp. Dijon-style mustard
5-lb. boneless smoked ham

1. Mix orange marmalade and mustard in a small bowl.
2. Place ham inside a plastic cooking bag. Spread top of ham with marmalade-mustard mixture. Seal bag with a twist-tie, then poke four holes in the top of bag.
3. Place in a crockpot, cover, and cook on low for 6 to 8 hours.
4. Transfer ham to a carving board. Pour juices into a sauce boat and keep warm. Slice ham and place on a serving platter. Serve with Orange Marmalade Sauce.

Serves 14.

Crustless Jack and Red Pepper Quiche

6 cups shredded Monterey Jack cheese (24 oz.)
½ medium onion, chopped
¼ cup thinly sliced red bell pepper
¼ cup margarine or butter, melted
8 oz. smoked turkey, cut into julienned strips
8 beaten eggs
1 ¾ cups milk
½ cup all-purpose flour
2 tbsp. snipped fresh chives, basil, tarragon, thyme, or oregano
1 tbsp. snipped parsley

1. Sprinkle 3 cups of cheese in the bottom of a 13 x 9 x 2-inch baking pan.
2. In a saucepan, cook the onion and red pepper in the margarine or butter until the vegetables are tender, but not brown; drain well. Place vegetables over cheese in baking pan.
3. Arrange turkey strips over vegetables. Sprinkle remaining 3 cups cheese over turkey. Cover and chill in the refrigerator overnight.
4. When ready to prepare, preheat oven to 350 degrees.
5. Remove baking pan from refrigerator. Combine eggs, milk, flour, fresh herbs, and parsley. Pour over cheese layer. Bake for about 45 minutes. Let stand 10 minutes before serving.

Serves 12.

Bloody Mary Crêpes Filled
with Crab and Tomatoes

Crêpes:

¾ cup Bloody Mary mix
2¼ cups milk
3 eggs
1 cup sifted all-purpose flour
6 tbsp. vegetable oil
Dash salt
¾ tsp. paprika
3 tsp. chili powder
Dash Tabasco
6 tbsp. unsalted butter
   (approximately)
Crab and Tomato Filling (recipe
   follows)
¼ cup grated Gruyère cheese
4 sprigs fresh dill (for garnish)

1. Combine all ingredients except butter in food processor or blender; process for 30 seconds. Scrape down sides and process 1 minute more. Pour batter into large bowl and seal with plastic wrap. Let rest at room temperature for 30 minutes. The mixture will be quite thick.

2. When ready to make crêpes, stir batter to recombine ingredients. It should have the consistency of heavy cream. If it is too thick, thin it with a little milk. Place a paper-towel-lined plate near stovetop.

3. Set crêpe pan, preferably with a nonstick surface, over medium heat until hot. Melt about 1 teaspoon butter in pan. Holding pan in one hand, pour 3 tablespoons of batter into pan. Tilt pan to coat bottom evenly. Set pan back on heat until crêpe starts to bubble, about 30 to 40 seconds. Loosen sides of crêpe with spatula. Invert pan to turn crêpe onto the towel-lined plate. Cover crêpe with another paper towel. Add butter to pan as needed and repeat until all the batter is used.

4. Place one portion of filling in the center of each crêpe. Fold the crêpes in thirds and place them 2 inches apart on a nonstick cookie sheet. Sprinkle with Gruyère cheese.

5. Heat filled crêpes in oven for about 15 minutes.

6. Serve crêpes garnished with fresh dill sprigs.

Note: Extra crêpes may be frozen for later use.

Yields about 18 crêpes.

Crab and Tomato Filling:

2 8-oz. pkg. cream cheese, at
   room temperature
¾ lb. fresh crabmeat
4 shallots, peeled and minced
2 tbsp. chicken bouillon
1 cup sour cream
2 ripe tomatoes, peeled, seeded,
   and coarsely chopped
¼ tsp. Tabasco sauce
¼ cup dried dill weed

1. Preheat oven to 350 degrees.

2. In a large mixing bowl, beat cream cheese with a fork until smooth. Mix in crabmeat, shallots, bouillon, sour cream, tomatoes, Tabasco sauce, and dill.

Honey-Lemon Muffins with Peach Butter

Honey-Lemon Muffins:

2 tsp. baking soda
1½ cups buttermilk
1 cup (2 sticks) butter, softened
1½ cups honey
4 large eggs
4 cups all-purpose flour
2 tbsp. grated lemon rind
Sugar

1. Preheat oven to 375 degrees.
2. Grease two twelve-cup muffin tins or four twelve-cup miniature muffin tins. Combine the baking soda and buttermilk in a small nonmetal bowl.
3. In a large mixing bowl, beat the butter and honey together. Beat in the eggs, one at a time. Gradually fold in the flour; then fold in the buttermilk mixture and the lemon rind until just blended. Do not overmix.
4. Spoon the mixture into the prepared muffin tins and sprinkle the surface of the batter generously with sugar. Bake for about 20 minutes for regular muffins (12 to 15 minutes for miniature muffins), or until the muffins are golden brown and a cake tester or toothpick inserted in the center comes out clean. Cool on wire racks and serve with Peach Butter (recipe follows).

Yields 2 dozen regular muffins or 4 dozen miniature muffins.

Peach Butter:

1 cup (2 sticks) butter, softened
2 large, very ripe peaches, pitted, peeled, and finely chopped
1 tbsp. confectioners' sugar
¼ tsp. ground cinnamon

1. In a small bowl, combine all the ingredients and blend thoroughly.
2. Mound the butter into a serving pan, cover, and refrigerate. Bring to room temperature before serving.

Yields about 2 cups.

Choconut Fondue

2 12-oz. chocolate bars with nuts
1½ cups heavy cream
3 tbsp. brandy
½ tsp. vanilla extract
Assorted fresh fruit cut into bite-size pieces
Marshmallows

1. Break up chocolate and place in double boiler over low heat.
2. Add heavy cream and heat slowly, stirring constantly until chocolate melts.
3. Stir in brandy and vanilla extract.
4. Transfer to a fondue pot.
5. Serve with a platter of bite-size fruit such as bananas, pineapple chunks, strawberries, and marshmallows arranged in rows on a platter.

Serves 12.

CHAPTER ELEVEN

Stocks

Stocks are the basic foundation for cuisine—they are the most important ingredient for sauces and they provide texture and flavor. Brown stock is the most heavy-bodied, followed by chicken stock, which is slightly lighter. Fish stock is the most delicate and the lightest of the stocks.

Stocks are economical to prepare. Beef and veal bones are available at your local butcher shop and at many supermarkets.

Chicken wings are also available at super markets. The cooking process—the blending of vegetables and bones cooked slowly with water—produces rich stocks that will enhance every recipe in which they are used.

This chapter includes useful recipes for Brown Stock, Chicken Stock, Clarified Butter, Court Bouillon, Demi-Glacé, Fish Stock, Lamb Stock, and Veal Stock.

Brown Stock

2 lb. meaty beef shanks,
   sawed into 1-inch slices
2 lb. meaty veal shanks, sawed
   into 1-inch slices
2 onions, quartered
1 carrot, quartered
Water
2 ribs celery
1½ tsp. salt
4 parsley sprigs
½ tsp. dried thyme
1 bay leaf

1. Preheat oven to 450 degrees.
2. Place beef shanks, veal shanks, onions, and carrot in a baking pan. Brown well in oven, then transfer to a large stock pot. Set aside.
3. Add 2 cups of water to baking pan. Deglaze the pan over high heat, scraping up the brown bits. Add the liquid to the stock pot with 14 cups cold water, celery, and salt. Place remaining spices in a cheesecloth bag, tie the top, and add to the pot. Bring to a boil and skim off the froth. Add ½ cup cold water, bring mixture to a simmer, and skim froth again.
4. Cover and simmer the mixture for 5 to 6 hours, adding boiling water to keep ingredients covered, until stock is reduced to about 8 cups.
5. Strain stock through a fine sieve into a large mixing bowl. With the back of a wooden spoon, press hard on solids. Allow to cool. Chill the stock, then remove the fat. Store stock in covered freezer containers.

Note: Frozen Brown Stock may be kept for up to three months.

Yields about 8 cups.

Chicken Stock

5 lb. chicken parts (backs, necks, and wings)
Water
2 medium onions, peeled and quartered
2 leeks (white part only), cut into 2-inch pieces
3 carrots, cut into 2-inch pieces
3 celery ribs, cut into 2-inch pieces
3 cloves garlic, peeled and crushed
2 bay leaves
4 sprigs Italian parsley
3 sprigs fresh thyme (or 1 tsp. dried)
2 tsp. coarse salt
10 black peppercorns, crushed

1. Rinse chicken parts under cold water. Place them in a stock pot. Add enough cold water to cover. Bring to a boil, then reduce heat to a simmer. Skim off scum as it appears.
2. Add remainder of ingredients. Cook partially covered for 3 hours. Skim and add boiling water as necessary to keep solid ingredients covered.
3. Strain stock through a sieve into a large mixing bowl. Allow stock to cool uncovered. Ladle stock into 1-quart covered freezer containers. Chill overnight.
4. The next day, remove and discard fat from the top of containers. Store stock in freezer.

Note: Frozen Chicken Stock may be kept for up to three months.

Yields 5 quarts.

Clarified Butter

1 lb. butter

1. Melt butter in a heavy-bottomed saucepan over low heat.
2. Skim off froth, then carefully pour clear yellow liquid from saucepan, leaving the milky residue. Discard residue.

Note: Clarified Butter will keep for two weeks in the refrigerator, or may be stored in a covered freezer container for one month.

Yields about 1½ cups

Demi-Glacé

8 cups Brown Stock (see recipe), chilled and skimmed of fat

1. In a large saucepan, cook the stock over medium-high heat until it is reduced to about 4 cups of Demi-Glacé.
2. Allow the Demi-Glacé to cool. Transfer to small freezer containers, cover, and store in the freezer.
3. To use Demi-Glacé, dip a spoon in hot water and spoon out the desired amount.

Note: Frozen Demi-Glacé keeps indefinitely.

Yields about 4 cups.

Court Bouillon

4 cups dry white wine
2 tbsp. white wine vinegar
8 cups cold water
2 carrots, chopped
3 shallots (white part only),
   thinly sliced
½ tsp. crushed white
   peppercorns
2 coriander seeds, crushed
2 tsp. salt
1 bay leaf
4 sprigs parsley
1 sprig thyme
1 small sprig fennel

1. In a stock pot, combine wine, vinegar, and water. Bring to a boil.

2. Add carrots, shallots, peppercorns, coriander seeds, and salt.

3. Place bay leaf, parsley, thyme, and fennel in a square of cheesecloth and tie corners together at the top. Add to stock pot. Bring to a boil, then simmer for 20 minutes.

4. Remove stock from stove and allow to cool at room temperature. Strain through a sieve, and store Court Bouillon in covered freezer containers.

Note: Frozen Court Bouillon may be kept for up to six months.

Yields about 10 cups.

Fish Stock

4 tbsp. butter
1 small carrot, sliced
2 small onions, chopped
2 leeks, cut in rings
2 lb. fish scraps from cod,
   halibut, flounder, or sole (or
   a mixture of these)
10 cups water
2 cups chablis wine
2 tbsp. fresh lemon juice
10 parsley stems
2 stalks fresh thyme
½ cup chopped fennel
4 celery stalks
1 bay leaf

1. Melt butter in a stock pot. Add carrot, onions, and leeks and sauté, stirring constantly, until transparent.

2. Carefully wash the fish, removing the gills, and add to the vegetable mixture. Add water, wine, and lemon juice.

3. Place the parsley, thyme, fennel, celery, and bay leaf together in a square of cheesecloth. Tie corners together at the top to make a bouquet garni. Add the bouquet garni to the pot and bring all ingredients to a boil. Skim off all the foam that rises to the surface. Reduce heat and simmer for 30 minutes.

4. Strain the stock through a sieve lined with cheesecloth; then return stock to the stove and boil for 15 minutes more.

5. Remove stock from stove and allow to cool at room temperature. Refrigerate or freeze in covered freezer containers.

Note: Stock will keep for three days in the refrigerator. Frozen Fish Stock may be kept for up to two months.

Yields 3 quarts.

Lamb Stock

2½ lb. lamb bones and
  scraps, chopped
1 onion, chopped
1 carrot, chopped
13 cups water
2 stalks celery, chopped
2 cloves garlic, peeled and
  mashed
2 bay leaves
2 sprigs fresh thyme
4 sprigs parsley
1½ tsp. salt
½ tsp. black pepper

1. Preheat oven to 425 degrees.
2. Place lamb bones, scraps, onion, and carrot in a baking pan. Brown in oven for 40 minutes. Turn and baste with accumulated fat every 20 minutes. Drain off fat, then transfer bones and vegetables to a stock pot.
3. Add 1 cup of water to baking pan, and simmer on top of stove for 1 minute. Scrape bottom of baking pan to loosen particles, then pour mixture into stock pot.
4. Add about 12 cups water, celery, garlic, bay leaves, thyme, and parsley. Bring to a simmer and skim off the froth. Add salt and pepper. Cover loosely and simmer for 4 hours.
5. Strain stock through a sieve lined with cheesecloth. Allow stock to cool, then remove all fat from surface. Store in covered freezer containers.

Note: Frozen Lamb Stock may be kept for up to three months.

Yields about 2 quarts.

Veal Stock

2 lb. 3 oz. veal knuckle
  bones, chopped
8¾ cups water
1 onion, studded with 1 clove
  peeled garlic
1 carrot, chopped
1 leek (white part only), chopped
1 rib celery, chopped
1 bay leaf
3 sprigs parsley
1 sprig thyme
1 sprig chervil

1. Blanch bones for 1 minute. Drain and place in a stock pot. Cover with about 8¾ cups water; then bring to a boil. Remove scum from surface; then add onion with garlic, carrot, leek, and celery.
2. Place bay leaf, parsley, thyme, and chervil in a square of cheesecloth, tie corners at the top, and add to stock pot. Cover and simmer for 3 to 4 hours, or until liquid is reduced to about 4½ cups.
3. Strain stock through a sieve lined with cheesecloth. Allow to cool, then remove fat from surface and store stock in covered freezer containers.

Note: Frozen Veal Stock may be kept for up to three months.

Yields about 4½ cups.

Index